A Long Journey

and some things learned along the road

By Mavis J. Longfellow

A collection of stories, letters, poems, and essays written over many years by a Maine woman now 90 years of age

"To try to make the world in some way better than you found it
is to have a noble motive in life!"

ANDREW CARNEGIE, *The Empire of Business*

A Long Journey ,
Copyright © 2020 Mavis J. Longfellow

ISBN: 978-1-63381-242-0

Cover illustration by Anna Brown

Designed and produced by:
Maine Authors Publishing
12 High Street, Thomaston, Maine
www.maineauthorspublishing.com

Printed in the United States of America

With love, I dedicate this book to my wonderful, unique family. Many of them urged me for a long time to write a book, and I have them to thank for the courage to finally do so.

I am also deeply grateful to my daughter, Anna Brown, for painting the beautiful scene on the cover of my book. I feel that she captured the symbolism of the road in the fall of the year, referring to my long life's journey.

Just as going home for a visit with family brings people back to a connection with their roots, so (hopefully) my book will be a legacy that will benefit my children and their families, and other readers, in much the same way.

As people live their lives, they gather knowledge through experience. They learn some truths that no one ever taught them. Hopefully, they learn ways to cope with life. Unfortunately, when they die, the wisdom that they have gained dies with them. If preserved somehow instead, knowledge that they have gained might help others, and save them the possible pain of having to learn those lessons through their own experience. I hope my readers, especially family members, will find some truths about life here, and will enjoy what I have humbly tried to pass on through my essays, stories, and poems about life.

CONTENTS

PREFACE

This book is not intended as an autobiography, although it does tell a lot about me, and about lessons learned over 90 years of living, in Maine. It is a collection of stories about how different life was during the depression and World War II, told through my experiences.

I have lived during the Great Depression, lived through WWII, grown with the social revolution which began in the sixties, and seen many changes over these many years. I had 65 years of marriage to the same man, and we raised six children. I like to show with my stories how times have changed.

Sometimes we face situations when it seems there are no words. I have at times written letters to people whom I love, trying to comfort them or give them a lift. Those letters are here, along with other letters (several to my grandchildren) in one section. Each one has its own story. In some cases I have used a fictitious name in order to protect that person's privacy, particularly in these letters. However, I have used the real names of family members and neighbors, for instance, in my stories, and in cases where privacy is not an issue.

I love to juggle words so that there is a theme, with rhyme and rhythm, if not a specific meter, and call it a poem. I have those scattered among some of the prose articles. Since 2009, I have written verse about Christmas to send with my Christmas cards. I have grouped those here, along with other holiday pieces.

As a guest columnist, I have had a few articles printed on the editorial page of our local daily newspaper. I have listed those titles on the next page, since they are included in this book. "Nothing succeeds like success," so I had the courage needed to write this book. I hope that it is entertaining, and perhaps more.

I chose "A Mother's Hands" as the introductory article, because I think it best shows where I am coming from. In it, I briefly refer to several aspects of my life that I explain later in my articles, in more detail. Since this book is a collection of separate articles, and these many items were all written at different times, over many years, for different purposes, there are duplications of the same subject here and there.

One time, my husband or I casually mentioned what might be written on our gravestones. I said that mine would read, "She tried." We laughed about it, but truthfully, I have tried. I have tried to be part of the solution instead of the problem. I have tried to set a good example. I have tried to do what I consider right and not wrong. I have tried to follow the Golden Rule and the rest of Biblical teachings, reflecting my beliefs. In spite of good intentions, we humans—including me—sometimes fail, unfortunately.

Most of us would like to help others as the opportunity arises. What I really would like to earn, and to have carved on my stone, is "She made the world a better place." I deeply desire that my life and my writing will have made a small difference. Life is wonderful, but at times everyone could use a boost over the rough spots. Perhaps I have given someone hope, or ease, or comfort, or courage, or have pointed out the way to go on. I can only humbly hope so. In any case, I hope my book is enjoyable. I tried.

Over the past year, the local newspaper, the *Kennebec Journal*, has printed seven of my articles. I have included them here, scattered among the other pieces. These are the names of those printed:

"A Mother's Hands"
"Courage in Hard Times—My Dad"
"Guilty, and on Drugs"
"We Need to Do Better"
"Better than Pearls and Opals"
"Move Mountains and Count Your Blessings"
"Christmas and Peace"

SECTION 1

Through the Years

This section contains stories, poems, and essays—thoughts and comments about my 90 years of living in Maine, from 1930 on. That's a lot of living! Hopefully I learned a few things throughout the journey.

A Mother's Hands

I looked at my hands this morning because they ache, they are numb, and they have lost most of their strength and dexterity. They look to be every bit as old as they are. Then I thought of how well they have served me until recently, and of what they have accomplished or have been a significant part.

From the time we draw our first breath, our hands are in training for a lifetime of use. Mine never did learn to draw well or write beautifully, but not for want of effort. In childhood my poor hands nearly froze sometimes in Maine's snow and frigid temperatures. Oh, how they ached! But we kids would soon be back playing in the snow, with dry mittens and short memories for pain. For a while, my young hands showed scratches, since I enjoyed playing with my cat. One of the scratches got infected. The doctor said we could call it "cat-scratch fever."

I struggled for years on the piano and never did accomplish much. I didn't have real lessons, anyway. The Hawaiian guitar, grandparent of today's steel guitar, was easier, and it was enjoyable to play duets with my brother. Every week we took the city bus from our South Portland home, where we lived for four years during the war, into Portland and handed over $1.00 each for our joint lesson. After a couple of years, we bought two electric guitars from Sears Roebuck for $139.50 each. When our Gram was in her last illness, she asked us to play "Whispering Hope" for her.

My youthful hands earned a little money as I scratched around in Mrs. Dyer's garden, pulling weeds and planting flowers that her hands could no longer manage. That earned me a few cents an hour that summer when I was 12 or 13. Another summer, nimble fingers picked strawberries on one of the farms in Cape Elizabeth, because all the young men had gone to war, so the women and old men hired

3

kids, whom they hauled to their farm in an open-bodied truck. Three cents a quart, for boxes heaped up, was the going wage for us.

At our 1949 wedding, my husband placed a gold band on my finger, which I was privileged to wear for more than 65 years until we were parted by his death. In 1949 he placed it there, and he was the one who replaced it the couple of times that I had to remove it from my finger.

I had an old treadle sewing machine when I was first married. I made a few clothes for myself and for my young children on that antique machine. Later, we bought an electric machine which I still enjoy. Among other items, I made a dress for a daughter for her college Chorale, helped make two bridesmaids' dresses, stitched up insulated curtains for my home, and then began my quilts. I made six quilts the tedious hand-quilted way for my six children, and then began making some for my grandchildren. I have fourteen grandchildren and six great-grandchildren. That's too much work for these old hands in my remaining years. I'll make as many as I can, though.

How many yeast rolls have I kneaded, shaped, and baked? How many vegetables cut up for stew? How many dishes washed, filled, and washed again? How many cakes beaten 200 strokes, carrots scraped, potatoes peeled, turkeys stuffed and roasted, and hot apple pies set to cool on the shelf? I usually had homemade snacks ready each day when the kids got off the bus.

How many diapers were folded, changed, washed, hung out to dry, and folded again? How many were fitted to tiny, warm, squirming bodies? Those were the days of cloth diapers, diaper pails, and big safety pins. A mother's hand would automatically slip between the baby's body and the sharp pin in case the pin slipped, resulting in a painful stab. Every mother wishes she could save her child from pain, and would even take that pain upon herself. Usually that is not an option, but moms do what they can.

How many hours did my arms hold, rock, and soothe my babies? There is no bond that can compare with the one that exists between mother and child. I still remember the peace and love of those times when the crying had stopped, and the innocence and beauty of my sleeping child flooded my heart.

For 27 years at the old greenhouse, my hands tucked little plants into seedling boxes each spring and hurriedly tamped them in. The boxes were heavy—the soil, too. During the winter, we had taken hammers in hand and nailed up the seedling boxes from wooden shook, working as a family. Later, when the customers came, my "cash register" was a wallet, a receipt book, and a pencil to add up sales.

When we built the new greenhouses, I helped on weekends and at the end of often difficult weekdays that I had spent teaching third grade. After I got home from school and the kids arrived on the bus, we all drove over and joined the tired family crew. Only two children still lived at home, but the older ones also helped when they could. The present co-owner of the business, son Scott, was fresh out of college, and was there working from the beginning. (He still is there, along with his wife as co-owner, son as general manager, another son occasionally, and a daughter when possible. His sister is design manager.) One thing I did was to help carry the A-frames and stand them in place in the cold winter air. That winter of 1977 was a cold one. I sometimes took supper to the crew, and we all worked late. Finally back home, the kids did their homework while I corrected my pupils' papers and prepared for classes the next day, washed the dishes, and fell into bed.

We retired after ten years and then took ten years off, but after that I got my hands back into it at the office for another few years, working sometimes until late at night. We had several cash registers by then, as the business grew, and one of my jobs was to reconcile them. These hands were reliable and seldom made mistakes. They finally learned in the office about clicking with a mouse on the computer.

I hope, and I sincerely believe, that my hands have given pleasure, relief, enjoyment, comfort, sympathy, and happiness at times. I caressed my babies and my husband to express love, and also my parents in their last illnesses, and tried to lighten their load, because I loved them. My hands helped babies learn to walk, and delivered their first solid foods. They detected fevers, soothed lame shoulders, rubbed away cramps, scratched itchy backs, and smoothed brows of sick or weary children until sleep came. I pray that my hands do not fail me

5

any further now that they are old. A mother's hands should never stop serving, but go on, and on, and on. I say, "Once a mother, always a mother"—then hopefully a grandmother, even a great-grandmother.

Everything I have accomplished in my long life pales in comparison to my highest calling. Above all, I am a mother. A mother needs her hands!

We Had "Nothing"...
Or Is It We Had "Everything but Money"?

"Mama! Mama! Brubba 'fat-bellied' me again!"
Barely out of diapers, I was learning early one of the facts of life—namely that brothers like to tease their little sisters. Guy was more than two years older than I, and just delighted in my consistent response. Sometimes it was "Mama, Brubba 'chatterboxed' me!" When we were a little older, he once chased me all around the yard, holding a short wire that he told me he had charged with electricity. I didn't have much of a temper, but that time I remember swearing, cursing him. I was so angry, and more than a little scared—afraid that he really could give me a shock! Cursing Guy that time was very unusual, and was because I had been pushed beyond my limit. Our parents trained us well, especially not to swear. My brother even became a Baptist minister, now retired.

I was born in 1930. That year our country was deep into the Great Depression, and many people were suffering. The whole country was crushed, beaten down, on its knees, at rock bottom. There were no jobs available. Many people who had money lost it when the stock market tanked and the banks closed.

My parents had been married nearly five years. Dad's father had died young, at the age of 45. Dad was fresh out of high school at the time, and as the oldest son, he was in charge of the farm, his mother, a younger sister and brother, and a cousin who lived with them after her parents died.

My mother naturally wanted to have a home of their own when they married, but for several years they lived either with Gram, Dad's mother for whom he always felt strong responsibility, or in a two-room house or camp across the road on the property, where I was born. My brother and I find it humorous these days, trying to figure out when and why we lived with Gram while Unk and Aunt Viola lived in the little house, and then the other way around. Gram was a good woman, and so was Mom, and they never quarreled. They loved each other their whole lives, but there was that fact of life concerning two women working in the same kitchen…

Dad built a small three-room house with two porches about a mile away soon after I was born, even though he had little knowledge of or experience with carpentry. He didn't finish off the interior. There was no insulation, or inside walls, or finished ceilings. There was a low-ceiling attic, but no basement. The house sat on posts. My brother and I wonder about this, too. Did Gram own that land where he built the house? Was it because of the depression that he didn't finish off the house and move in? In any case, we continued living on Gram's farm and rented the new place to a family who had no place to live, until I was five, possibly six, and in school.

Before I was born, my father decided to study for the ministry. He stayed with his sister in Boston and worked at "The Spa" while attending Gordon College. My mother and brother stayed with him at least part of the time. He had three semesters finished when he realized the odds were against him. The Great Depression was crippling the whole land, and he and Mom both came down with scarlet fever. A second child was on the way—me. He left college and went back to the farm.

Guy and I grew up in a close extended family near our cousins, Arlene and Melva, until I was 11, in 1941, when the next chapter of our lives began. There were a few other children in the neighborhood. The Damren family lived in the little house where I was born, and Alta and Jerry played with us. Harold Towle lived less than a half mile away. Alta, Jerry, Harold, and I were in the same class at school.

Of my earliest years I have few memories. Mostly I remember living on Gram's farm, and playing with our cousins. We ate berries from the bushes, and pulled rhubarb and chewed on it, and we four cousins often played in the barn. Sometimes we jumped into the loose hay from a slightly higher loft. I remember feeling as if I were flying, and almost believed I could! One day we decided to climb on the ladder to the top loft. We all made it up okay, but when we got ready to come down, I panicked and just couldn't step off the edge of the loft onto the nearly top rung of that ladder and descend, as the other three had done. When they saw my predicament, they went to the house and got Mom and Gram, who both climbed the ladder (as I remember it) and coaxed me to climb down while Mom held onto me. I have always remembered the lesson she pointed out to me after my scare. She said, "You should always think before you do something like that, about how you are going to get out of it!" I guess "Look before you leap" would sum it up.

I have a vivid memory of the summer day we were playing out in back of the barn and a bee got caught under my dress and stung me on my stomach. I guess that must have been my first experience with bees and hornets, as I remember the horror of the awful pain and how unbearable it seemed.

Yet another time we were playing around an old car that was abandoned at the back of the property. Somehow my finger got shut in the door, which was old and rusty. I couldn't get my finger out because the door wouldn't open. Again the kids ran to the house and got the womenfolk to come to my rescue. It seemed like a very long time before they came, and actually it was, under those painful circumstances.

Then there was the cold morning that I was out on the porch and picked up a frost-covered hammer and innocently put my lips and tongue on it. Of course it froze to my mouth immediately, and my mother, with Gram's help, had to swab it repeatedly with a hot wet washcloth before the heavy hammer could be removed with a minimum amount of blood but a maximum amount of crying—mine!

I stuttered quite badly, and I remember well the uncomfortable stress of trying to get those certain sounds out of my mouth. It was a problem for years, and caused me a lot of embarrassment and pain. When I was called on to stand by my desk and read in school, I would look at the book with dread to see what sounds I was going to have to start with, as that was the hardest part. Sometimes it was okay, but there were some letters that were more difficult than others. The letter D at the start of a word gave me problems for years. My mother finally helped me to outgrow it, over several years, by singing the words whenever I was where I could do that.

These may seem like bad memories, but I mostly had very happy times. My mother was very warm and loving. She sang to me and with me, read to me, and called me her "little sunshine when it rains." How many mothers today clean their children's fingernails before school? Ours did. She told me that she said a prayer every morning when we went to school, and that she would not dare to send us off otherwise. When I was young, I had platinum-blond, almost-curly hair, and she tried to coax it into Shirley Temple curls, not too successfully. If we were sick, she tended us, applied poultices, warmed a flannel cloth for the chest by the open oven door, and applied Vicks VapoRub. I can almost feel the comfort of that warmth. To take out a splinter, a needle was sterilized by holding it against the hot stove. A cut would require iodine, but we much preferred mercurochrome, because it didn't sting! Gram used to tell us, "No sting, no cure!" We had nothing for sore throats or coughing. Mom mixed sugar and butter to soothe the throat. I loved it, but oh, the fat and calories!

Gram, too, provided comfort for her grandchildren. She had lost her youngest child at the age of four, after an appendectomy. After her husband died at the age of 45, she made the statement that she would never again complain about little things. I guess such bereavement puts things in perspective. As a very young child, I would sit on her lap and she would rock as she sang or chanted, "Wizshy-boo, wizshy-boo, wizshy-boo-boo." Her signature crooning was as effective and soothing as any lullaby, and all of us grandchildren remember it. Her lap was a loving and safe place for a child to be.

It was great when Dad's sister, Aunt Hazel, with Uncle Paul, would arrive from Cape Cod for a visit. Such a trip took all day back then. Pauline and Carolyn Story were our younger Massachusetts cousins, four and nine years younger than I. Their ages more nearly matched those of Arlene's and Melva's younger brothers, Alton and Gary.

The Judkins family was a close family. Gram, and Aunt Hazel, Dad, and Unk and their families laughed and told stories to the delight of us children. We would sometimes load into the back of Unk's truck for a trip to Westport Island, where they had grown up, for clams and crabs and a glorious picnic. We could dig the clams ourselves. There were other times that we had the seafood feasts at home.

We had a room called the milk room, which stayed cooler because it was on the north side of the house. Most always, a salt cod fish hung on the back of that door. Sometimes we kids would strip off a piece and eat it raw when no one was looking. Cooked, it made wonderful fish hash.

We were still living at Gram's when I started school. Arlene was one year and Guy was two years older than I. Like most five-year-olds, I felt very eager to be going to school, yet very nervous. After all, I had new clothes and a new lunch box and pencil case. Guy and I waited for the bus that morning under the maple tree, with Arlene. When the bus came along, the driver took a look at me and told my mom, "Sub-primary kids don't go until next week!" (That's what kindergarten was called then.) You can imagine my disappointment as my brother and cousin boarded the bus, and I went back to the house to wait another week. I had screwed up my courage for nothing!

I enjoyed school more than a lot of children do. I always wanted to do the right thing, and I tried hard to get good grades. I was always—and I still am—a basically shy person. I am uncomfortable to be in the spotlight. In school I often blushed when called upon to recite. For one thing, we had to stand when the teacher called on us, whether or not we knew the answer. I had the kind of intelligence needed to do well in school, but I never thought I was better than anyone else just because of my good grades.

It was important to me to do well, though, and I spent time checking over my homework to find errors that I didn't want the teacher to find. I never got over blushing. When Mom would visit school, which mothers did some in those days, I was so embarrassed. She and a friend would observe in our classroom most of the day and go home with us on the bus. The teacher would call on me often, to be polite. I wasn't embarrassed about Mom, but just because I was on the spot as her daughter. I suppose the basis of shyness is lack of self-confidence.

When I started school in Belgrade, Maine, we had three grades in each classroom. Before lunch each day, Miss Williams, teacher of the youngest children, marched us with our towels in a double line down to the basement, where the bathrooms were located, to take care of necessities, and especially to wash our hands. On Monday, we each brought in a clean towel from home and kept it in our desk all week, hopefully remembering to take it home for laundering on Friday.

My grandfather Tozier, my mother's father, was ill at his house in New Portland that first year I was in school. After Christmas, my mother and I went up to visit them so she could help care for him. Wouldn't you know, I came down with measles while there! They took my temperature with a glass thermometer on which, in my childish ignorance, I bit down. It broke! I think my mother was more worried that we had broken something of theirs of value, than about whether I had swallowed any of the mercury! Probably she didn't realize the danger. Meanwhile, back home, Guy and Arlene were having measles at Gram's house, and they, too, were very sick.

I enjoyed our visits to New Portland throughout my childhood. I especially enjoyed their wind-up record player (Victrola) and great collection of records. Once I broke one of the records and felt so bad that I just could not admit that it was I who did it. Another time I put on my best dress and danced for everyone to the music of one of the records. I had made up some fancy, although repetitious, little clogging steps. I wonder now how I had the courage to do such a thing!

For years we looked forward each week to when Carl Carter would drive up the road in his big old truck, on his route through surrounding towns selling fresh vegetables, fruits, candy, etc. Thursday was a big day for us, hoping Mom would be able to spare a couple of pennies for candy for us. We liked best the so-called Monkey Shines. They were two little kisses and a small trinket or toy, wrapped up like a candy bar. Carl was a farmer, a big man, a nice man, who stuttered badly. I can hear him now, when asked about the price of bananas, how he would stammer out, "F-four p-pounds for a quarter." After I married and moved to the Litchfield Road in Farmingdale, I discovered that Carl and his family lived on our road, only a mile or two away.

It was a different world when I was a child. Very few people during the depression had luxuries or conveniences. Much of what people have today hadn't even been invented. I often wonder how we got along without Scotch tape and Kleenex, plastic bags and paper towels! We had no electricity or indoor plumbing, microwave, radio, TV, or telephone for most of those years. The outdoor toilet was the norm for rural families. The use of often decorative chamber pots, pails, or "thunder jugs"—whatever you want to call them—by women and children at night required the daily added housekeeping chore of emptying and cleaning them. They were a fixture under every bed. Down in the shed, in our "outdoor" privy, we nearly always had real toilet paper, but at my grandparents' house in New Portland, they had an old Sears Roebuck or Montgomery Ward catalog. The paper was not at all absorbent, but crinkling it up before use improved it. Sometimes they had corncobs, old and dried, instead. They didn't have "two-holers," but four or five seats, some sawed out to fit a child's anatomy, some an adult's size.

"Use it up, wear it out, make it do, or do without!" was the motto. We saved everything, including string and rags. We had a rag bag, and a man came around to buy any that we had collected. We never threw away anything that had any value. It was a way of life, and such roots run deep. I still save my leftovers to make an appearance a second time on the table.

My parents drank coffee only once a week, on Sunday morning, during the bad times. (Guy remembers it as twice a year, and maybe that was true for a while.) We children were allowed a cup occasionally, too, probably diluted a bit. The rest of the time they drank water, milk if they wanted, and quite a lot of tea. A teabag was never discarded after making just one cup. The second cup was almost as strong, if you steeped it longer. I still do that once in a while, not out of necessity, as in those depression times; it's just that ingrained habits die hard, if ever. I still hate to waste anything.

The use of kerosene lamps required the weekly filling, washing of the "globes" or "chimneys" of the lamps, and trimming the wicks straight across for an even flame. That was often my Saturday job. If we needed warm water it was heated on the woodstove. Telephoning, only if very important, was done at a neighbor's. The weekly ironing was done by heating three or more flatirons (*made* of iron!) on the woodstove, using one until it was too cool, then putting it back to heat again and using a hot one.

Our first radio was a car radio, acquired in the late 1930s, and set up with a car battery in the house. We listened sometimes as a family, and possession of a radio made us feel truly rich. I remember listening to several of the late-afternoon soap operas like *Stella Dallas*, *Lorenzo Jones*, *When a Girl Marries*, and *Ma Perkins*. Evenings or Sundays brought *The Jack Benny Show*, *Fibber Magee and Molly*, *The Green Hornet*, and *The Shadow*. These are only a few of the more wholesome shows on in those days.

My father carried water for us in two pails from our spring, quite a long hike, summer and winter. In the winter, a path had to be shoveled after each storm, and it was slippery going; in the summer, the mosquitoes were terrible. The water was good. He built a cover over the spring to keep out foreign material. The spring was in a bog, and if a storm washed surface water into it we had to boil the drinking water to purify it. I well remember the taste of that boiled water!

The two pails of water sat on the shelf at the edge of the rectangular iron sink, and the dipper hung on the end of the cupboard over them. There was a wash dish that stayed in the sink. Water was saved and reused whenever possible; its final use might be to water plants.

A container of eggshells, soaked a long time in warm water in the kitchen stove warming oven, would serve as fertilizer for the indoor plants.

Washday, every Monday, required extra water and extra trips to the spring. Water was heated in a big copper boiler on top of the stove. Some clothes were boiled on the stove before the washing. The clothes were scrubbed on a washboard, then put through a wringer cranked by hand, into a big tub of cold water, rinsed, then put through the wringer again. They were hung outdoors in all kinds of weather. As children, we found some humor in bringing in clothes off the line that were frozen stiff into their hanging shapes! (My father's union suit comes to mind.) Clothes were usually ironed, or else "aired" near the stove, before being put away. Unk made the joke that Gram wouldn't let anyone use even a washcloth unless it had been aired!

Living near a bog, we could not go out after dark because the mosquitoes were so thick all summer long. Inside the house, as you looked out the windows in the evening, the window screens were just black with mosquitoes parked there, hoping to get into the house. As it was sometimes necessary to open a door at night, they would get in and be thick enough to require that my father spray the rooms to kill the bloodthirsty critters before we tried to sleep. I don't know what that spray did to my parents' health (they both died rather young of cancer), but my brother and I were instructed to pull our sheets over our heads and not breathe the spray for the first few minutes. We are still alive at ages 90 and 92!

We had no car during much of the depression, but would borrow Unk's or great-uncle Steve's, though not too often. Unk was good about picking us kids up and going for a ride, which often resulted in a treat—an ice cream cone or penny candy. I don't remember how we got groceries. I do know that we ran up a grocery bill at Gowell's store, at which, out of the goodness of his heart, George Gowell somehow managed to keep a lot of people in town from going hungry during the depression. Dad paid him back every penny as soon as he could.

Farmers were better off than some others during the depression, since they could grow a lot of food in their gardens. Canning preserved it for year-round insurance. Many had meat, too, from their own livestock or from hunting.

One day the census taker came in and asked a lot of questions. It must have been in 1940, when conditions across the country had improved a lot. One question was, "How often does your family eat meat?" I clearly remember my mother answering, "About once a week." Of course, she cooked everything with salt pork, or sometimes bacon ends, which she didn't count as meat, and we had plenty of eggs and an occasional chicken to roast. When we lived on Gram's farm (before 1936), there had been pigs or beef creatures slaughtered for a supply of meat. Later there were beef neck meat or flank, beef tongue or heart, hot dogs, fish "muddle," fish tongues-and-cheeks, and lots of Saturday night baked beans. All country folk that we knew had Boston baked beans every Saturday night, cooked all day in the woodstove oven. They were served again Sunday morning. The pork would be cold then, and the fat pork was consumed as desired. I loved it, and would still eat it if I didn't know better. The beans were brought out a third time for Monday noon, since that was washday with no time to fix a big meal. We had three hearty meals most days, which we referred to as breakfast, dinner, and supper.

Dad had a specialty that he cooked once in a while. It called for lamb as the meat, and it had rice and onions. He called it something funny—maybe "slumgullion."

One year, we raised a batch of ducks. Their eggs were large and rich, and the ducks were good eating, too, when their turn came.

A neighbor "loaned" us a cow for the summer after we left the farm. Since we had no barn, she was hitched to a post in the ground, where she could eat the grass. (No need for a lawn mower down back!) She was milked outdoors. Earlier, we'd gotten milk from Gram's or Unk's cow.

My father always raised a big garden involving a staggering amount of work before crops were ready, and my mother canned hundreds of quarts of the produce. I am amazed when I think of the labor involved in that, but we had vegetables every day all year, and some fruit, too.

Canning was done in hot summer weather, of course. My father would pick the vegetables in the morning before work. We kids might help shuck the corn, shell the peas, snap the green beans, or prepare the tomatoes. Once in the glass jars, with the kitchen woodstove stoked to its hottest and the canning kettle ready, the produce was duly processed in that boiling-hot kitchen for two hours or so, according to the prevailing instructions of the times. Most things were canned in quart jars, or sometimes two-quart jars, and some in pints. The canner held seven quarts at a time.

During the depression, jobs were very scarce, and people were lucky to find any work. Unk had his own truck and got a job working on the roads. A few men were hired to work with him, and my father was one. Sanding the roads in the winter was one of his jobs. He would stand in the truck body on the load of sand and throw out shovelfuls behind the truck, or ahead of the truck if they were going downhill. It was very hard work. Pay was 35 cents an hour, which for a 48-hour week came to $16.80, not exactly a living wage, but certainly helpful for those times. The trouble was he seldom got a full week of work! The jobs had to be shared by several men, to spread around a small amount of money. If he was called out in the middle of a cold stormy night to clear some roads, two hours would bring in 70 cents! That meager job was what we had for income throughout the 1930s.

For a bit extra, my mother did make butter once my father had built a small tie-up where he kept a cow or two. Churning the cream to make the butter was another job on which we children helped. Cream was skimmed off the milk and poured into the churn. We children often turned the crank of the churn. When that was done, Mom rinsed the butter well with cold water on a kneading board, added salt, and pressed the butter into a mold. It sold for about 35 cents a pound, as I remember. There was a saying, the origin of which I don't know: "Go easy on the butter, boys, it's forty cents a pound!" Whether the cream had been sweet or sour, the butter was good. So was the buttermilk. So was the cottage cheese, made from the skimmed milk after it had turned "bonny-clabber" (had soured and formed curds.) It was set on the back of the stove to cook very slowly. Every bit of the milk was used.

Due to a childhood experience, Dad had an unusual fear of fire, and didn't want to build barns and outbuildings too near (or attached to) a house. He always wanted to build a nice house across the road from our "temporary" home, where there was an old cellar hole and foundation. He really wanted to own a dairy farm. Looking toward the future, and hoping to have a house there, he built his small barn across the road, at quite a distance, and walked to it to tend the animals.

Because of that fear of fire, he would get up and get dressed when a thunder shower came close, no matter what time of night it was. Sometimes in the daytime we would all go sit in the car for safety during a close shower, as the house had no lightning rods.

He put up a swing for us near the future house, which I enjoyed a lot. I also spent time watching the hens and chicks that he kept near the barn. They are such quaint little animals!

Dad never did build that new house, but did get as far as digging a trench to the tie-up from another spring higher up on a hill, farther on beyond the barn, and laying pipe for watering the cows by gravity feed. He also dug a hole near the house foundation where plumbing would hopefully eventually enter the house.

Life for a little farm girl back then was far different from the busy life of a youngster today. I often took walks, sometimes alone as I got older, over in the field to the brook, or in the winter to the area where the brook spread out and froze, where I would skate. We also skated on the lakes, sometimes at night with many others, with the light and warmth of a big bonfire. I only remember doing that a couple of times, probably when I was older.

I played with my dolls and my doll carriage. I had a cat that would submit once in a while to being dressed in doll clothes and to riding in my doll carriage. I also liked paper dolls. When Guy and I played together, we might pretend that marbles were people, and a matchbox or small Velveeta cheese box would be their car. They had great imaginary adventures. One year, we each built "cars" big enough to sit on but without mobility. We had no wheels or much of anything to resemble vehicles. Mostly they were just a couple of different-sized boxes with a stick for a gear shift. Imagination had to play a big part. Eventually we owned a cart, skates, skis, and sleds. Dad built Guy's sled, and mine was from a "secondhand store." We had hand-me-downs, and Christmas presents. I wasn't good at any of the sports. I enjoyed skating, anyway, and would pretend that I was Sonja Henie, a famous skater/actress at the time. I would get very frustrated with my skis and call them "old sticks!" We built snow forts and snow tunnels, and of course snowmen. We drew pictures by lamplight sometimes, on brown paper bags cut open and spread out. There was no money for drawing paper. We treasured books.

Our dad had some standard tools in the shed. There were often scrap pieces of wood around, and we were allowed to use any bent nails that he had discarded, to make things. We pounded on bent nails to straighten them enough so that we could make whatever we decided on. I made a couple of wooden dolls which were very rudimentary. I had a great time walking on stilts that I had made for myself. I got pretty good both at making them and walking on them.

18

I mentioned that our house was not finished off into rooms. We had curtains hung where walls would be, to provide some privacy. Guy had asked an important question all children come up against, about a certain jolly fat man in a red suit. My mother told him she would talk with him that night after I went to sleep. I overheard her say that, so I was determined to stay awake and listen. I pretended to be asleep and got an earful through the curtains! I didn't let on, but played the Christmas game through two more Christmases. I was only six. They also talked about other things that night that he was curious about, but which didn't make much sense to me at that age.

My mother had meningitis in 1938. We didn't know what it was for many years, until a doctor told her in later life that she had had it earlier. We only knew that she was very sick. She was bedridden for five months. Gram stayed with us a lot, but she had not begun visiting around with her children, so still had her own home to take care of. It's odd, but I don't have many memories of life being very different then, so Dad must have taken pretty good care of us. I did cook a little, as in getting my own breakfast, and I did dishes sometimes. A couple of Mom's friends came in a few times to help out. One of them, Teeny Damren, was a fun-loving sort. She did the laundry and put starch in Dad's shorts to be funny! Elsie Greene spent the day, and had me practice my sewing. I was only eight. She made me take out a whole line of stitching in a quilt I was attempting to make (but never finished) and do it over. I didn't think my sewing was that bad, and I hoped she wouldn't come again! Mom's old country doctor, Dr. Williams, who called on her a very few times, could not diagnose her trouble. He said she had a nervous breakdown, and he wanted her to gain back her strength. He advised her to take whiskey medicinally. She could hardly bring herself to follow his advice, as she had never tolerated having any liquor in the house. She looked upon drinking as a sin. Finally Dad got her a bottle of whiskey, of which she took just one teaspoonful in a glass of water three times a day! She was absolutely mortified when a man (a friend) came in to visit us and the whiskey bottle was sitting on her bedside table! She wasn't well for several years, but nerves and her age were both part of the problem.

Since there were no vitamin pills, we kids were given cod liver oil in the winter if there was money to buy it. That was so hard to swallow that we followed it with a spoonful of shredded coconut to take away the taste. To this day, when I eat coconut I taste cod liver oil! In the spring, folks commonly took sulfur and molasses. That didn't taste as bad as it sounds. I wonder how much good it did as a tonic.

There was plenty of work to be done in country homes in those times, and we kids had our regular chores. One was to bring in wood from the woodshed to the wood box, carrying it up a good flight of stairs and across the back porch to the kitchen. Guy did it regularly, and I did it at times.

Another was to do simple chores in the garden. Potato bugs were a problem every year, and we would carry a little jar of kerosene and knock the bugs off into the jars. That is not very interesting work, but it would perk up near the tomatoes when I'd come face to face with one of those huge, fat, ugly, green tomato worms with black horns!

We had to help with the haying, and I still hate the extreme heat of those torrid summer days. I also found the itchy hay and chaff very uncomfortable. Going swimming afterward, or having some home-made root beer, chilled in the cool water of the spring (remember, no refrigerator), were worthwhile rewards. I remember the awful taste of the "switchell" Dad sometimes made to drink in hot weather. It was made with molasses and ginger in water, and I think he added vinegar! It was vile, and I never drank it. He thought it helped in hot weather when a person was working hard and sweating a lot.

When haying season arrived, Dad would mow the hay with the mowing machine, sometimes with Mom's help. Although she never got a driver's license, she could drive the car or tractor on the farm (nervously). He would make sure dogs and cats were safe in the house, to avoid cutting off any pets' feet. After the hay dried, we would rake it. I enjoyed riding on the hay rake when it was my turn to do it. He had positioned a post to serve as something to hold onto to keep us from falling off. The big C-shaped tines would rise up when I kicked the lever and let go of their collection, leaving long rows of hay. Later, Dad and Guy scooped the windrows into individual stacks, ready to load on the rack. Guy and I would build the load in the hayrack, moving each of Dad's forkfuls to an appropriate spot, and then tread it. The hay had to be dry to ensure good quality hay free of mold, and to prevent spontaneous combustion in the barn. Not having a regular barn, Dad built his hay into a haystack.

I can still see my mother's tortured red face as she worked, too. She tried valiantly, but reacted badly to the conditions, especially the heat; but we all had to keep on in order to get the hay in before the next thunderstorm appeared in the west. It was all hands on deck for various farm jobs year round!

We had an ice cream freezer, the kind where you pack ice or snow and salt around the inside container and turn the crank for a long time until the ice cream is frozen. In the early years, there was ice in the sawdust in the silo in Gram's barn all year long. Later, we made ice cream only with snow and salt. The best part may have been licking off the dasher. I remember those pains between the eyes— the brain freeze—from the extreme cold of delicious homemade ice cream.

My mother must have baked biscuits every day. We always had them available. She took pride, though, in using bakery bread for our school lunches. Poor children would be more likely to bring home-made biscuits for lunch. So she would put the card in the window to signal the Nissen or Harris or Cushman driver that she wanted him to stop. Her biscuits were good, though. Like potatoes, they were often eaten three times a day. Occasionally on a Sunday night, after a big noon meal, we would have hot biscuits with butter, and molasses poured over them, for supper, with a big glass of milk. There might be applesauce or a canned fruit, too. Homemade desserts were always available. Cookies were usually molasses, oatmeal, hermits, or sugar cookies. Cakes were not frosted unless for company. Our choices were sugar cake, spice, chocolate, or gingerbread. I just loved the chocolate cake with cream poured over it! Remember, we had a cow, and that meant not only milk, but also cream. Yum! We had pies and puddings, too. My father liked suet pudding—yes, actually made with suet!

In the late summer that I was ten, my folks were working over in the field across the road one day, and Gram was at our house. I had an old bicycle—I don't remember where I got it—and was riding it up the road. At that time, there was little traffic on our country road. As I rode back toward the house, I hit the sand at the edge of the road, and the bike twisted and threw me off face first onto the tarred surface of the road. I must have passed out, and when I came to, blood was oozing from a gash on my very sore nose. The bicycle wheel and frame were bent, so I had to walk the bike home, limping and hurting with other gashes on my arms and legs. Gram saw me come in. She went across the road and waved down my folks, and then mopped me up. My nose was broken. Doctors were not called in those times unless death's door opened, so it healed in time by itself; but my mother did often rub down over my nose to be sure it was healing straight. Didn't *that* hurt! I've had the scar ever since, but it doesn't show under my glasses.

For recreation women sometimes spent a day with a friend or neighbor, sister or mother. Going for a car ride was another relatively inexpensive way to get away for a while. On a Sunday, Dad would sometimes take his mother and us for a leisurely ride, when a car was available. One such time, when I was a baby, the car stalled on railroad tracks. Lo and behold, a train was coming! Dad and Gram hurried out of the front seats, and Dad took Guy out of the back. My mother, still sitting in the backseat, was passing me out to Dad when the train went by—on the other set of tracks! That was a close call!

We went to New Portland only occasionally, some forty miles away, to visit my mother's family. We kids loved their feather beds, an old Edison phonograph, a modern wind-up Victrola, and their collection of records. My grandmother made the best baked beans and yeast rolls in the world! There were uncles and aunts and cousins there, too. Living on a farm, they had barn cats, with lots of kittens each year. Once, we each brought home a kitten, and those pets were important in our lives. We had cats during most of our childhood.

Quite often, if the weather was good on a summer Sunday, we went for a walk in our woods. These were very pleasant times, as Dad was relaxed and not weighed down with his heavy workload. Work was his life. He didn't cut corners, but just kept on plugging with whatever had to be done. He seldom had anyone other than us to help him. Talk about having a work ethic, he personified it! Whatever work he did was never shoddy, even if he considered it temporary. "Whatever is worth doing is worth doing well!" But Sundays were special.

One trip through the woods was not very enjoyable for me. Our cow had managed to get out of the pasture, as sometimes happens, and daylight was fading. Dad called us children and our dog, Trixie, to come along, and we circled up through the woods where Dad thought she had likely gone. This walk was different: I was barefoot! Dad hadn't noticed, and I hadn't told him. The going was rough! I got scratched up some, and bruised on a few sharp rocks, but no real damage was done, except to my comfort. Memory fails me now, but I suppose we found the cow.

When I was nine or ten, Gram developed diabetes. She had always been a somewhat stout but healthy woman who was seldom sick. She had to learn to give herself two shots of insulin each morning, one in the arm and one in the leg. Probably these days she would have been able to take oral medication and watch her diet and avoid those injections. There was no choice back then—she had to take the insulin. She could do the leg by herself, by pinching the flesh with one hand and administering the injection with the other. When it came to the arm, she needed an extra hand, and one of us kids usually pinched up the flesh while she gave herself the shot. By that time in her life, she was "visiting around" with her three children instead of living alone on the farm, and she was with us a lot. She was given eight all-day menus, which she followed religiously, weighing out to the gram every morsel and not cheating! Oh, once in a great while, since there were foods that she liked a lot that were not included on her menus, she would help herself to a sample from our food with the comment, "I'll just have a piece as big as a mouse's ear!" We tried not to eat treats in front of her, since she couldn't have them.

Soon after that, my parents thought *I* had developed diabetes. Diabetics then did not have glucose meters as they do now, but instead they had to test a small sample of urine each day. We placed a test tube in a dish of water on the stove, the tube containing about an inch of urine, and measured drops of a blue chemical solution called

Benedict's Solution (or was it the other way around?) and boiled it for a certain length of time. If the solution remained blue, there was no sugar in the urine, but if it turned any of several shades of green, sugar was present and the diet or amount of insulin had to be changed. The rest of us tested to see if we might have diabetes, and I showed positive! For probably two years, they deprived me of sweets, until a doctor told them that a blood test was the only way to diagnose the disease, and that I was not diabetic! Good news indeed! I had been limited to half a Dixie cup of ice cream at a time, probably a quarter cup, and that not often. Sometimes, if the family was having ice cream, I would choose a different treat, like stuffed olives, since I did like them. When my urine test had turned green that first time, it was the Christmas season, and we had more money by then so we had candy and goodies. Maybe that was an actual wake-up call anyway, because in my adult years I developed the disease. I may have been pre-diabetic all my life, and I always loved candy and other sweets and ate a lot of them! I had terrible eating habits.

After Gram developed diabetes, Dad made regular trips to Waterville to the larger grocery stores every week when she was staying with us. There were special foods on her menu which were not usually served on our table, and he saw that she got them. He must have been making a little more money by then, because I remember he would often take Guy and me to the Opera House Theater in Waterville for whatever movie was playing. We called it going to the pictures, or to a picture show.

I'm sure movies only cost a few cents then, and they did not need letter codes to warn parents about inappropriate content for children. They were sometimes violent, but were screened for language and such. Even actors who played married couples in the movies (and in sitcoms in the early days of TV) did not share a bed—they had twin beds! Ah, those were the good old days! Dad very much enjoyed the serial movie that would go on week after week, always leaving the hero in a hair-raising situation at the end of every episode.

After the movie, if he had a few cents in his pocket, he would buy hot dogs for us. They cost a dime each, as I remember, or was it a nickel? We never asked, but just waited to see if this was a week when we could have them. The vendor had a cart not far from the theater. The hot dogs had fried crumbs of salt pork on them, in addition to whatever we wanted for condiments. I can still almost taste them! Ever since those treats, if I want a very special hot dog at home (not very often!), I add crumbled bacon to take the place of that salt pork. Salt pork was a staple then, but I never buy it now, even to bake beans. How times have changed!

We did not have the things that cost too much. I envied our friend and neighbor, Alta, because she sometimes brought American cheese sandwiches to school for lunch. Some of the kids at school had Whoopie pies (which we called chocolate cream sandwiches) to snack on. They looked so good! When Aunt Hazel and Uncle Paul would bring oranges or bananas for their girls when they came to visit, if I saw them, I just wanted to taste them—so badly. Such tropical fruits were out of our reach for a few years. Having apples, tomatoes, and plums, we got vitamin C, but more would have been better. Our father and mother both labored long and hard to provide garden produce for us and to preserve plenty for our winter meals. My point is that we seldom had treats, but never went hungry.

As I said, the house Dad built, in which we lived from 1936 (we'll say) until July 6, 1941, was not finished off. The floors were cold, since there was no foundation, but he banked the house with boughs, sawdust, and/or snow. We did not suffer from the cold. The wood fire in the kitchen stove was allowed to go out overnight, but the parlor stove in the living room held large chunks of wood that would usually last all night. There were times that Dad would get up and stoke the living room stove and start the kitchen fire early. He always fired up the kitchen stove before the rest of us got up, but it would take a while to warm up the house. I got pretty good at doing most of the process of getting dressed in the mornings—under the bedcovers! No, we did not suffer from the cold.

We always changed our clothes when we got home from school to keep them clean and new longer. We had school clothes and home or play clothes. Probably I would have three, four, or possibly five good outfits, but Mom always felt bad that she could not provide me with new clothes every new semester, which she thought the other girls had. One year, when I was about eight, her sister-in-law, Aunt Pearl, made three new dresses for me. I can remember them still! We had appropriate clothes for the cold, snowy weather—always! Our clothes might be old and mended—even patched—but they were always clean and ironed.

By today's standards of comparison we did have "nothing," yet we had everything we needed. We had food, clothing, and shelter. We never went hungry, and Dad's efforts kept us warm. Our parents tried to provide healthy food. In the 1930s, these were good hearty foods, paired with the physical work most people performed daily that worked off the calories. Our lack of red meat probably was a good thing, since we had other sources of protein.

We had parents who loved us and tried to bring us up to be good Christians. They had admirable values and did all they could for us. They taught us things we would need to know, and they did things with us. They sacrificed their own comforts for us whenever they saw a need. Those were hard times, but instead of "nothing," we had a great deal. We had all we needed, except for money. I would even say we had a surplus of the things that count!

Field of Memories

It was not a special field; it had no wheat waving in the breeze or other claim to beauty or fame. Actually, it could hardly even produce a decent crop of hay. It was the long field next to the house where we lived when I was a child in the 1930s.

The end of the field nearest the house was where Dad planted his big garden, and Mom canned enough produce to last all winter. It meant a lot of work—spring, summer, and fall—and my brother and I were assigned tasks with which we could help. One necessary job that we could do found us walking down a garden row holding a tin can with a little kerosene in it. With a small stick in the other hand, we would knock the potato beetles off the plants and into the can. You never heard the term "organic gardening" back then, but I guess we would have passed the test. However, when it came to those ugly, fat, green tomato worms, someone else had to take care of them, not me! Just looking at them gave me the heebie-jeebies. It still does.

Anyone who has never had the pleasure of eating pie made with wild field strawberries—or strawberry shortcake with flaky biscuits or cake topped with sweet wild berries and real whipped cream—has missed out on a delicious treat. I don't know whether those beautiful cultivated berries were available in stores back then, but they were not to us, anyway, because of the tight budget necessary in the depression years. So, when the field berries were ripe, my brother and I headed for the bounty in our field, each carrying a small bucket—a lard bucket, I think we called it. We found the best spot for picking, and settled in. Picking enough for a family of four takes a while because the berries are so small. When one of us had picked enough to cover the bottom of the pail, we would shout to the other, "I've got my bottom covered!" Then we would laugh and giggle at our daring joke. Hulling the little berries takes about as long as picking them. We helped on that, too. When we reaped the tasty reward at suppertime, the tedious work was forgotten.

The third product the field yielded was frogs! Of course frogs may not commonly be a commodity for sale, but for a year or two ours were. We lived near a village where tourists came in the summer. Many of them were fishermen, so they needed bait. It was my brother's project, but as long as I could help by catching frogs, I could have some of the profits. I got pretty good at it. There were a lot of them in our field, possibly because it bordered a bog. I must have been too young to understand exactly what was going to happen to the cute little green-with-black-polka-dots frogs once the fishermen had bought them, or I probably would have resigned my job in horror. But ignorance is bliss, and I was thrilled to have enough money to buy something I wanted—a doll carriage.

Our family cats and our dog, Trixie, are buried on the knoll in that field. Our pets were very important in our young lives. We children each had our own kitten. Since we lived in the country, the animals stayed outdoors a lot. In the morning, after Dad got up, he would open the back door when it was time for us kids to rise and shine, and the two cats would race into the house. My brother's cat would jump up on his bed, and my cat would come to my bed, both of them purring happily.

For just a plain old field, this one is extra-prolific in precious memories of times gone by.

Courage in Hard Times—My Dad

Whenever I think of my father, I remember first his strong work ethic, which stands out in his remarkable character. The man worked from dawn to dark during his whole adult life, except on Sunday. He worked alone mostly, the exceptions involving my mother nervously driving the tractor while he manned the accompanying rig, or vice versa. We children also played our part, especially at times like haying season.

Like Atlas, my father assumed the weight of his world at the age of 19, when his father died suddenly. As the oldest son, he accepted his role as head of the family. From that day until his mother's death at age 69, he was considerate of her needs and her comfort.

When my father and mother were married, he brought his bride to his mother's home. Dad built a small house about a mile away a few years later. He had little experience as a carpenter, but still he did it all himself. That was in the early years of the Great Depression. Building that house should have given them a home of their own, but the trouble was, he couldn't finish the house off inside. I guess he ran out of money, the depression being in full swing. It was late 1935 or 1936 that we finally moved in, with the house still not finished.

There were no walls between the rooms, just the studs, and heavy curtains took the place of walls. The absence of insulation, wallboard, or sheetrock meant that visible frost formed on the inside of the house along the boards that, with the outside shingles, were our only protection from the cold. Dad banked the house as soon as snow came, to keep the cold air from coming up under the building, which had no basement but sat on posts. We had a wood-burning cookstove in the kitchen, and a wood-burning parlor stove in the living room, which kept us warm. Dad stoked the fires as needed, often getting up in the middle of the night to take care of his family's comfort.

Country folk, who burned wood for fuel, knew the truth of the old saying that wood warms you more than once. Trees are cut down, logs hauled out of the woods and sawed to lengths to fit the stoves; those chunks are split, the wood stacked carefully to dry, and then armloads are brought into the house daily, before actually chucking the sticks of wood into a stove. Every step in the process is hard work. Dad did all of that every year to keep us warm.

His stamina was remarkable. He never backed away from a job that needed to be done. He was even cheerful about it. A haying day, which summoned all family members to the field, usually turned out hot. If we complained about the heat, he always said, "Oh, no. It's just a nice summer day." About winter's slippery roads, his comment was, "It's winter driving." Sometimes, when the haying was done for the day, he drove us to the lake to cool off and wash away the scratchy, itchy hay chaff.

We didn't have electricity or running water at home until after the war, in 1945, when we finally finished off the house. Before that, Dad carried water in two big pails from the spring—day after day. In winter it meant shoveling a path and still managing slippery walking. In summer, mosquitoes lined both arms as he carried the pails out of the woods and uphill to the house. Washday required extra water to do laundry.

Dad was a stoic and didn't believe in showing excessive emotion. He didn't coddle himself, and he had an extreme belief in what that meant. For instance, he never wore scarves or hoods to protect his neck from the cold. He said if you don't harden up your body, you become "soft and weak, like a hothouse plant."

He didn't drink, smoke, curse, play cards, or sing. Work and family were his life—and church when he could go. Somehow he never had much exposure to music and had little appreciation for it. I never saw him tap his foot in time to a lively tune. This lack of musical enjoyment I consider to be another hardship in his life, because that added dimension could have brought pleasure.

Dad and Mom made sure to teach my brother and me to live right, as they saw it. Dad said that although there isn't much any one person can do to change the world, there is one thing that everyone can and should do. That is to set a good example. We objected, "Who would pay any attention to what we did?" He answered wisely, "You might be surprised at who might be watching." He tried to convince us young teenagers that it is okay to be different—in fact, probably necessary in order to live a good Christian life. He said we didn't need to be one of the "crowd," that is, the popular kids.

He tried to live according to the Bible and didn't work on Sunday if he could help it. He tried not to buy anything on Sunday; we had "Blue Laws" anyway, so most stores were closed. He kept his beliefs private, though, and didn't try to convince others.

I remember the walks in the woods on our land. He had that country feeling of being one with Nature.

In the only period in his life that he had spare time while we children were still around, we four played Parcheesi sometimes. That was in South Portland during the war years. We also had family discussions there after a nice Sunday dinner as we sat around the table. We young people participated, as well as our parents.

During the war, Dad worked in the South Portland Shipyard, where he made what seemed like a lot of money. During the '30s there had been few jobs, and his work on the roads yielded a pittance for a full week of 48 hours. In the late '30s he left home and went to Massachusetts, where Fort Devens was being upgraded for war. He worked as a carpenter. He then moved to South Portland, where the four of us lived during the four war years.

The crash and depression had discouraged people from trusting banks. The banks failed and people lost money. My folks kept their savings in war bonds, and in cash pinned securely in my mother's clothing! For a while, Dad worked double shifts to make more money. People enthusiastically joined the war effort in those years. The shipyard made Liberty warships, and Dad did his part.

When I was married years later, our new home needed renovation. Dad was our carpenter, working during his off seasons and accepting only enough pay to cover his expenses.

In their later years, my folks enjoyed picnics at the coast, and we joined them when we could. If we couldn't make it, they sometimes took our children anyway and stopped for ice cream on the way home. Dad always made sure to bring a treat for the kids when they visited us.

Two goals he wanted to accomplish in his life: to build a large boat that was seaworthy, and to have a herd of dairy cows. He was a farmer at heart. Another wish, on which he never got the chance to work, was to build a new house for us across the road. Returning home after the war, he worked as a carpenter and began addressing his goals. He was in the dairy business for a few years, and he almost finished building the boat before he died.

He died ten days before his seventieth birthday, after a long battle with painful cancer. He even did that stoically. His doctor remarked, "Oh, the depth of that man's soul!"

Well said, good doctor!

Mavis J. Longfellow, daughter of Roland B. Judkins, 1903–1973

A New Easter Bonnet

I think of my mother a lot, especially during the Easter season. She grew up as poor as you can imagine. Soon after her marriage came the depression years, taking away any hope of having money for things she wanted. She felt bad when I, a little girl, couldn't have new clothes for a new school year or other occasion. She was a very loving mother, a very giving person, in spite of not having material goods. She was outgoing, she loved to be with people, and she was eager to help wherever she could.

She was a Christian, and Easter meant much more to her than new clothing. But the holiday was especially hard for her because "everyone" had new clothes and showed them off at church on Easter Sunday morning. (You have no doubt heard the song "Easter Parade.")

Women all wore hats and gloves to church, but there never seemed to be a time when there was money for a new hat for Mom. She would sometimes make herself a new dress. Women often used printed grain bags for fabric to make clothes. The company that sold grain to farmers for their animals purposely provided them, and they even had some pretty prints. They were eagerly utilized by farmers' wives and families. Still, they were not silk or satin. They were utility grade, perfect for aprons and such.

Then came the war years, when my father worked in the ship-yard. We attended church regularly. She would buy herself a new suit *and* hat, and maybe shoes, and feel good going to church on Easter Sunday. As you know, Easter comes earlier some years than others, and that could mean she had to wear a coat that covered up her new finery. Usually, though, a suit with a warm jacket was warm enough. I don't remember many new coats.

My mother accepted her poverty for her first forty-one years, and she was not a frivolous or shallow person. But she did long to have things that she saw other women enjoying.

Her self-image suffered all of her life. She hadn't been able to extend her education; she was needed at home because she was the oldest daughter. But she was intelligent and was a self-taught person, and she was elated when someone would ask her if she was a teacher, for example. It indicated to her that her lack of education didn't show.

She would have dearly loved opportunities to be more social. She enjoyed our four years at South Portland, living within walking distance of the Methodist church. They had an active women's group, which she eagerly joined. Those may have been the best four years of her life.

Later, when my brother left home after graduating high school and went in the service, he had accidently left a greasy hand mark on the door frame after working on his car. She missed him so much that she refused to clean off the stain.

She was a very helpful person, and after I was married and had a big family, she would wash my stacked-up dirty dishes when she visited me, and then would take home clothes that needed a button sewed on or a ripped seam repaired. She would then bring them back mended, washed, and ironed. Due to our seasonal business, which kept us so busy, she and my father took our young children to visit with them at their house for a few days every spring. They also took all the children on some Sunday picnics during the spring and summer. Often we all went.

My mother had a big heart and loved many things about life. Music was one joy for her. I see her in my memory, sitting at her piano, singing loudly and enthusiastically, "When the Roll is Called Up Yonder, I'll Be There!" I'll bet she got that right!

We need to count our blessings. If we are made of the right stuff, as she was, we will overcome our own adversities and be thankful for what we have, and will find something left over within to help others. We will really appreciate a new Easter bonnet—or whatever pleasure for which we have waited so long.

Mavis J. Longfellow, daughter of Margaret Tozier Judkins, 1900–1971

Country Ingenuity

As the saying goes, necessity is the mother of invention, and that is more likely to be true when you throw in a couple of other ingredients, like a dash of poverty and more than a sprinkle of country life. When I was growing up during the Great Depression, we lived on a small farm. I often think of the many times my parents found ways to do what had to be done, and they came up with some pretty good ideas, too. Some experiences are quite humorous, looking back; the whole picture brings a glow of nostalgia.

When Mom and Dad finally began life on their own little farm, he had no tractor and very little money. He managed to get an old Ford truck from which he put together a homemade tractor, which served very well. It was involved directly in a lot of work over the years.

My mother had to help with those jobs that required two people. She had been around horses all of her life, and like many women of her generation, she never learned to drive a car. In order to help Dad, she tried hard to learn to drive that tractor. She suffered with a case of nerves whenever she had to get behind the wheel. One time, she was on tractor duty and Dad was behind. Maybe they were picking rocks out of the field and hauling them away on the "drag" that he'd made for just such jobs. Whatever they were doing, she had to drive alongside a stream. When she got a little closer to the brook than she wanted or intended to be, she lost her cool and reverted to her earlier life. "Whoa!" she hollered. "Whoa!" She jumped clear of the tractor, leaving the engine running. Of course it ended up in the brook, where it rested until Dad got it hauled out. He was good about it, but she felt badly. We all, including Mom, laughed about it for years, though.

Haying was a big job, without much machinery to help. Sometimes my mother would drive the tractor while my father sat on the mowing machine, but sometimes he would do it alone and put a big rock on the seat of the mowing machine for weight. He rigged up a post on the rake to hang onto, for Mom, or sometimes my brother or me, as we rode the rake over the rough fields while he drove the tractor. It took the whole family—all four of us—to haul in the hay. Mom would drive, and my brother and I would tread the scratchy stuff and build the load as Dad pitched the loose hay onto the hayrack. He had a small barn then for a couple of cows, but no place to store hay, so he built a monumental haystack, which served quite well.

My mother worked very hard, particularly on washday. She had always wrung the clothes by hand, but my father made it easier by building a bench with a hand-cranked wringer in the center, with space on either end for her copper boiler and a washtub. She took clothes from the wash water on one side, after scrubbing them on her washboard, and then turned the crank to put them through the wringer, into the rinse water on the other side. She used the wringer again after the rinsing. Then the clothes were hung outside to dry, regardless of weather. I can still picture clothes frozen in shape when they were brought in.

Washday was no picnic for my father, either, because he had to haul all the extra water uphill from the spring, a pail in each hand. Usually he made a trip in the morning and sometimes one later, but washday demanded more.

After the war, my parents had saved enough money to build a dairy herd through Dad's work at the South Portland Shipyard. He built a new barn. He solved the need for water in the cows' automatic drinking cups in the tie-up by digging a pipeline by hand to a natural spring on a nearby hill on our land. There was always plenty of gravity-fed water—no pump needed.

He bought a few cows here and there as opportunity arose. One of my uncles, who lived forty or fifty miles away, wanted to give him a calf, to help him. How were we going to get the calf home without a truck? Well, our car was old, and we had some determination and imagination. It is not easy to put a diaper on a calf, but Dad did the next best thing. We put down a protective covering over the backseat and the floor where the calf would stand. Dad pulled a grain bag, or gunny sack, up over the calf's hind legs and fastened it over her back.

I sat in back with her, keeping the sack in place and trying to keep her calm all the way home. That was a memorable trip!

Often I recall those days before our modern conveniences of today. When I use my washer and dryer, I think how different my life has been from my mother's workload. There is no doubt in my mind that pleasures were sweeter and victories more gratifying when they came hard. Appreciation for life itself seemed deeper. It seems that folks' faith in God was stronger the harder their lives were. People were grateful for perceived blessings, meager though they seem today.

Pity the Powerless Child

I remember one of my childhood birthdays. It was probably my eighth or ninth. During the day, something made me angry; what it was is long gone from memory. I announced that I was going to run away from home! Then I spent the rest of the afternoon in a crawl space under the house. It was like a cubbyhole, where we sometimes played.

It got dark, and I got hungry. The family was in the warm house, probably eating supper. I silently crept up the stairs to the back porch and into the closet there. There was a window up high, which looked directly into the kitchen. I saw them all sitting around the table. It must have been a Saturday, since they were enjoying baked beans.

There was a birthday card standing up on my plate! I don't recall the conversation, or anything about going into the house and taking my place at the table. The incident was over and done with.

How wise my parents were, and how well they knew me. Yet, how hard it is to be a child! There is so little a youngster can do to satisfy needs and deep desires. They have to do as they are told, and they have little power to fulfill individual idiosyncrasies. That changes only gradually as the child matures and gains judgment enough to choose his own behavior. Until then, he or she needs to be under the guidance of knowledgeable and loving parents. Bringing up a child, and molding his character, is an all-important job.

Backyard Visitor

The fawn, innocent of fear,
Appears first, like a newborn calf,
Only dainty.

He is curious about our backyard,
This side of the trees,
His cover.

The doe is near, no surprise,
In the dappled sun/shade
At a safer distance.

She appears as on a pedestal,
Silent trumpets announcing her majesty,
A halo around her.

Big sensitive ears, transparent in the sun,
Their veining visible,
Her main feature.

Some sound or flicker unheard, unseen by me
Sends them into safety, fading from my sight
Except for flicking ears and tails.

With all their grace and beauty,
They have real poverty. They cannot afford
Curiosity!

From Depression to World War II

In the late 1930s, the Depression was still not over, but more people were finding jobs and the economy was looking up. The country was recovering under the presidency of Franklin D. Roosevelt and his federal projects. War in Europe had America worried that we would eventually get involved, and preparations were beginning. Our dad learned that there were jobs to be had at Fort Devens in Ayer, Massachusetts, which was being readied as an army base. He had no hope of getting any job in Belgrade better than his work on the roads. He had recently been cut to three days of work a week, so in the fall he struck out to hire on as a carpenter at Fort Devens. He arrived in Ayer with no money, and no place to sleep at night except his car, until he got a paycheck and a room. I was very happy when I got letters from him a couple of times. He was soon able to buy a more reliable car. He bought presents for us for Christmas and brought them home. My present was a Mickey Mouse watch!

Gram came to stay with us when Dad left. Guy was just barely a teenager when he took on the farm chores with some help from Mom. Life didn't change much for me, with my father away. However, Gram was with us when Dad took Mom to Ayer with him for a week or so after Christmas. When she left, I went down to the woodshed and cried.

One time, I went skating with other people on the big lake in Belgrade. Gram scolded me for skating home alone across a wide portion of the lake where there were currents not solidly frozen. She realized the danger; I didn't.

Mom must have gone with him a second time, too, in the spring. That time Gram made me continue to wear my winter jacket after the weather got warm. People worried that you would catch cold, or worse, if you removed your long johns or coats too early.

Guy and I played a Halloween prank one year. We didn't have trick-or-treat back then. We saved a big empty flour bag from the pantry, filled it with hay, and tied a long string to the top. We hid beside the road, down over a bank, with the bag of "flour" visible in the ditch.

Reggie Hammond came along on his way to take Phronie Guptill on a date. Just as he got out and reached down to pick up the bag of "flour," Guy pulled the string and yanked the bag out from under his hand! He thought it was a good joke, and told us to do it again when he brought Phronie back down the road! The trick worked again!

There was a very strong earthquake in the middle of one winter night while Dad was away. I was so frightened! My mother got up to make sure the stovepipe hadn't shaken loose, which might allow a house fire to start. She remarked that it was scary, as though walking around would start the earth shaking again! We had another quake that same winter or spring, in the morning as we were getting ready for school. Earthquakes still frighten me. There is such total lack of control.

Most kids didn't take dance or music lessons in those days. Guy took piano lessons—free—from a young music teacher who owed our mother a favor. She had used Mom's piano to practice on earlier in life. Mom had bought herself a piano when she first left home and went to work, because she loved music so much. She took a "correspondence course" to learn to play. She could read music and played hymns and such songs well enough to sing by. Anyway, I listened in on Guy's lessons, and practiced with Mom's coaching. I didn't get far, but I learned the basics about music, and it served as a basis for all the musical opportunities I enjoyed through the years—a very important aspect of my life.

When I finished the fifth grade in the spring of the year that Dad left, we went on the schoolwide picnic on the last day of school, to a nice beach at the lake in the neighboring town of Smithfield. This was an annual outing, and we went by school bus. Mom went with us, as did some other mothers. There was a roller skating rink nearby, and I tried it out and had fun. I enjoyed those school picnics so much!

Going swimming was always one of my favorite activities, although I didn't get to go often very early in life. We lived there among the lakes, but had no access. Finally a family who had a summer home near us kindly invited the neighbors to walk down their long field to their boathouse, pier, and small beach. We didn't go when the owners were in town, but they didn't spend much time in Belgrade anyway. How I enjoyed those times, and how I hated to leave when it was time to get out of the water! When Teeny Damren or someone would take the neighborhood children swimming during the day, we had to walk from home, and of course it was usually a hot summer day. After cooling off in the water, we'd get all sweaty again walking back home.

One time when Aunt Hazel and Uncle Paul and their girls were visiting, it was a hot day and we decided to go swimming. Uncle Paul didn't have a bathing suit, but Mom suggested jokingly that he could use one of hers. Uncle Paul was a good sport, and he loved a joke. He took her up on the offer, and off we went to the lake. No one else was there. After much laughter and fun, we suddenly realized there was a water snake in our area, near the shore. Uncle Paul grabbed a nearby stick to use as a club, and ran—in a woman's bathing suit, mind you—along the shallow water near shore, splashing wildly with his club, chasing the snake out of our vicinity. I can see it all still, the club in both hands up over his head, this bald man running with his short, slightly bowed legs in Mom's green, white, and yellow boldly flowered suit. Hilarious!

In those days people took baths and shampoos less often than is today's habit, relying on auxiliary sponge baths. In the summer, when convenient, we sometimes bathed in the lake, using Ivory soap, which would float! (No one ever thought in those days about the harm to the lake.) One time, Dad took his dirty work pants along and scrubbed them in the water. He left them there, sort of out of sight under an overhanging tree branch, soaking for a full week until he went back again. I don't remember whether they got very clean, but at least my mother didn't have to scrub them by hand in the washtub that week. It was a good thing that the area wasn't used much by other people: the pants were not stolen. Probably they were old and patched anyway!

By the time school was out in the spring of 1941, Dad had found a good job at the South Portland Shipyard, considerably closer to home than where he had been working in Massachusetts. He found and rented a small four-room (plus bath) apartment over a grocery store, and on July 6th we moved in. There was a real honest-to-goodness bathroom, and a kitchen with running water, an icebox, and a gas stove.

There were back stairs off our kitchen for the third-floor tenants, and beyond that was a spare unheated space Dad used for a shop.

Dad built a beautiful bookcase with glass doors in that shop beyond the back stairs. He brought an old walnut table from Gram's house and made the bookcase out of that. It now sits in my living room, and I treasure it greatly.

The woman who lived with her young family and her husband on the third floor, over us, would frequently stop on her way up the back stairs and stand in the doorway and talk and visit. She was a large, red-haired woman of Germanic heritage, good-hearted and likeable. I babysat for them occasionally.

It really wasn't much of an apartment; but for the times, and compared with the conditions we had lived in during the depression, it served well enough for our four years there—the war years. If our landlord had been more generous about sending up the heat, we would have been quite comfortable!

While living in South Portland, we attended a Methodist church which was within walking distance. Gram went, too, when she was with us, and Dad, too, except later on during our four years there, when he worked two eight-hour shifts daily. I sang in the choir, my first experience as part of a musical group. During two summers, I went to the Methodist youth camp for a week. I must have been 12 and 13. I enjoyed those opportunities a lot.

When Gram was with us, she washed all the dishes as her part in helping out. I helped Mom do them often when Gram wasn't there. Usually Mom washed, and I rinsed and dried. Those were good times for a mother and daughter. It was during one of these times that I got the "birds and bees" talk. Often we sang together. I had just learned to harmonize, singing "You Are My Sunshine," which I had heard done by a girl in my sixth grade class. I took it from there. I practiced taking alto, tenor, and bass parts at home on the hymns we knew from church, and Mom and I would sing our favorites in harmony while doing dishes.

When school began that first year, Guy and I started Hawaiian guitar lessons together. We would take the bus to the studio in Portland and hand over $1.00 each. After a couple of years, we bought electric guitars. Those made beautiful music, and I was asked a couple of times later on, after Guy had graduated, to provide intermission music at a school entertainment. When Gram had cancer, a few weeks before she died, she requested that Guy and I play "Whispering Hope," which we did. Guy sold his guitar early on in adulthood. I kept mine, but never played it. I finally sold it in later years. Improvements on the old Hawaiian guitar have produced the present steel guitar, the playing of which can involve foot and knee pedals. I do still enjoy the music when it is played right.

The first summer we were in South Portland, Dad rented a garden plot and raised lots of veggies, which Mom canned just like on the farm! Actually, that was probably 1942, since we moved in so late in the growing season in 1941. I think it was only one year.

Since Dad and Mom did not trust banks, with their savings they bought Liberty War Bonds at $18.75 each, which at maturity in ten years were worth $25.00. Dad's good wages (for the times) were closely guarded, and they tried to save all they could for the future. They were very afraid of losing it somehow, due to the depression experiences, and so their cash savings, which belonged in a bank, were tied up in a handkerchief and pinned inside my mother's bra! We didn't waste money or spend recklessly, but we did enjoy some indulgences that we hadn't been able to in the past. When we moved there, I had never eaten a real meal at a sit-down restaurant, and had never owned a dress that cost much over a dollar.

Still, recreation was often without cost. That first summer, we went to Crescent Beach in Cape Elizabeth almost every good day. We went for long walks, at times all four of us, but usually Guy didn't go. As a family, we sometimes played Parcheesi, a board game for four. After Sunday dinner we often had discussions, sometimes of a Biblical nature. We went to the movies some. I remember reading *Uncle Tom's Cabin* for my ninth grade English class. Although my mother liked to read, she never had much time for it. So I read it aloud to her so she could enjoy it, too. My English teacher said she considered it quite a "juvenile" book for me! I still think she was wrong!

When the day's housework was done, and Mom's and Gram's aprons had been changed for fresh ones that would be worn the next day, and it was not yet time to start supper, I would sometimes sit with the two of them and listen to our wind-up phonograph. The particular times that stick in my memory must have been during the short days of late fall, because we listened to the music as darkness gradually crept in, and felt no need to turn on a light. We all enjoyed "When You're Gone I Won't Forget You" most. I still have the record, and a lot more of those old-time recordings.

That first summer in South Portland, I had my tonsils out, something I had needed for a long time. My hearing had even been affected slightly. I recall lovingly how Mom lingered that night by my bedside in the hospital because she hated so badly to leave me. I didn't mind, though, and all went well. Years later, after I was married, I learned that my husband had *his* tonsils removed that same month and year.

I had an attack of appendicitis—I'll always believe it was that—when I was 12 or 13. The pain was bad. The folks called the doctor, who made a house call. I was scared that I would need an operation, so I wouldn't admit the extent of the pain to the doctor. He was pretty sure that it was my appendix, and the abdomen was rigid, but my denial of bad pain made it doubtful. He said to paint the abdomen area with iodine, and if it didn't improve, to bring me in. Right after he left, the symptoms began to fade. He left me a bottle of Pancreo-Bismuth, an early form of Pepto-Bismol.

My teeth needed work badly. As a child, I had ulcerated teeth a few times, and at least once, had an extraction. It got infected because I used my finger to feel the wound, even though I had been warned not to do that. Dad and Guy had to chase the dentist down at some evening function to get medication for me. One Sunday on a trip to New Portland when I was about six, Mom got the bright idea of having her dentist friend there work on her children's teeth. Old Dr. Clark was glad to do it, even on a Sunday. The drills he used at that time were powered by a foot treadle, so were very slow, and the process was extra-painful! Some five years later, in South Portland, I went many times to have work done, being anesthetized with self-administered gas.

When school started, I was the tallest one in my sixth grade class. I stood crouched over because I didn't know how to carry my maturing body, and I felt conspicuous. It was bad enough to be "the new girl." I applied myself to my school work and did well. I socialized some with the other kids, but had few close friends.

Near our apartment was a building called Whitehall. Within was a mini convenience store/sandwich shop, and behind closed doors, a pool hall. There was a good-sized dance hall, too, and many a night we could hear its music way into the wee hours. Our folks were quite disturbed that Guy played pool there a lot, but I think he was with other kids his own age, and that it was not your typical pool hall—not considered a "den of iniquity." (It may have been that, later in the evenings, though.)

I first tasted two of my lifelong favorite foods at Whitehall—potato chips and Italian sandwiches. We girls would go into the shop and buy a small bag of chips each and go walking along the sidewalk for something to do. I don't know when potato chips were invented, but I do know they tasted so-o-o-o good, and new to me! Italian sandwiches are strictly a State of Maine product. In other places they use a different bun, or use mayonnaise and lettuce, or do something that makes them different. They have remained basically the same as they were in the early 1940s. The bun is important. It is (at its best) moist, and either six or twelve inches long. Then the meat was usually salami, and that is one thing that is different—now ham is the chosen meat, but salami and other meats are usually available, and also tuna or veggies. The cheese is a soft American alongside slices of tomato, green pepper, and onion. Dill pickles may be either thin long slices or rounds. Salt and pepper are applied unless one specifies otherwise, and then a special flavored oil with vinegar lubricates it. There you have a truly delicious sandwich!

I wasn't very happy during those four years in South Portland. Part of it was my age, of course, and a teenage tendency toward depression. We weren't in a big city, but it certainly wasn't rural. I was a country girl and always felt "different." Dad taught us that, as Christians, we *should* be different. No doubt he was right; but teenagers, struggling with self-image, are unhappy if not accepted. Guy was in the eighth grade when we moved. Later, he went to work at the A&P store, and spent a lot of time there, to his credit. He had friends and did things with them. They were good kids. He was better suited to life there than to the more isolated rural style of living.

I had some friends, but I just never was "popular." Of my new friends, Mavis Jones was one. I was amazed that another girl had the same name I did. I was even more amazed a year or two later when another Mavis came to our school. There were three of us in one class!

Mavis Jones and I corresponded for a long time, through our marriages, births of children, her divorce and remarriage. The Trask girls were other good friends, and I exchanged Christmas letters every year with Alice. Sadly, both Mavis and Alice have died. Alice and Mavis bought friendship rings for the three of us when the war was over and we moved back home.

I liked going by city bus into Portland to the movies or to the library. I often went with my friends, but sometimes I went alone. I loved Gene Autry movies, but also had crushes on other good-looking actors like Van Johnson and Henry Fonda (father of Jane Fonda). In those days, they didn't clear the theater after the movie was over, but began the next show right away. Sometimes I stayed through two shows.

A few times, I took the bus alone and spent time in the library in Portland. Once or twice it was to the art museum. I loved to read, and was one of those people who can't put down a book, and who are somewhat oblivious to their surroundings while reading. I know that helped me to do well in school, and it also improved my vocabulary and helped me with composition. I was quite religious, and read my Bible often. I read it all the way through one year. It was a Christmas present that year, at my insistence.

I belonged to the Campfire Girls while living in South Portland. I don't remember doing much, but I did earn some beads. I gathered quite a long necklace of pretty wooden beads of different shapes and colors that I earned over time. I think I still have them somewhere.

The other thing that guaranteed success in school was the time I spent doing homework, then checking it over, and maybe even checking it again the next morning during homeroom period. With few friends, and no television at that time, I put extra effort into schoolwork. I guess I was a "nerd." (Guessing not necessary—I was!)

There were other activities, too. Radio was big in most homes before television, and listening to radio shows was one way I spent my extra time. I also kept diaries in which I recorded everything dear to my heart. I worked one summer in our landlady's flower garden, which she enjoyed but was not able to tend. I picked strawberries at a farm in Cape Elizabeth, but that didn't last long. It was hard work, and we only got paid three cents per quart, rounded up.

At the shipyard, Dad chose to work the afternoon/evening shift, getting home near midnight. I suppose that shift paid better wages, but it precluded any family activities after school or in the evenings. Sometimes I would wake up when he got home and hear him laughing at the antics of our cat when, for instance, while undressing he would lay his sock across the cat's back. (That cat used to eat raisins. Also he would "fetch" a crumpled piece of paper that I had thrown down the stairs! Guy's friend from Belgrade, Oliver Yeaton, who visited us, named the cat Tugwell.)

I remember one Christmas, about our third year there, when we celebrated by opening presents after Dad got home in the middle of the night, and then we immediately struck out on the long car trip to Carver, Massachusetts, to take Gram to stay for a while with Aunt Hazel and Uncle Paul. I must have slept most of the way; at least I have no memory of it.

I entered sixth grade that first year in South Portland, then moved up to seventh and eighth grade at Reynolds School for the next two years. There we had three "old maid" teachers, and the situation was a horror. One teacher was pretty okay, but another was old, somewhat deaf, and her eyes darted constantly from side to side in a very distracting manner. The boys delighted in putting things over on her. We didn't do anything interesting in her English classes, but guess what! I actually enjoyed learning to diagram sentences! (I told you I was a nerd.)

The other teacher was the principal. She was very old (or at least I thought so then) and cranky. She would rail at us as a class for sitting with dull and uninterested (bored) expressions. She used a ruler to slap hands. I used to have bad dreams about her, even though she never got after me. One time she had one boy, a poor student, standing beside his desk, as we had to do when called on to recite. Her question for him was to repeat the steps for solving a math problem (as I remember), and, in all fairness, she had told us what those steps were. The boy couldn't remember them, so for each step, she would quote it, strike him with the ruler, and make him repeat it. Don't ask me how many steps there are—it's all gone from my memory! I don't think hitting me with a ruler would help me remember, though!

It was quite a long walk to Reynolds School, probably about ten minutes. One day a week we had to walk an extra distance to Lincoln School for a half day of home economics. We took cooking and sewing, and I still have some of the recipes. We made dolls' dresses, and finally one for ourselves.

We had one bitterly cold morning one year, but I walked, bundled up, to school anyway. Not many kids showed up, and we were sent home. Our home thermometer showed 42 degrees below zero! Your breath freezes on the scarf which you have pulled up over your nose. Your eyelashes freeze, too. I remember my woolen snowsuit had a sheepskin jacket lining. I watered the plants for the teacher that morning, and spilled some water on that lining. It's a wonder I didn't freeze going home.

High school, which I attended the last year we lived in South Portland, required a daily walk of one mile each way. The city bus was handy for inclement weather. A ride anywhere was only a dime, with free transfers to other bus routes. The nearby bus stop was almost across the street from our apartment.

My parents couldn't afford to send me to any college, but would try to find funds if I chose to go to a Bible college, so I figured I'd better prepare for secretarial work, without college. I also entertained thoughts of possibly becoming a home missionary, one who travels from church to church offering assistance with Bible schools, Sunday schools, and other projects in this country, not in Africa or some other place overseas. I had been interested ever since meeting the young people who ran our Vacation Bible School in Belgrade when I was younger. However, I chose to take commercial courses in high school.

I have always been very proud, though, of earning such good grades in a good-sized school. Each spring, South Portland High School celebrated Recognition Day for the students with the best grades. I had the highest grades in all of the school's classes in each of my subjects. It was a real achievement. When I graduated from Belgrade High School as valedictorian of my class, it was a small class of only fifteen pupils.

The war effort demanded some sacrifice and afflicted some hardships on all of us. Dad was not going to be drafted because of his shipyard work building Liberty Ships. Let's see—he was 38 years old at the time of Pearl Harbor on December 7, 1941. We experienced rationing of scarce goods and were allowed to buy only as much of certain products like meat, sugar, coffee, butter, and gasoline as the stamps we were issued allowed. We had a card with the letter B on it to put in the car window, which designated our status on the gasoline quantity we were allowed. We wouldn't have been able to take car trips back home to Belgrade, to New Portland to visit Grammie Tozier, or to take Gram to Aunt Hazel's to stay for a couple of months, if Dad hadn't saved up his gas allotment by taking the bus to work. We still couldn't go often. Before rationing began most everyone stored up such things as sugar and coffee ahead of time. It was referred to as "hoarding," and it was considered selfish. We didn't do much of that. All I know is that sugar turns rock-hard if stored very long! I don't remember any real hardship attributed to rationing, but planning ahead was necessary.

People were asked to donate old aluminum kettles and such salvage as they could spare, and it was kept on the town square, a mountain of pots and pans, until collected to be used in the war effort. We kids made balls out of the aluminum foil that certain candy bars and gum were wrapped in, along with any other foil, and donated that.

At that time, foil was not commonly used as a kitchen food wrap. I don't think it was even available then. Waxed paper was the common food wrapper, and my mother saved waxed-paper bread wrappers for reuse. Plastic was not on the market yet.

To prevent attack in this country, we kept window shades drawn at night. Car lights had the top half of the light painted black. This was to keep the lights from showing upward to attackers in the air. Any particular area would not be recognized as a city unless a lot of light showed. We had air raid practices, lots of posters and slogans to keep up the patriotism, and radio broadcasts from correspondents overseas to keep us up to date. Homes boasted stars in the window, one for each son who was in the military forces. Sadly, a lot of stars were replaced by gold stars signifying that one of those sons had made the supreme sacrifice. My friend Alice's oldest brother, Billy Trask, a tail gunner, was shot down and listed as missing in action. He never was found.

We experienced a phenomenon in World War II in which the country buckled down to real effort, real cooperation, real patriotism. From young men enlisting, and "Rosie the Riveter" going to work in a shipyard or factory in order to free up another man to fight, to everyone's uncomplaining acceptance of hardships due to the war, there was a common effort. There were real hardships for many, perhaps most, like those caused by young men having to leave wives and children and family, and of course the horrific experiences of war that they went through, and the tragedies of those who didn't come home.

In South Portland, Mom really enjoyed the social contacts she was able to make with the church ladies and first-aid classes, etc. Her life in Belgrade was far too lonely for a person like her, and she would have enjoyed moving to South Portland permanently after the war. Guy, also, didn't relish going back to Belgrade. He had one more year of high school, but the small school Belgrade could afford didn't offer the advanced courses that South Portland did. He was invited to live with a friend and his family in South Portland to finish his last year of school there, but in the end he moved back with us and helped Dad get established in the dairy business that he had always wanted.

Dad could have joined with another man who wanted to start up a shipbuilding company after the war. Guy has always felt Dad made a poor decision in pursuing the dairy dream. But some people are called to be close to the land, in a country setting; and the siren call of more money or less work, with its accompanying politics and rubbing of elbows with lots of people, just doesn't tip the scales enough. Dad just wanted to go back to our roots, and so did I.

When the Thunder Crashes By

Are the animals afraid in the forest?
Do the birds all tuck their heads beneath their wings?
When the lightning sears the sky and the thunder crashes by,
Are the babies scared and trembling at these things?

Do the babies cry and shiver near their mothers,
When the storms approach with cold and angry winds?
Do mothers try their best to soothe their babies 'neath their breasts,
When Mother Nature roars instead of sings?

Yes, I think they are afraid in the forest,
And I know my fellow man is suff'ring too,
Even though he makes no cry when his sorrows I slide by,
Saying blithely, "There is nothing I can do."

We are all sometimes afraid, in need of comfort,
When the storms of life become too much to bear.
When life's lightning sears the soul and its thunder takes its toll,
It's so good to know a friend is always there.

You, too, could be a friend to one who's frightened,
Could clasp him by the hand and calm his fears.
Through the lightning, wind, or storm, you could be the one
    who's strong,
And calm yourself by seeing to his tears.

A Small Farm, a Small School, and a Small Town

Right after school was out for the summer in 1945, we moved back to our Belgrade home. Home still had no rooms divided off, no running water, no bathroom, and no electricity—just the way we had left it four years earlier, when the depression years were over and the war years were beginning. But we were home, and I was to have my own room, with the wallpaper I chose. I have always loved the aqua-blue and rose-peach of a sunset, and that was my choice of colors for my room. I savored the dream with every sunset a long time in advance. It actually came to pass!

Just as soon as we moved in, we wired the house for electricity and set about finishing off the interior. Guy remembers that he dug the ditch by hand for water pipes to the spring, and then we had water at the kitchen sink. The back porch was enlarged, new steps were built, and the front porch was closed in as a sun porch, providing an extra room.

I was really happy to be home. I decided that I was going to enjoy my three remaining years of high school and not be such a nerd. Sometimes an assignment was done at the last minute, with much more reliance on study hall.

The Belgrade Grange put on weekly dances at Belgrade Depot. The high school kids went, as well as many older folks. I really, truly enjoyed going to those. Right away I learned to do the popular square dances and just loved it! Usually the band would play a square dance, then a waltz, then a foxtrot, and then repeat the sequence all evening. I didn't have to sit many of them out, but was asked to dance most of the time. My folks let me go as long as I came home with the same person with whom I had ridden to the dance—usually a neighbor, always pre-approved. I'm sure they felt better when Guy was there also. The other rule was that I was not to go outside the hall during the evening, as so many did, especially at intermission. That was where the drinking and most of the smoking—and other such unsupervised activities—went on. I was happy to oblige, as I had no interest in either drinking or smoking.

Jumping ahead, on the subject of alcohol, to a time several years later, after I was married, I drank spiked punch at a party, not knowing that it contained alcohol. I thought the bitter taste was grapefruit juice! The steps I had to walk down loomed as steep and dangerous, whereas I'm sure they were quite normal. I was loud, too. I had had enough punch that I shouldn't have driven. One of the older ladies said she wished I didn't have to drive home. She surely could tell that I was somewhat under the influence, but I thought she meant because it was dark and I was alone. I glibly informed her that I was okay—I was used to it! The next day I realized the truth and was quite angry that I had been allowed to make a fool of myself among people whom I had wanted to impress favorably, not this way. I have always treasured having a good reputation and have always intended to guard it. I suppose those serving the punch thought I knew that it was spiked. Also, did I mention that I was a couple of months pregnant with my second child?

But back now to my high school years.

At the end of the year that we came home from South Portland, Guy graduated in a class of eight students. His friend, Oliver Yeaton, was one of the graduates. Although I had always liked him, I had never had a crush on him. He and Paul Meservey were Guy's friends, and they hung out together all that year. I really enjoyed the times they were at our house, and that was often.

One evening, Oliver invited me to go to the senior prom with him! That night of his invitation, I stayed awake all night, I think, because I was so excited! I enjoyed the prom—my first real date—and Oliver and I continued going out all summer. He and Guy both went into the service in the fall. I wrote to Oliver often, and pined dramatically but sincerely. When it was all over, I didn't want to go with anyone again, not for a long time. I continued going to the Monday dances and really enjoyed being an unattached teenaged girl.

I played guitar in the school orchestra my junior year. The next year, Mrs. Atherton had me play a small portable piano instead; I think it had two octaves. She had been displeased because at Dexter, where the towns got together one year for a music festival, I had delayed things quite a while when the electric cord for my guitar wouldn't reach the outlet, and I hadn't thought to bring an extension cord. She did forgive me, though, and actually depended somewhat on me.

As our music teacher, Mrs. Atherton provided this small school with an opportunity, for those who were interested, to enjoy music and improve their musical education. We put on school shows, went to Dexter, Maine, to join with other choruses and bands, and I felt grateful for the experience. When I was a senior, she stood before the combined school one day and announced that her health was forcing her to cut back. She said that she would continue in our school if we wanted her to, but if not, she would retire. She called on me to answer for everyone, in front of everyone! I stood up beside my desk, recalling silently the snide remarks and complaints I had heard about her (there are always some of those!) but realizing the value of the chance she was giving us for the musical experience. I had to answer her question, so I said that we certainly didn't want her to stress her health, but that we recognized the opportunity she was providing for us, and that I thought her services were valuable and appreciated. She agreed to stay on. No one ever told me that I gave the wrong answer.

A local woman, Pauline Plourde, whom I believe was a Girl Scout leader in town, got a few of the girls together. We put together a musical show which we performed at the Grange Hall. We made costumes out of blue crepe paper for ourselves, in the style of old-fashioned Southern belles' long gowns, with "pancake" hats to match with ribbons tied under our chins. That was fun as well as a good experience. Mrs. Plourde became a sort of mentor for several of us girls.

I believe I was in at least one play or presentation every year all through school. I was an angel in a Christmas pageant one early year, and a neighbor told my mother that I looked pretty. Mom didn't repeat the compliment to me, which would have done me a lot of good because of my lack of self-confidence. Years later, she told me, explaining that she hadn't wanted to give me a "swelled head." At the close of eighth grade, we had a graduation ceremony. I had a dusty-rose dress, which I remember well. I received the Good Citizenship medal and had to walk down the long aisle and up on the stage to accept it. Of course, that was in South Portland.

Junior year brought Junior Speaking, for which we each had to memorize and present publicly at the Grange Hall an entertaining short story, poem, etc. The only one I remember (including my own) was Edgar Allan Poe's "The Tell-Tale Heart," spoken by Paul Meservey, who had a rather deep, rich voice. We had some talent in that small town.

I always hated looking out at the audience at that moment when the lights go down, the curtain goes up, and I'm on! I then see all those upturned faces, with the many eyeglasses reflecting the low light, and know that everyone is looking at me!

There may have been other such times in high school. For seniors, of course, there was graduation. I was valedictorian, with a grade point average of 95.6, or something like that. The salutatorian designation went to two people who both had 85.6. You have to remember that mine were commercial subjects and theirs were college preparatory courses. I wrote my own speech on "Our American Heritage," and our English teacher, Mrs. Kinney, coached us.

An interesting aside regarding graduation: There were fifteen of us, and one of the girls was pregnant. She was not allowed to sit on the stage and participate in the graduation ceremony, but sat in the audience, in the front row, with other people. She got her diploma, married the baby's father, and they stayed married and had more children. Unwed mothers were not accepted then.

Erma Clement, the teacher of the youngest children in the school, taught kindergarten, first grade, and second grade. The building was set up with the high school rooms in one end and three rooms for the lower grades, three grades to each room, in the other end. Erma wasn't musical, and she asked me if I would come in on my recess time sometimes and sing with her kids. I was happy to do it, and I don't remember feeling self-conscious. I taught them "Where

Is Thumbkins?" and sang other songs with them. I rather enjoyed the time I spent there.

Because I had good grades, I suppose, and could thus afford to miss some of my classes, I was hired by the town to substitute for Erma Clement when she was sick; it seems like it was for three or four weeks, but it might have been less. Erma prepared some things to help in keeping the children busy, but didn't expect me to actually teach. I didn't have any problem with it, and I kept up with my own assignments without attending my classes during that time. Actually, I don't remember if I was paid by the town, and if so, how much. Funny, the things that your brain lets slip away.

Another time I saved the town some money by subbing when another teacher was out sick. That was for only a few days, and there were two of us girls who supervised the children. Those were third, fourth, and fifth graders. No problem!

When I was a sophomore, the town did pay me to tutor a neighbor girl who was nearly blind. She was a state ward living in our neighborhood briefly. She was an emotional basket case, but she was fairly smart, and we got her through with passing grades. She was a year younger than I. I worked with her two or three times a week, reading to her, explaining, and helping with her assignments.

She would burst into tears for no reason. Once, she confided to me that the man in the family where she stayed was abusing her sexually. I know she could have been lying, but this same man had made a pass at me while we were dancing at the Grange Hall one Monday night. So I believed her and told my mother. Mom called the state worker who was in charge of her case, who investigated. She didn't find any proof of his wrongdoing, but I believe he was guilty.

My mother, a good Christian woman, regretted that the children in our neighborhood were not getting any religious training or education, as the nearest church was some distance away and the parents were not churchgoers. She decided to open a Sunday school in our home. She taught the older children in the living room, after opening services when we sang hymns (we had a piano, which Mom played), and accepted their pennies to be used toward expenses. I taught the younger ones in the kitchen. We had cookies and milk, too. We had ten or twelve children most weeks. One of those children told me recently how valuable that experience was in her life. She remembers coming to our house as a child on Sunday mornings. She said that I was her only Sunday school teacher ever. I wonder if I saved any souls. Probably not—I'll do well if I save my own! That's enough of a job for any one person!

I was not always in the mood on Sunday morning to go about such noble work when I wanted to sleep in. After all, Sunday morning comes right after Saturday night, and by this time I was dating pretty regularly. I can't recall when our Sunday school ended—whether it continued until I married and moved out, or just until I finished high school.

With my grades and ability, I should have been getting encouragement to attend college, but no one ever spoke to me about it. I knew that my parents couldn't afford to send me, but would manage to do so if I chose a religious college, but I wasn't sure I wanted to go anyway. Girls didn't have many career opportunities then except office work, teaching, or nursing, so there was little I could do with a college education that I couldn't do without one. I know now that education is valuable for one's personal growth, affecting all aspects of life; but I didn't know that then. Anyway, I am not sure I had the self-confidence to go away to college at that time.

Going back briefly to 1945, I remember the year we came home from South Portland as a happy one for me on the whole, but it had a traumatic aspect. There had been no deaths in our family, of anyone I was close to, that I could remember. I had never had to face up to the loss of a loved one. When Gram died in November of that year, it hit me hard. She was diagnosed soon after we moved home, with cancer of the colon, I think. The doctors gave her three months to live, and they were just about right.

She chose to live with us while she was "recuperating." She wasn't told that she had cancer or that she was dying. When she died, we were not supposed to tell anyone what she had died of. Don't ask me why, but having cancer was some kind of disgrace to be hushed up, I guess. She thought the surgeon had removed a tumor. She didn't have bad pain. We set her up in the living room on a twin-sized bed with a commode beside it. Her brother from Massachusetts, Uncle Bert, who over the years came to Belgrade to visit her for a few weeks over several summers, built the potty-chair for her.

Soon after we got back to the farm, Dad began work on his plan to finally get into the dairy business. (Call it his dream, or one of three dreams. He also wanted to build a house across the road on the old foundation; and third, had drawn up plans to build his own sailboat.) He was a man whose life was mostly work. He took Sundays off, but most of his waking hours other days were spent working, sometimes slowly, always carefully, nearly always alone, on and on. His hopes for a dairy farm just barely came to pass, and his situation seemed doomed from the beginning. He bought Jersey cows, whose milk is very rich with cream. Just about then the health gurus decided that fats in our diets needed to be reduced, so milk with less butterfat than the milk Jersey cows give was then more desirable. Soon after that, the dairy companies that had been collecting his milk from his small tank began driving out the small farmers. They began buying milk only from the big dairy farmers with large storage tanks. Dad would have had to buy equipment and make changes that were not possible for him, and he would need a new barn and more cows. So his dream had to be abandoned.

He went to work as a carpenter, and in the Belgrade area there are still many summer camps, homes, a famous restaurant, and a horse barn that show the strength and beauty of his fine workmanship.

When Guy went in the Air Force that fall after his high school graduation, it was very hard for Mom to have him go. His greasy hand print on the door frame stayed there, a reminder of him. It wasn't wartime, but to a person who had never traveled and never had much worldly experience, it was almost more than she could take. He was an MP in Biloxi, Mississippi first, and then went to Korea, where he worked on radios. After that, he spent a while in Japan before his time was up. While in Korea he had a religious experience in which he felt called to go into the ministry. Once out of the service, he went to Gordon College, as Dad had done so long ago. In due time, he became a Baptist minister, and that has been his lifelong vocation.

Most of the Belgrade girls worked summers in the tourist trade in the village of Belgrade Lakes, but my folks didn't want me to. The summer after my junior year, I worked for Clarence Chase, who had a vegetable stand. It sat in a lonely spot down beyond the cemetery, where the Oakland road joins the cemetery road. It was fun in a way, but a bit lonely sometimes.

When I graduated from high school, I took a test to qualify for employment by the State of Maine, and I soon went to work at the State Bureau of Taxation. I took dictation in shorthand, but I preferred the recording machine from which I wrote the letters for some of the men. I was a good typist. I had ability with figures, too, so they put me to work on big charts, or worksheets, recording unorganized territory taxation figures that had to add up, both across and down. Work was quite different then, before computers. My take-home pay was $27.20 a week. I thought I was rich! I remember thinking, "This is just about like school, only I'm getting paid!" I gave my folks a small amount for room and board, since I was now a working girl.

Wedding Bells

Those Monday night dances finally yielded a serious candidate for my particular interest! A young man, home from the war, sat across the hall and smoked his pipe during intermission. He asked me to dance once, then more often, as we were getting acquainted. His name was Lawrence Longfellow.

His brother, Alden, also came to the dances, and they showed up most Monday nights. Alden had worked on the Penney Farm in Belgrade before the war, when he must have been in high school. Some of my friends knew Alden, and I found that the Longfellow family, who lived in Farmingdale, was respected locally. Alden made it a habit to be the first one on the floor for the square dances, with his partner. He was an enthusiastic square dancer, trying to swing all the girls off their feet! Lawrence was a bit more reserved about it, which was more my style, and still fun.

I let Lawrence know through my cousin, Arlene, that I would accept an invitation if he wanted to take me to my junior prom, which was coming up. I got three other invitations while waiting for him to ask me! Meanwhile, he finally asked me to go to the movies. *The Yearling* was showing in Augusta. He picked me up and met my parents, and they liked him. We enjoyed the date, and he finally invited me to the prom. It was formal, and he endeared himself to me when he inquired if picking me up in his father's delivery van (panel truck, or utility vehicle) would be okay. It was either that or his uncle's Model A Ford—an ancient antique! Of course I said it was all right. On later dates, we did go in that Ford quite often.

An aside goes well here, about buying my formal dress for the prom. It was hard to get to the stores to shop because of Dad's work schedule. My folks agreed to let me take a day off from school and go to Waterville on the train, having walked to the nearby depot from school. I stopped in Oakland and looked at a used dress that had been advertised for sale in the paper. I decided against that one and went on to Waterville. I bought a lovely blue dress and imitation pearls to match, and made it back to Belgrade. I never had done such a thing alone before, although my mother and I had made some trips by train.

Monday night dances continued, and Lawrence and I danced together a lot. When the dance was over, I would notice the fragrance on my clothes or hands of the Yardley lavender soap that his mother favored and provided for her family's use. Memory of him lingered on in lavender when the evening was over.

That's how it all began.

Lawrence was very different from anyone I knew. He had some remarkable qualities: a high IQ and good insight; he was very creative, was generous beyond expectations, and had a memory better than that of anyone I've ever known. He fit perfectly the description of a "rugged individualist."

He also had good character, which was so important. He didn't drink. He soon stopped smoking his pipe, partly because of me but mostly because of setting an example for his brother. He went to church fairly regularly and had done so since adolescence. He had been part of the church youth group. He was good-looking, with very deep dimples in both cheeks. He had an eyelid that drooped, especially when he was tired, but who cared? He also had a blond streak in his hair, in the front. Quite distinguished and unique! I recognized that he had some fine qualities, and he liked to do things for others. He was honest and fair, and thoughtful. In short, he was a good man. I was happiest when we were together.

On one of my early visits to his folks' house, I eventually needed a bathroom facility. Now Lawrence knew that I lived in a home with an outdoor toilet, as did he, yet my gallant host made me wait while he went upstairs to borrow his sister Ruth's spray bottle of cologne, with which he sprayed every inch of that bazoozi until it reeked! That's the kind of man he was!

We met in March of 1947, during my junior year at high school. We dated through the summer, and all of my senior year, and all through the next year.

Because it was quite a distance between his folks' house and mine, he would sometimes have me stay over with his family instead of driving me home to Belgrade. I slept in the room right next to his parents' bedroom. Sometimes, if we were nearer Belgrade, he brought me home and stayed at my folks' house.

One time that proved embarrassing. Lawrence was a playful sort, and since my room was next to the living room where he bunked on the couch, he knocked on that wall between us just to say good night to me. Ours was a very small house, not at all soundproof. Well, the dog heard and barked her fool head off! Dad got up and pulled on his pants and came out through the living room to see who was knocking at the front door. Lawrence 'fessed up, and that was that!

Another night, we were out very late to a dance in another town, and on the way home we had car trouble and the engine died. We had his car, a 1937 rust-colored two-door Olds. He tinkered under the hood for a while, but to no avail. There were no nearby houses, no telephones, so what were we to do? (Remember, no cell phones!) He thought we were near the Penney farm road, where Alden had worked earlier. Lawrence felt he knew them well enough to wake them up and get help in getting me home. Well, it was considerably farther than he had imagined, and it was very dark. We walked and walked, and then walked some more. We saw an animal ahead of us at one point, and we were afraid it was a moose, which could be dangerous. It turned out to be a horse out of the pasture. What a relief! It was a very long time before we finally arrived at the Penney Farm, and George was actually getting up that early to start the milking. He gave us a ride to my folks' house, and by then Dad was up. As my date was bringing me home at such an unseemly hour, Dad's words to Lawrence and me were: "Made quite a night of it, didn't you?"

Lawrence, home from the war, set about going into business with his father, enlarging their greenhouse operation. Some crops were grown outdoors also. These included field-grown pansies, which are very labor-intensive. The black flies during that season were horrendous! Another major crop was glads—gladiolus bulbs which yielded a huge crop of beautiful cut flowers. They were laborious, too—planting the bulbs, tending the crop, cutting the flower stems, and walking back and forth to put them into cans of water at the end of the rows. In the fall came digging bulbs, drying bulbs, shucking bulbs, and stacking boxes to store for the winter.

The greenhouse business was seasonal, but during the winter, wooden seedling boxes were made in which the seedlings were to be planted and sold in the spring. This job was almost like a family party, done in what had once been a henhouse (a project of Lawrence's in the past), cleaned up and heated with a metal barrel woodstove. Each person, including the children, was set up to a bench, given a hammer, small nails, and the shook from which the boxes took shape. There were two sides, two ends, and two bottom pieces to be nailed together to make each box. Today's seedling boxes are so very different! They are half the size or less, made of lightweight fiber or plastic, and filled with a very light "artificial" soil mix.

By telling this now, I may be getting ahead of myself, but I spent a lot of days during our "courtship" period at their house and place of business, helping with the work. We would often go to the movies or somewhere after the day's work was done.

Lawrence had been on the front lines on active duty in Germany during the war. His war experiences, like those of so many young men who went when their country called, were unimaginable. It does things to people who have to be part of such horror. Once off the front lines and back in France, at Officer Candidate School, he was in much less danger but still experiencing the molding of his character by the military discipline and the war terror he had seen. It affected the whole remainder of his life, as well as the lives of his family.

When the war in Europe was finally ending, he was kept on in the army of occupation. He was then a second lieutenant. As an officer, he had many assignments. For instance, at three different times he was in charge of a concentration camp which had been turned into a prison for German prisoners of war. He also was in charge of moving a trainload of displaced persons once. Young men like him had to grow up fast in those times.

I was still a teenager, although more mature than most. Girls my age were swooning and fainting over Frank Sinatra. I had some pretty adult philosophies and values. But was I ready for marriage?

Was he the right choice for me? Was I wrong to decide that I wanted to be the one he chose? Should I go away to Bible college, knowing he would probably choose someone else while I was gone? It was a big decision.

His life experiences compared to my lack thereof, along with an age difference of seven years and ten months, the fact that 19 is usually too young for marriage, plus our natural personalities—my desire to please and do the right thing, and his need to take charge—set us up for certain dynamics in a wedded partnership. To have a successful marriage would take some luck, a lot of love, and strong characters determined to be fair and to work toward success.

Added to that was the expectation by both men and women then that the man would be the head of the household, make the decisions, handle the money, and tell his wife pretty much what to do. Men were supposed to "control" their wives, and only a weak man let his wife "wear the pants." He was in control of the purse strings if he was a real man. For our wedding vows, I promised to "love, honor, and obey" him, while he promised to "love, honor, and cherish" me. In later years, "women's libbers" raised everyone's consciousness of a woman's worth as a person, and how unfair it is for a man to expect a woman to obey him. A woman knows she is equal to any man. Men of my generation learned to give lip service to that, but some couldn't completely abandon the old ideas; they were ingrained.

Lawrence stayed in the Army Reserves, and that has made a huge difference in our lives over the years. I mention it now because that was one of his sources of income.

Lawrence finally proposed in April 1949, and we were married on July 2nd that same year at my parents' house in Belgrade with only our two families present. That number made more than a houseful! So began a new chapter in both of our lives, the two of us facing the world together and building our futures as one. We were so very happy!

If I Could Be a Fairy

Gardens seem so heavenly, with fairies everywhere,
Sliding down the beanstalks and combing carrot-hair,
Playing "ring-a-rosy" around a cabbage head,
And borrowing some corn silk to make a featherbed.

If I could be a fairy, or cherub, here today,
And had my choice of playgrounds, I know where I would play.
I'd choose a dewy garden with care, and there remain,
For joy is in the sunshine, and in the drops of rain.

But then when it came winter, I'd have to choose again.
I'd pick a sunny patch of green near some bright windowpane.
I'd slide down spider plants all day and climb the ivy stair;
I'd comb some green plumosa fern instead of carrot-hair.

I think that Heaven must have plants, to go with streets of gold,
And all the other happy things of joy, as we are told.
The fairies know a lovely place—a garden where plants grow;
And people, too, will find it's true, for Life is there, you know.

Our Faith in the Wind

No man has ever seen the wind
That makes the tall trees sway.
EFFECTS of wind are what we see
When March winds have their way.
SOME PEOPLE MIGHT CALL THAT FAITH,
      since we can't see the wind, but only its effects.
The air we breathe we cannot see,
And yet we know it's there.
EFFECTS of air keep us alive;
We breathe it everywhere.
SOME PEOPLE MIGHT CALL THAT FAITH,
      since we can't see the air, but only its effects.
We've harnessed electricity.
Ben Franklin knew its power.
EFFECTS of it are powerful
And we pay for it by the hour.
SOME PEOPLE MIGHT CALL THAT FAITH,
      since we can't see electricity, but only its effects.
So why should there not be more things
Unseen, that we can feel,
EFFECTS of God's hand everywhere
Which suggest that He is real?
SOME PEOPLE MIGHT CALL THAT FAITH,
      since we can see only His effects.

Married Life and the Old Burns School

Lady Luck was with us that year. Farmingdale had built a new consolidated school, leaving three one-room schoolhouses vacant. The town sold them at bid, at just the right time for us. The Burns School was across Litchfield Road from the Longfellow brick house and greenhouse business. It was built in 1916. The lot was about three-fourths of an acre in size. Lawrence's mother had taught school there, as had a few other women over the years. All the Longfellow children had gone to school there through the eighth grade.

When we moved into the schoolhouse, the desks were still there and the slates were still on the walls! There was no running water, no bathroom. I had no kitchen sink. The only things we bought right away were the electric range and the bed. There was an old table there in the schoolhouse, and a couple of chairs. I still use a small bookcase that was left there. We scrounged a couple of unused pieces from our families' attics, and that is all we had at first, as we proceeded to make a home out of the old Burns schoolhouse.

At the inexperienced age of 19, I set about drawing up plans for making the building over into a one-and-a-half-story home for us and a big family of children. (Lawrence had said he wanted eight children.)

We needed a carpenter, of course, and my father kindly offered to work for us for a lower rate than he usually got during times when he had no regular work available. Year after year in his slack seasons, he would drive the twenty miles or so, bring his lunch, and fix up our home the way his daughter wanted it—with advice from time to time about things a carpenter would know. It was after 1960 that we were finally able to make use of our upstairs.

We offered to have him eat with us, but he said that if he did he would feel he needed to wash up, comb his hair, and take more time, so he preferred to just open his lunch pail. That's the kind of man he was.

I plunged into married life fully determined to be the best wife, mother, and homemaker possible. Magazine articles of those days urged wives to build up their husbands' egos and look after their happiness. Such a life was to be viewed as a career in itself. I really tried, and even without conveniences to work with, I enjoyed my new role in life.

We had some very enjoyable times that summer. We took a few trips, to New Hampshire and to Quebec, to name a couple. We went down to the Cape (Cape Elizabeth) to visit (sister) Arlene and Roy Maxwell and their land on the Back Shore. We went on Sunday picnics with my folks, and had lobster. We went to New Portland to visit my grandmother and family. We went to a lot of places and visited a lot with Alden and his girlfriend, soon to be his wife, Esther Benner.

In spite of a few newlywed adjustments, and learning about each other, life was good.

Late in the summer, Lawrence decided to sign up for active duty, since he was in the Reserves, to go to an army school for four months. It would mean good pay, and would be a good experience for the two of us. I quit my job, even though my office manager had chosen me as the person that she wished to train to use a new (pre-computer) office machine. We gathered the squash that he had grown that summer for a cash crop, and stored it in the henhouse. We wound up the other fall chores, packed a few essentials into the Olds, and headed south. It was the last of October, and we were going to Fort Benning, in Columbus, Georgia, for four months. It was my first trip beyond Massachusetts.

It was hard for Mom to have me go so far away. The Longfellows invited us, and my father and mother, for supper the night before we left. It was a bit hard for me to leave, too, but my husband, my "lord and master," was with me, and where he was would always be home to me. And…I would have him all to myself! For four months! It was like a second honeymoon!

Alden and Esther had been married October 8th, just three weeks before we left. They had no house but were going to build one, down over the hill, on the other side of the brick house. Alden asked his brother if they could live in our house while we were away. We were glad to help them out, as they would have had to live in the brick house with his parents all winter. I will admit, though, that I felt a bit selfish about someone else using my new wedding gifts and my few possessions, which I so valued. As I spent my winter in Georgia, using someone else's apartment and equipment, I actually said to myself as I cleaned the oven that I would take good care of the items I was borrowing, and hope that my things at home were being treated with equal care. Of course they were, and I was glad we could help.

We found a second-floor apartment on arrival in Columbus, on Halloween, and had trick-or-treaters at our door before we got moved in. The place consisted of a nice bedroom and a separate kitchen, separated from our room by the hallway and doors on both rooms. The bathroom had to be shared with a quiet gentleman who lived down the hall.

We had cockroaches—some of them very big! After all, Georgia is a "tropical" state! In the kitchen, Lawrence squashed one small one on the wall over the table and then drew its outline on the wall around the body with a pencil. I can still see that drawing in my mind's eye! I still have to laugh.

I remember that winter as a happy time for learning to cook and keep house, with lots of time for writing letters and reading. I got up and got our breakfast early; but when he left for the day, I usually went back to bed for a nap! A few times I walked the mile or less to the shopping area, especially around Christmastime. It was amazing to me to not need a coat, but only a sweater, and to admire the flowers in people's gardens—in December! I learned from a book how to do tatting, and I made a pair of pink earrings for my mother for Christmas, as an extra gift.

We took an evening class in astronomy together, which was very interesting. One night he had evening duty and couldn't attend class. I took the bus and went by myself. On the many evenings that we spent alone—just the two of us newlyweds—he often had homework. We played cards a lot, and rummy was our favorite. He usually won, but I continued to want to play.

Then it was Christmas. We had bought a small tree, which sat in the window on a little table. We bought only a few ornaments, but to me it was beautiful! We exchanged Christmas cards (seems odd now). On mine he described for me his visions for our future together—a home and children. I can't remember what we gave each other for presents. There was a fireplace in our room, which we had not used, but we decided to spend Christmas Eve in front of a nice fire, on a blanket on the floor. I put on the pretty robe that my co-workers at the Bureau of Taxation had given me at a farewell dinner at the Augusta House when I left. Even though it was my first Christmas away from my parents and home, it was our first Christmas together. I was warm and happy.

It was a lovely evening. Later on we heard voices and looked out the window. There was a fire truck down there! We never knew for sure, but we assumed the chimney had caught fire due to our celebration with an unused fireplace. No firemen came to the door, though, so maybe it wasn't our chimney after all.

Lawrence had a week off at Christmastime. He wanted to take me to Florida during that time, but almost gave up the idea because he had a toothache! However, early in his army training he had spent time in Florida, and he dearly wanted to visit again. So we went, and the toothache was bearable. It actually got better each day.

That first night in the soft, warm Florida air was so nostalgic and at the same time so exciting for him that he scarcely slept at all. The week went by quickly, as we visited some of his old haunts, and I gazed in wonder at orange groves and palm trees and all the beauties there. Florida has remained dear to me ever since. I have always remembered with special affection the Bok Tower and its carillon bells. We have visited there several times over the years since. Edward Bok is quoted as saying he wanted to make the world a better place. He certainly did that!

The time in the South passed quickly, with both of us writing frequent letters home and receiving replies; my organizing a cookbook, learning to cook for my very particular husband, and getting plenty of rest; and the two of us getting to know each other.

My husband was impractical when it came to opportunities to

be generous. He wanted to buy a new van for his father and drive it home. He felt very strongly about it, and he wished he could manage it. I don't remember what suggested it to him. I knew that we just couldn't afford to do it, and that we would need any money we could earn. He knew I was right, and gave up on the idea, although reluctantly.

We headed home the first week of March, and made a trip out of it. One of the early adventures happened in Kentucky. I was in charge of reading the map, thereby choosing our route. I was new at the task, and got us off on a mountain road with dangerous switchbacks and no guardrails. Memory insists that it was raining, also. (Rain makes a better story anyway!) We would come suddenly upon places where the edge of the road had collapsed into the depths below. It got dark, and there were no towns and few houses. Where were we going to find a place to stay, and were we going to be able to get there safely? Or would we disappear down over one of those steep drop-offs?

We finally came to the town of Hazard, Kentucky, and there were rooms available! The next morning, we sat up to a counter at a diner and had a hearty breakfast. We were fascinated by the conversation of the two waitresses behind the counter. Not only their exaggerated Southern drawl, but also their colloquialisms were charming. For instance, one said to the other as they conversed, "He was my onliest brother." Afterward, we used that word to each other on occasion and enjoyed the shared memory.

We stopped at a park in Tennessee where there was a "Lovers' Leap," a swinging rope bridge, and a "Fat Man's Squeeze," among other attractions. I can't recall the name of the park, but I have pictures.

In Virginia and North Carolina, we wanted to drive the Skyline Drive, but when we got there we found it closed, probably not open during the winter months. That husband of mine drove around the "closed" sign, and said we'd go a little way on it, or until we had to turn back. Well, we drove the whole length, and never saw another car! What if we had had a breakdown or other emergency? There was snow, but the road was plowed. Anyway, the scenery was beautiful, even at that time of year. The road is in the Blue Ridge Mountains, and in later years we made three or four trips along it.

We also toured a few spots in Washington, DC, although I confess I don't recall much about the city from that trip. I remember *walking* down from the top of the Washington Monument instead of taking the elevator, an experience which was an option. There were nearly six hundred steps.

In New York I remember Central Park and the Bronx Zoo. A gorilla spit at me from his cage! Travel is so educational!

When we got home, Alden and Esther moved back to the brick house until their new house was finished. We socialized with them regularly, living so close. She worked at the State House also.

I say "also" because when I got home, my old assistant office manager at the Bureau of Taxation wanted me to come back to work. The girl they had hired to replace me had messed up those charts I referred to earlier, of taxes in the unorganized territories. She didn't have the math skills or the ability to use an adding machine accurately. I had to go over all of her work and get those columns to add up vertically and horizontally, which took me just about all summer! I got pretty fast and accurate on the adding machine!

We did lots of things together, the two couples. Work on the farm was a big part of it. I hated being away every day to go to work, even though I knew we needed the money I brought in. We talked it over and agreed that, feeling as I did, if I stayed home I could put in more time on the farm work and help to bring in money in that way. When the job I had been asked to do for the State was completed, I stopped working and settled down to being a good wife and homemaker, and my husband's helper.

I soon joined Lawrence's church, Old South Congregational. I had never been baptized and needed to be, as part of church membership. To please my mother, I was baptized by immersion (the Baptist way) at the Hallowell Baptist Church. Two deacons from Old South had to be there to witness my baptism. My folks and Lawrence were there, too. I got Dr. Bradshaw (who had married us) to come down from Bangor to baptize me. It was an emotional experience for me, being a religious person.

In 1950 trouble began in Korea. Reservists were being called up for active duty. I was terribly worried that he would have to go. I didn't think that would be fair. He had gone through so much, and so recently! He wasn't called then or anytime later, but that was when I realized that life isn't fair. Nowhere are we promised fairness.

Life went on. It was a quiet country style of life with work paramount and family closeness as the cementing factor.

As an extreme example of things our foursome did together, the following poem stands out in memory. This happened right after we returned from our winter in Georgia, and the squashes' winter in the henhouse.

Rats, Youth, Love, and Laughter

Two country brothers worked the farm,
Year—nineteen forty-nine,
Chose two girls for their blushing brides,
And life was really fine!
> They needed money—extra cash—
> To start their two homes, new.
> They planted cucumber and squash.
> Need more sales than a few!
Their bounty sold all summer long,
But extra squash was stored
Within the henhouse (no hens then),
Best place they could afford.
> In winter's cold, the fire's warmth,
> Some squash succumbed by now.
> Some rotted and attracted rats.
> Mess had to go; but how?
Now rats are vermin, bad on farms;
There were many gathered here.
To free them now would not be wise,
They'd spread out far and near!
> Where was the famed Pied Piper, hmmm?
> He'd pipe the rats away!
> 'Twas just the men and their good wives.
> Yes, they must save the day!
The stinking stew of slimy squash
Was home to rats, and oh!
You had to watch your step in there,
'Twas slipp'ry, don't you know!
> They plugged all exit holes, rat-chewed,
> That rats used night and day,
> And they were blocked from all escape
> As squash was moved away.

The four were armed with baseball bats
And shovels, brooms, and hoes.
They manned four corners, war to wage,
While holding tight the nose!
       First shoveled corner—there's a rat!
       Hullabaloo began!
       "There's one! Get him!" "Wa-hoo!" "Oh no!"
       A shriek, loud laughter, WHAM!
"Oh, Judas, gone! There's one! Look out!"
Oh, did those women dance!
The next half hour, squash all moved,
The rats had no last chance.
       They didn't kill all rats that night.
       Hated killing anyway!
       Protecting farm and family
       Took courage, one might say.
They hated killing, but hated rats,
Stepped forward all the same.
When duty called they answered clear—
And made of it a game!
       Their youth, high spirits, helped them do
       What must be anyway.
       They laughed—'twas funny, fearful, too!
       Remembered 'til this day!

Strawberries Are Ripe on Longfellow Hill

"The berries are ripe!" comes the word on The Hill.
"We need to start picking today.
Come early; it's hot out; many boxes to fill."
Women, children, and men on their way.

      Now Alden is driving the mail every day,
      And Lawrence the Star Route and KJ.
      So Esther, in shorts (looking pretty always),
      And Mavis, and big kids fill trays.

The berries are Sparkles, so juicy and red.
Choose a row and pick clean as you go.
The women bend over to reach the raised bed,
Though kneeling is better, they know.

      The baskets fill slowly, or quickly sometimes.
      Trays of six, carry back to the shade.
      Turn the berries on top to look juicy and fine
      To tempt that good buyer; sale made!

The children have set up their stand on the lawn
In the shade 'neath the maples, so cool.
There's even a breeze—it's been hot since the dawn.
At strawberry time, that's the rule.

      Grandfather may visit these tykes by the road;
      The berries and kids he will watch.
      But both are just fine; they soon need a new load.
      Berries sell for a dollar a box.

Down the hill now comes Lawrence, with boxes in tow.
He looks for good picking, and fast.
He finds it and starts, further end of the row.
No bending—he kneels. Help at last!

He's known for fast picking; his record is old.
He skips poorer bushes for now.
 His goal: to fill boxes and get them all sold;
The question remaining is: "How?"

Now sharing in life is an admirable trait,
But with some things the urge you may quell.
He was told by his father, a lesson most quaint:
"When you find a good berry bush, don't tell!"

It's noon and the housework has not yet been done,
No laundry, meals cooked, and such deeds.
For lunch there are berries! and leftovers (fun!)
Then caring for children with needs.

Not easy, our lives, but from tragedy spared.
We now reap rewards many fold!
The FAMILIES we nurtured (our lives showed we cared)
Are our rewards—or pure gold!!

Although this is about life on the farm several years down the road, it illustrates our working together, with everyone doing their bit.

On Esther's suggestion in later years that I write another poem, I searched my memory for something I could write about that would interest her and her family, as well as have meaning for me and mine. Our children and their lives, and their love for us in return for our love and labor for them, have turned out well. These factors have been the backbone of our own lives. We now can rejoice in the rich rewards we earned and are now reaping, through having large families, even though it wasn't always easy while the children were young. I hope I have struck a note close enough to the truth to bring pleasant memories and also gratitude for our blessings, regardless of the early costs to us.

"Those were the days, my friend; we thought they'd never end..."

My Life's Mission Fulfilled

That late fall, after our winter in Georgia, we decided it was time to start our family. Of course, our house wasn't anywhere near finished and we didn't have much money. The greenhouse business wasn't profitable enough to support two families, even though Lester, Lawrence's father, kept giving us breaks and extras. However, we didn't think we had to have a lot of money or perfect conditions to bring up our children. Also, I wanted to give Lawrence his first child before he was thirty.

It was early summer, 1951. Lawrence had signed up as a Reservist for a two-week mountain-climbing course in Colorado Springs, and we left by car right after attending Guy's wedding in Boston, and visiting Aunt Hazel and Uncle Paul the next day. We didn't have home pregnancy tests back then. I was "suspicious," and before we got to Colorado I was feeling very sick, especially as we drove into higher elevations.

We did a little sightseeing, but I couldn't enjoy it much. We were happy that I was pregnant, though, and that trip to Colorado remained among our fond memories.

We kept our good news secret for a couple of months. When we told Alden and Esther, we all got a surprise: Esther and I were both pregnant! None of us had talked about plans for a family, yet our due dates were only about three weeks apart. People wouldn't believe that we hadn't planned together.

Lawrence had to go to summer camp for two weeks, being in the Reserves, so I went to visit my folks in Belgrade while he was away. I was in the habit of going up there to do laundry anyway. Before long I told them my good news. My poor mother looked as if I had hit her with a baseball bat! She'd had difficult deliveries with her babies, and she keenly felt and suffered with every ill feeling her children experienced. I knew she dreaded the birth for me. Still, I didn't get discouraged. That morning sickness was debilitating, though.

I enjoyed my pregnancy a great deal, in spite of the sickness. I was happy, and I found the experience so very interesting. I read up on pregnancy, delivery, and child-rearing, notably Dr. Spock. I bought a large rectangular clothes basket and padded it and covered it with a pretty fabric. We didn't know whether to expect a boy or a girl, but I used both pink and blue fabric on that little bed. I redecorated that same basket for each of my six babies. Esther's sister was also pregnant, and we three hemmed squares of flannel for receiving blankets. We made little gowns that opened down the back. I bought a large enamel-coated baby's bathtub, belly bands, undershirts, cloth diapers, a diaper pail, and very little else. Esther and I were given a joint shower, so we got most of the necessities as well as a few other treasured gifts, like a baby record book.

In due time, our daughter, Anna Mae, was born. (Lawrence had suggested calling her Scarlet, but I never knew whether he was joking.) She was a large baby at nine pounds, seven and a half ounces. I was given an epidural for the birth. Dr. Fay was even more old-fashioned than the other local doctors and kept me in bed for four days. It was such a wonderful experience when the nurse brought Anna in to nurse, her dark hair dressed up with a little pink bow. Lawrence was as proud as could be. He got off the elevator and looked in the nursery window where the nurse was showing him his daughter. From my room down the hall, I knew he had arrived when I could hear him exclaim that she was the prettiest baby there! (His voice carried well!)

Mom was there to help us when we got home, and the very first night we had a major blizzard, which went down in weather history. It had been snowing on the way home from the hospital. Lawrence had put plastic sheeting over a couple of windows and doors to keep the cold drafts away from his new daughter, and had plenty of wood for the fire to keep us all warm. Anna woke up at just about 2:00 a.m., and her proud father walked in deep snow over to his folks' house, rapped on their bedroom window, and informed them, "Time for the two o'clock feeding!" Now that was a proud and happy daddy!

The next day we were snowed in, with Litchfield Road not

plowed all the way. After a few hours, we were pleasantly surprised to see my father driving in. He had been able to get there by taking Maple Street off Route 201 in Farmingdale and following it to its junction with Litchfield Road, a bit below our house. Before leaving Belgrade, he had to walk in hip-deep snow to his barn to feed and milk his cows. Then he struck out in this major storm to see if we needed any help with his new granddaughter.

Alden and Esther welcomed Nancy just three weeks later. She was as dark as Anna was fair, and weighed just a bit over six pounds.

No parents were ever happier or more proud than we were. We would sit and gaze at Anna in pure admiration. I enjoyed the whole experience of all those months of guarding my baby until birth, then the miracle of childbirth, and then the actual little person, so innocent, so new, so wonderful, and mine.

A funny thing happened one night while Mom was with us. I was so very tired, but still had to nurse the baby when she awoke. Mom said she could help by changing her diaper and getting her back to bed. During the night I decided to bring her out to Mom and take her up on her offer. I brought her out and passed her to Mom, only to hear her say, "What have you done with the baby??? This is a pillow!! Where is the baby?" In my sleepy state, I led the way back to where the baby's basket sat beside my bed, sleepily blocking Mom's way as she tried to get by me. As we crossed the big heat register in the living room, she almost burned her bare feet! The baby was sound asleep in her basket. I guess I had dreamed that I had fed her and needed Mom to get her back to bed.

In a very few weeks, I was needed at the greenhouse, as spring season had begun. We had a high chair/table and chair/stroller combination that we had bought, and sometimes I used the stroller wheel assembly to transport her in her basket, or I would carry her over to the greenhouse in her basket, park it on a bench, and try to keep her comfortable. A friend of mine from my work days at the State House brought her baby and visited us. Her little boy was in a snowsuit, and my Anna was in just a diaper! When we first took her to New Portland to show her off to my mother's family, she had a great big black fly bite in the middle of her forehead, which she had gotten at the greenhouse!

Anna was a little princess, with good behavior and motherly, helpful ways. We were always so very proud of her. She had many talents, from a very young age.

We planned for the children to be about two years apart in age. Scott Wilson was born just about on schedule. I had similar problems with morning sickness with this pregnancy, too, only I was not two-thirds of the way across the country, in high elevations, with a new experience, as I had been with my first. Again I had an epidural. Scott had a little difficulty breathing that first day, so they put him in an oxygen tent overnight. They assured me we had nothing to worry about, that it was done just to make it easier for him. I think it was his first allergy attack, of which he has had many throughout his life.

He was only a couple of ounces lighter than Anna had been, at nine pounds, three and a half ounces. We were so glad to welcome him—our first son; we now had a daughter *and* a son! He was fine, and we went home five days later. My mother was to spend a couple of weeks with us. I can remember as we drove up to the house seeing Anna peeking up over the windowsill, on tiptoe, to get a look at us as we came in! That's one of those things that stick in your memory.

Again, Esther and I had our second children, both boys, only a few days apart. She was first this time.

As an infant, Scott had to be fed every two or three hours around the clock for weeks! Oh, well, he was well worth every minute of it! Besides, time spent nursing the baby was time spent resting for me, as I made it a habit to lie down myself. Often it provided a nap for both mother and baby, which didn't help to get much work done!

Those were precious times that meant so much! Having a large family was not easy, but I'm so very glad that we did it.

Every single year when the Christmas season rolled around, we and our children, our entire family, went to cut down a tree in the woods. It didn't matter if I was pregnant or had a small child to carry; all of our children and Lawrence and I braved the cold and snow. It gets dark so early in December that we would have to hurry when the children were in school, and know where we were going to hunt for the best tree before it got dark. Usually we could do it on a weekend, though. Scott's birth was nearest to Christmas of my six children. I was, of course, quite uncomfortable by tree-selection time *that* Christmas. Lawrence knew that there was a fir tree that was big enough, in the field across from the brick house, down near the sawdust pile. We went by tractor and trailer down the lane to keep up our new annual tradition.

Children are so different, and boys are different from girls. I had to learn that Scott was not going to be like Anna. He walked earlier than she, but she talked earlier than he—that sort of thing. He was more mischievous than she was, being a boy. Nevertheless, he grew up to be a wonderful person. We loved and enjoyed him tremendously all through childhood, were proud of him, and just so glad he was ours! He has always shown special abilities to an unusual extent.

Lawrence began taking Scott out with him at a very early age, which grew into their working together as Scott became older. Lawrence later was quite sure that he worked Scott too hard and too many hours all through his childhood. Still, Scott didn't seem to mind, and he did have time for play. The greenhouse was a ready-made playhouse for boys when it was not full of plants. The boys used to make roads in the dirt benches, and I can still hear their voices giving engine sounds to the various trucks, tractors, and other toy vehicles that they played with. He greatly enjoyed looking at the "tractor book" each month, which is what he and I called the *Farm Journal.*

A clipping on our wall throughout their childhood said that a person becomes what he thinks, reads, and keeps on his mind (not a quote). I tried to teach them that. I strongly believe it.

I would add that a child needs to be flexible and buoyant because parents are far from perfect. In spite of our mistakes and shortcomings, we must have done something right because a finer family of children, now grown, would be hard to find.

By the time we had six children, the older ones were helping out quite a lot. I have always said that I was glad we had a girl first, as Anna was like my right arm. She was a valuable "second mother." She had good judgment at an early age and always seemed willing to help.

Wayne Lester Longfellow was born a couple of years later. This birth preparation, labor, and delivery were different from my first two. But oh yes, I still had the morning sickness!

I am a humble person, not given to boasting, but what I did was a phenomenal accomplishment of which I am rightfully proud. I had heard about a new theory called "natural childbirth," which was built on the assumption that much of the pain of labor and delivery are due to fear and misunderstanding of the physical process. Admittedly, the body goes through tremendously hard work and stress, but knowledge and attitude can render the woman's interpretation of her experience as "labor"—work that her body is doing to bring forth her reward, not just torture that she has to endure.

I purchased Grantly Dick Reed's book *Childbirth Without Fear* and studied it. I borrowed a book from the library on Progressive Relaxation, and lay down every day to exercise and to practice this type of relaxation. I learned to recognize tension in my body and to let that tension go. I identified groups of muscles, which I tensed and then relaxed in progression. It takes practice, but I got pretty good at it.

I read *The Power of Positive Thinking* by Norman Vincent Peale. I made a list of relaxing, positive words to repeat to myself to keep up my spirits, like *serenity, tranquility, peace.* I committed to memory the Bible verse which seemed to give me courage and strength: "...They...shall renew their strength. They shall rise up with wings as eagles. They shall run and not be weary. They shall walk and not faint."

Realizing that I was a local pioneer in this method of childbirth, and that my doctor and nurses would not be knowledgeable or sympathetic, I knew that I would have to do it all alone. Husbands and others were not allowed in the labor or delivery rooms. Would I be able to do it without a coach?

I talked to Dr. Fay and got his permission to go ahead with my plan. We decided that I should probably have an anesthesiologist in the delivery room in case I needed him. The doctor let me know that he considered it so much nonsense and that I must have a subconscious self-punishing wish to suffer. The nurse who attended me during labor asked to see my book on natural childbirth. When she brought it back, she said, "I guess it's all in how you get yourself to thinking." In many things we do in life, I guess there is an element of self-hypnosis. That's not a bad thing if it helps you to rise to greater heights.

I will not say that the labor was painless. I will say that I did not have unbearable pain. I did not need anesthesia.

The joy and pride with which I greeted our new baby boy that afternoon were beyond measure. He was a few ounces heavier than Anna or Scott, at nine pounds, eight and a quarter ounces, and just as near to being perfect. They were all beautiful!

Wayne was my most placid baby. They all cried quite a lot for the first six weeks, and only a little less until they were about three months old. Those were hard times due to lack of sleep, upset hormones, and some little worry. A baby is a tremendous, although wonderful, responsibility. I decided not to have Mom come down to help, although she would have liked to. Certainly I could have used some help at such a time, with three children now; but no matter who it might be, another person in the house adds a certain element of stress, and I felt we could manage alone. I had plans for doing the necessary chores.

Anna had turned four while I was in the hospital. (I had bought two new dresses for her birthday present, and I hated to miss her big day. I missed my kids each time I had to stay in the hospital, as they weren't allowed to visit.) A four-year-old can't do much work, but they can bring you things and help out in little ways. We got by nicely. Since Wayne was a little more patient and polite than some babies, he could wait fairly easily while I got the meal on the table, for instance.

Polio had been a terrible scourge, especially for children, for years. It was a big worry to parents. At last a vaccine was developed, of which we took advantage with gratitude and relief, when our town held a clinic, giving free vaccine to all children. As we walked into the building, Lawrence took Anna by the hand, and I held Wayne in my arms. Scott walked along with us. There were two lines of children being vaccinated. Lawrence took Anna through one line and I took Wayne through the other. Then I had Scott come through my line, and he got his shot. The trouble was that he had already had a shot in the other line! I was so stricken I could hardly speak! What had I done? What was going to happen to him? The whole process came to a standstill as the two doctors conferred. They decided that no harm would come to him. It has been many years, and I have worried frequently that there would someday be some residual event stemming from my big mistake. I'll never forget that horrible day!

A few days later we left home as a family on a winter adventure. Lawrence had arranged to take another army course, this time at Fort Knox, Kentucky. Anna was five years and eight months old. Scott was three years and nine months and Wayne one year and eight months. Anna was in kindergarten, and I was doubtful about taking her out of school. I hated to put her in a strange school for four months. Her Farmingdale kindergarten teacher, Mrs. Nelson, said she would send some papers for Anna to practice on, and Anna would be in school anyway for the months of September, October, March, April, May, and part of June, so she would be able to pass into first grade without going to school for those four months.

We packed our Bel-Air sedan with essentials quite carefully. We filled the trunk, then the floor of the backseat section up to the height of the seat. Then we continued putting things across the whole back section as evenly as possible to make a flat surface for the three children. They had pretty tight quarters, but we made it work. In those days, there were no seat belts or car seats.

We had only one pet, a little turtle, and he went with us. One night on the way down, we booked a room, but we forgot and left the turtle in the car, in his little home with the water in it (a bowl, I think) sitting on the dashboard. The next morning he was frozen in place! He thawed out slowly as we drove, and became quite active for a while. He lived for a long time with us during our four months in Kentucky.

The last night of the long drive down, we stayed in a room for visitors at the army base. Next morning, we began our hurried search for a home for the winter. We looked at several places. Anna and Scott decided they wanted a mobile home. I'm glad we didn't decide to do that!

It got to be night, and I was so tired and discouraged! We settled for a second-floor apartment in an old building in Valley Station, just south of Louisville. We moved in late at night. I felt I had to scrub the table and other things before I could prepare a quick supper. Then we had to decide on sleeping quarters and make beds. Wayne had a sort of cot instead of a crib, in the hallway. Somehow I trained him to stay in bed and not get up and wander off while we slept. He didn't need a crib, I guess.

Lawrence rented a television set at the base for us to use. Before we undertook this trip, we had recently purchased our first television at home.

We soon learned that we would be planning for our fourth baby in August. Of course, I didn't feel well, and I had a hard time getting us settled in and keeping us clothed and fed. We had to have the landlady, Mrs. Mahoney, come by for several reasons while we were there. She complained a lot, and told stories about past renters. She frequently voiced what we learned to consider her bywords: "Ain't people awful?"

The children enjoyed Christmas and each of their birthdays while we were there. We did quite a lot of sightseeing. Lawrence took us to the base for Thanksgiving dinner. We came back home in early March, ready to pitch in at the greenhouse.

Alice Priscilla was born in the summer after we got home again. I had not asked for an anesthesiologist to be on duty this time, and again I did not need anesthesia. My first impression of my new little girl was that she was so pretty! She was like a delicate and fragile pink shell or flower. She had fair skin, fine hair, big eyes, long lashes, and a rosebud mouth. She weighed somewhat less than the first three, just eight pounds and six ounces.

The older children were big enough to really help out quite a bit. They adored Alice (at least at first!) and entertained her at times. I loved having a new little one to nurse, rock, sing to, dress, and watch develop. When your child is little, she is all yours, and she adores you without question or judgment. I had no spare time, but I enjoyed her more than there are words to express. I see her now as a couple of years old, my little blondie in a blue corduroy one-piece playsuit, sitting in her little rocking chair. In her bathing suit, she looked like a little peanut!

Alice was born in August, and do you know when early tomatoes ripen? In August! The men grew market tomatoes many years, Alden every year and Lawrence a few years. They all had to be picked, sorted, washed or wiped, and packed in boxes. Lawrence was growing them that year, and I remember bushels of them day after day in my kitchen sink. I would put Alice on the couch with her little music box beside her and work on those tomatoes while stacks of dirty dishes waited to be washed.

The busiest part of the greenhouse season was from March to June. Black flies were horrendous during that time. Glad bulbs had to be planted during that hectic season, also. Then came strawberry season; the picking again was a family affair. At times there were other crops. Lester's glads were picked for selling, delivered or at the house. Lester and Lawrence usually did the cutting, and I (or the older kids) would carry each armload to the cans of water on the trailer at the end of the rows. We walked miles! One year he sold 4100 dozen glads! Pansies had to be transplanted (on hands and knees) in their winter beds for sale the next spring. In the spring they had to be dug (on hands and knees) and sold, six to a box. One year they sold 12,000 boxes! After frost hit, glad bulbs were dug. Lester (alone) then sorted, dried, shucked, and stored them.

I worked many hours every week on these farm jobs. Sometimes the children were with us, sometimes playing at Alden's house, and sometimes they were at our house with dependable oldest sister Anna. Apparently we took adequate care, and they became responsible, self-confident, and capable individuals. This is another example of the good luck we had in having a girl first, as she was so often the one caring for them. Esther and I babysat for each other. We only hired an "outside" girl a few times.

I had little of any social life except family, but I did go to choir practice and church. I even took a couple of evening classes at the University of Maine at Augusta, which was getting established. One or two of those years, Lawrence and I took a class together. I recall economics and math, and one other. This probably was mostly after 1960; it's hard to remember.

In addition to being a wife, mother, homemaker, and all-around farmhand, I also was substitute driver for Lawrence, who contracted to carry the Star Route (sacks of mail) from Hallowell to Litchfield post offices six days a week. He took the morning route, in which he delivered mail to houses along part of the route also, and I very often took one or both of the other two trips, from one post office straight to the other. The baby and young children would go with me, or sometimes one or more would be napping and left for Lawrence to check on, or they might be outside with him. Later on, he enlarged his mail route by taking on an additional route, for a Mr. Antworth. I didn't have to drive that one.

Somewhere along the line, Lawrence took on the job of substitute for Alden's RFD mail route. Esther had been Alden's sub, but when their family grew large, she found it was too much for her. Lawrence took it over to preserve the job for her return when the children got older. She never went back to it, though.

It didn't happen often, but there were some days when he had to do not only all of his jobs, but the sub job as well. That wasn't easy. On those days, he sometimes had me go with him to help by putting the mail into the mailboxes while he drove.

Another very important element of our family life had to be accommodated and absorbed when Lawrence took on yet another job. We needed the money, and to his credit, he was trying to support us. This job was to deliver bundles of newspapers around several towns to the paper boys and to the stores where papers were sold. What made it difficult was the schedule. For several years beginning in the late 1950s, he got up at three every morning, delivered the papers, and then continued on his Star Route, getting home in midmorning. That meant that he had to go to bed right after supper, and the house, with a wife and four children (more children later) had to be quiet so he could sleep. We tried—with no loud television, no musical instrument practice, no company. We had no social life.

I had each of the children take at least two years of piano lessons and then their choice of a band instrument. After a few years, when all but the youngest needed time and place to practice early, that wasn't always easy! When I think back, I hear the piano, the trumpet, the clarinet, and one or two more instruments, each in a different room, as the children attempted to finish practicing before supper in order to keep the evenings quiet for their father. Anna studied piano for ten years, Lorraine (nicknamed Dee) for five.

This was the world, our little world on Litchfield Road, into which little Lorraine Evelyn was born, one October morning, at 2:56 a.m. She weighed eight pounds and nine ounces. It was a quick labor and delivery. A precious, beautiful, perfect little baby was mine again. This new doctor kept me in bed only a day less than Dr. Fay did. I went home on the fourth day.

What a wonderful experience it is for a mother to see her baby when it is first born, and to hear its first cry! I was awake for the births of all of my babies and wouldn't trade any of that for the more common circumstance at that time of being asleep and avoiding the added minutes of labor. This experience is to me right up there among the highest thrills in life. Yet I have heard women say, "I don't want any part of it. Just put me out for the whole thing." What a marvelous blessing they miss out on!

The times when I held my baby and felt her precious little body against me were times of purest love. She was so completely dependent on me. I was her whole world. In her eyes, I could do no wrong. When she held my finger so tightly, and later on when she smiled, I would just absorb the wonder of that love.

Since children were not allowed to visit in maternity, Lawrence brought all four of them a couple of times to stand under my window where I could see them and wave to them. I remember that it was late October and they were not yet in winter coats. They looked like ragamuffins down there in the cold. Each year now when I get out my winter coat, I remember that if it is late October, then it's time!

At last our family was nicely rounded out, and complete, at the count of three boys and three girls. Daniel Adams Longfellow was born on a Saturday afternoon. He was my heavyweight at nine pounds, thirteen and a half ounces. Labor went well and I was successful in my natural childbirth methods. In fact, another mother was taking note of my quiet and peaceful delivery. She inquired of the doctor about the method and was able to deliver her baby that night without drugs.

I did notice a difference in my body's response to the stresses of childbirth. I was 34 and hadn't given birth for four years. But things went well. I was very, very happy with my new little boy, and quite sure he would be my last baby. He was born around 5:00 p.m. Lawrence visited us, and then he and Alden and Esther took the kids and went to a church supper in Readfield. I didn't mind—I had my little son there with me. We joke about it now on his birthday.

Lawrence and I had a situation in which his blood was Rh positive and mine was Rh negative. This is a setup that often causes problems in fetuses. If the baby inherits its father's positive blood type, the mother's negative blood causes her body to attack the fetus before birth. These days, babies or fetuses are treated if a problem exists. However, a blood test showed that I had no antibodies built up, and no harm had been done to any of our children.

Dan was a "good" baby, like Wayne, and was polite and usually placid. Of course, he had all those older siblings bossing him around, and as he got older, he had to hold his own and prove himself. The children had records that we gave them for Christmas, and he would stand up on the piano bench and dance to "Jimmy's Train." His sisters thought that was cute, and it was! He was quiet and mild-mannered generally, a wonderful little boy!

He was not yet five when I started my five years of college, which left me less time for him. He and I had a good relationship, though. I had always cooked a lot and had snacks ready for the children when they got home from school. When I started college (at age 39), there just wasn't time for that as often. Dan would ask me to bake something, and I wouldn't have the time. At an early age he learned to make no-bake cookies!

All the older children had taken piano lessons from Mrs. Colomy for at least two years. Dan had several months of her lessons, and then she had a stroke and had to give up teaching. He was shortchanged. He did, however, sing in the junior choir at church, sang in chorus at school, and played trumpet for a while in the band. I tried so hard to get him to continue as he got older, but it wasn't "cool" for an older boy to do those things, and he quit.

Music has always added enjoyment to my life. Like most people, I have my favorite kinds; like most elderly people, I have no love for the so-called music of recent years. I made sure each of our children got a basic musical education, and they built on it from there, some more than others.

The Fragile, Flickering Flame

At first the fragile, flickering flame
Needs fanning, shelter, help to glow;
But soon erupts in glory bright,
All fiery, strong, and set to grow.

So this, my baby, helpless, young,
Needs me just now, my help and care.
Oh yes, I'll gladly guard and watch,
My every thought—how best he'll fare.

A privilege and honor high
Is mothering this child at length.
For I must fan the flickering flame
Until he finds his fire's strength.

This time is dear, I'll not forget,
My precious, fleeting, building time,
When he's all grown, an upright man,
Then I'll remember he was mine.

Little Boy Dan and Me

I thought I knew what "happy" meant,
It means "content," I'd say.
It's like the opposite of "sad,"
No problems in the way.

"Oh, yes, I'm happy!" I would say,
"Because there's nothing wrong."
Now I know just what it means;
It's taught my heart a song.

No words can tell the purest joy
As mother holds her child,
Hears his first cry, sees his dear face,
And feels his body, mild.
That tiny body, warm and real,
Depends for life itself,
So helpless, sweet, belongs to me—
Within my arms real wealth.

No words describe this mother's joy.
There's love in his eyes, blue.
Then when he smiles I know he feels
Our mother/child bond, too.

It's the only time I'm perfect here,
In anyone's eyes, it's true;
And I am happy beyond belief;
He's my world and my Heaven, too.

Bringing Up a Family:
The 1950s, '60s, and Early '70s

With some exceptions, my memories of these two decades are a sort of blur of diapers, babies, fevers, pregnancies, farm and greenhouse work, housework, mail routes, paper routes, anxiety and depression, first days of school, trying to keep the children safe, getting meals, washing dishes, watching weight, church, Sunday school, choir, and marriage, not in any particular order.

It was not all work, by any means. This is from Alice's baby book (not a direct quote): We took all the children, including Alice, to Old Orchard Beach when she was fifteen days old, to Grammie and Grampa's (my folks); to Windsor Fair at three weeks, a picnic on Bailey Island at four weeks, New Portland at six weeks, Mount Abram and New Portland at eight weeks, and to the White Mountains at nine weeks.

When did we work? I wonder! Alden's family went on some of these trips with us.

My parents visited fairly often. Mom always looked for ways to help me. Since there were usually dirty dishes stacked up, she often busied herself at the sink. When our children got a bit older, my folks took them on Sunday picnics and bought them ice cream cones. They took those not yet in school to stay at their house the last few days of our busiest time, just before Memorial Day. They did that for several years, and it was an enormous help and relief. I hated not having enough time with my children.

The children had the usual childhood diseases. The most serious was the measles, when Anna was six and Scott four. We were at Wiscasset Hardware buying my first washer and dryer when the children came down with the measles! They were really very sick. Wayne was two; and in an effort to prevent his catching it, the doctor gave him a shot of gamma globulin. He had the measles anyway, but was not as sick as the other two were. The younger three had the measles shot when it became available, so they didn't have the disease.

When I was pregnant with Dan, the older five had two diseases in one winter—German measles and chicken pox. It is dangerous for a pregnant woman to have German measles, and I wasn't too sure that I had had the disease and thus built up immunity when I was young. I guess I had, because I didn't catch it. That was an experience, to have five children sick at once. They had mumps, too, but I don't remember much about it. Norovirus, or stomach flu, went through both families way too often, also.

It must have been in 1968 that so many bad things happened in our family, one after another. First my mother dislocated her shoulder—soon after she had recently recovered from a minor operation.

Our dog, Trouble, had been outside the night a rabid raccoon was killed on our lawn. We didn't know if she was involved or not. If so, she had been exposed to rabies. The warden insisted that she be penned away from the house for thirty days. She was so unhappy! She was okay, though—no rabies.

Next, Guy and Lucille were divorced after seventeen years of marriage, and four children. Our teenaged kids had a few teenage problems, like getting driver's licenses. But the worst of that summer's suffering was yet to come.

My mother found a lump at the base of her neck, by the shoulder. It was a swollen lymph gland. It was breast cancer that had spread; she had discovered it late. Her illness took about three years to claim her life, with many trips to the hospital for operations, radiation, tests—each event representing the turning of yet another corner toward the ultimate end. She was a bit confused from morphine but was kept comfortable most of the time. (Neither of my parents had dementia. They also died young.)

Mom took the whole illness with great strength and courage. I dread ever having to face what both my parents did before they could exit. She would have liked to watch her grandchildren grow up, but comforted herself that at least she had probably seen all the grandchildren; there probably wouldn't be any more. I had six children and was 41, and Guy had four and had remarried a younger woman with two children.

She died June 16, 1971. Her strong faith saw her through to the end. God was very real to her and led her by the hand every step of the way. He gave her strength, courage, peace, and acceptance.

This is a poem I wrote soon after my mother's death, in 1971:

Her Death

Death waits, relentless, determined.
It waits quietly by hospital rooms
Full of flowers and cards and glasses of ice water
And smiles meant to be cheerful.
Death waits, pitiless and persistent, unyielding.
And then there were thin green tubes
Bringing oxygen from the walls,
Constant reminders of Death's ultimate victory.
I said goodbye. Her arms still felt strong around me.
The green tubes got in the way as we kissed.
"You've been the best daughter anyone could have,"
　　she said.
"I'm awfully sorry you have to go through so much."
　　Heartfelt, from me.
"It helps just to know you care."
"I do; and if there was anything I could do, I would.
"I'll be up tomorrow, in the afternoon..."
Death must have laughed.
Tomorrow, in the afternoon, was too late
Because Death prevailed in its relentless claim.
But a blessing was hidden,
For that hospital room was not the domain of Life,
　　but the dominion of Death,
And to linger was to suffer.
Death brought consummation to her life,
But her death consumes me.

A Vital New Year's Resolution

The joy and rewards of raising a family are many. We had our share, and those times still give me a warm feeling. Unfortunately, while parents have joyful times, there are also sad, frightening, tragic times. We need to resolve to be constantly vigilant about keeping the children as safe as possible. We must constantly renew our efforts.

Bad things do happen, in spite of our best intentions. They happened in our family, as related below. (I will tell you ahead of time that things turned out okay in each case. We were blessed.)

Perhaps our most bizarre experience happened in the middle of one cold night. Our phone rang. It was my brother-in-law.

"Are you missing anything?" he began.

What we were missing was one of our daughters! I'm guessing she was six or seven. She was sleepwalking—not a habit of hers—and thought she was supposed to go down to her uncle's house to borrow some bath tissue. (Since we lived in the country, we did borrow from one another on occasion, to get by until the next trip to the grocery store.) She had unlocked the door and gone out in her pajamas, barefoot on snowy ground, and commenced the five-minute or less walk across the road and down over the hill. She was accustomed to going there often to play with her cousins. By the time she got there on this night, she had fallen and scraped her knee, was waking up and crying. "All's well that ends well," they say. We added a bolt lock, up high on the door.

When one of our six children was a baby, she was down on the floor, busily crawling around. I noticed a thread on her mouth and pulled it away. I was shocked to find that there was a needle on the thread, and it had been in her mouth! Where had it come from, when I was always so careful about taking care of such things?

Another time, I put my four-year-old daughter and two-year-old son down for a nap one afternoon. In a few minutes, my daughter came out to tell us that her brother was choking on something! We rushed in, and my husband picked our son up and tried to dislodge the item. He must have bumped the boy against the baby's crib, because a good-sized washer (flat round metal, like a coin with a hole in its center) appeared and skidded away on the floor. The crisis was over. Lesson to be learned: Be more careful about letting young children play with dangerous articles, especially when going to bed. I didn't know he had the washer, but I should have known.

Again, a time that could have been tragic involved one of our babies before she learned to walk. It was a Sunday morning, and I was busy getting my older children ready for Sunday school. The baby seemed to be behaving herself, playing quietly in a corner. She should have been in her crib or playpen. When we realized that she had disappeared, panic struck! Our upstairs rooms were not yet finished off, but the stairs were built. Even though she hadn't learned to walk, she had climbed up the stairs—her first attempt—and there she sat by a container of d-CON mouse and rat poison, her hands in the white powder and some sprinkled up and down her front. I rushed her to the emergency room, and the doctor examined her and decided that she had not eaten any of it. He was right—she was okay. Another blessing! Another warning: to try harder and not take chances.

Another episode—this one left me shaken for days. I guess our little girl was about three years old. It was summer, and she and her older sister were playing on the front porch, directly in my field of vision as I worked in the kitchen. We had a Volkswagen bus, and their dad was coming up the road in it, on his way home. Our little one saw him coming and was eager to welcome him. She slipped away, went down the few steps, and off the porch. Lawrence had the habit of driving in, swinging around, and backing into place beside the porch. That day, after doing that, he turned off the engine, opened his door, and stepped out as usual. There, crawling out from under the side of the bus, in front of the back wheel, was our little girl! Apparently, when he was backing the bus, she had been knocked down; but the wheels didn't touch her, so she was unhurt. Some of us would call that a miracle!

We thought we were being careful, and we were spared tragedy. You may call our outcomes miracles, or blessings, or good luck, but tragic outcomes are way too common. Please buckle down and increase your efforts to keep your precious little ones safe. Add it to your New Year's resolutions. It may be your most important one.

We Need to Do Better

We all know a lot of good people—caring people—in every age bracket. Most youngsters and young adults deserve praise and inspire pride. Parents want their children to grow up to be law-abiding, productive, good citizens. That said, the fact remains that we have a huge problem with crime—drugs, murders, and terrible mass killings.

Sick minds need to be treated earlier, to avert some of these tragedies. But there are other reasons given for some of the shootings, like hate. Not to place blame in specific cases, but a twisted childhood, with too-busy parents, can contribute to the basic causes of crime.

Moral standards have changed over the years. It is not just us old-fashioned folks who know this. The concepts of right and wrong have softened. To some, "right" now seems to mean anything you want it to mean, and it is "wrong" only if you get caught. Many people have high standards, of course, but in the past it seems more folks did the right thing simply because that was what they believed in, not through fear. Many of the children were brought up attending church, which helped boost parents' efforts. The church family was a strong part of the "village" involved in raising children. Lack of concern for others, seemingly more common now, is a long way from "Love thy neighbor" and "Do unto others…" Hate is the next step beyond lack of concern.

We need to do better—individually and as a society—to universally instill higher values in our youngsters. We might produce a more civilized world, in time.

We are not going back to the old days when mother stayed at home with the children and father brought home the bacon. Yet I believe it was better for the child to be with his parents, to learn their values. Now children may spend more time in school, day care, and with babysitters than with their folks. Most such workers and teachers do a very good job, but it is not the same as being with Dad and Mom, soaking up parental values. The children's loss needs to be addressed. Children need good examples to follow, and parents need to make sure they are *setting* good examples. We can be more likely to lessen hate in the world if we make sure our children do not learn it from us.

Think how it is now. Healthy play has been replaced with too much sedentary digital obsession and violence. Current heroes and heroines are a far cry from the good leaders young people need. Think of the low morals portrayed as normal behavior on the TV shows and movies that are "bringing them up." Think of the lyrics in their music. Youngsters are bombarded with these lower standards constantly. They see it as normal—the way life is—unless counteracted by watchful parents. If not trained otherwise, a child will grow up going after what he wants, and expressing hate, with little regard for how it affects others.

Again I give credit to those who are doing their best in today's world, but in general, I would urge parents to spend more time with their children, of any age. Talk to them. Look for teaching moments. Find opportunities to discuss the examples of poor behavior the child sees on TV. Point out and discuss better choices and the reasons behind your beliefs. You know what qualities you want to instill: compassion, respect and regard for others, good morals, honesty, perhaps lifelong faith—the list goes on. Help them to develop their conscience and to be guided by it. Remember that praise is a valuable reward for good behavior. Give them the praise and attention they need, or they will seek it elsewhere, too often dangerously.

Raising a child is not easy. It takes lots of work, unconditional love, constant learning, and a whole lot of sacrifice. It is about the hardest job you ever undertake, but at the same time it will be fulfilling. It will be one of the most important things you ever do—perhaps the most challenging *and* the most rewarding.

I know I am probably preaching to the choir, the people who least need to hear it, but our human society needs to become more—or better—civilized, to reach a higher plane than we have ever achieved.

As long as there are people, there will be crime, but all of us should do our best to make sure our children are not the problem. Improvement could start now, with us, one family at a time. We need to renew our efforts. There could be unimaginable value to mankind. Maybe we could eventually all learn to get along.

Just a Boy—Now Dark and Gray

When a baby is born, there is, in most cases, cause for rejoicing. Fathers are proud. Mothers experience profound tender and protective love. Grandparents and other relatives welcome the little one. Everyone is full of hopes and plans for this new little person's future.

Time passes, and the child grows and develops. Adults try to pass along their wisdom, in some families more than others.

Then come the teen years. Hormones rule. Rebellion, ranging from very mild in some young people to constant and severe in others, is a way of establishing a child's own identity. He experiments with a lot of ideas to find out just where he fits. With luck, supportive family, and by choosing friends who don't stray too far from adult expectations, some merge from this period in their lives relatively unscarred, while some get into serious trouble. Of course, most fall somewhere in between.

When drugs were becoming a bigger problem everywhere, too available alcohol and drugs beckoned with a loud siren call. Teenagers were very susceptible, and were getting into trouble because of them. Most of our own children were grown by then, past the teen years. But people whom we knew and loved were devastated to find out that their son was a user.

Deeply moved by sympathy for the mother, a good friend, I wrote this poem to express the anguish a parent feels when she sees her good-natured, sunny child become silent, sullen, seemingly "gray" and "dark." She loves her son so much that she can only grieve while he gropes in the dark to find his way, insisting on following his own way and refusing help. It seems forever that she must wait and watch, hope and pray.

Fortunately, there is usually a happy ending, but waiting for it is hard indeed.

Just a Boy

Dark, dark, is my boy, the smile gone,
The sun-bleached hair, the child-fair skin,
The man-child body, so newly strong,
The waking man who bears the world—
       My boy, my beautiful boy!
He wants no help. Oh, God! How can I help?
Life is too much for you,
So young, without help, not wise, just a boy.
Yet you seek your own help,
       Wrong help—no help;
Help that only makes you less, that makes you worse,
That makes the world heavier when it leaves.
It makes you dark, and gray.
What's wrong with our world? It is bright and happy,
       Not dark and gray.
At times it gets heavy, but we know of real help.
Join our world—on your own, all your own.
Take what's good, and fair, and fine,
In our world, where you have love, and light.
       And be a man, your own man!

Family Camping

O ne of our favorite activities, from about 1960 on, was camping. With Lawrence's busy schedule in later years, he couldn't go with us during the week, but could on weekends. The kids and I would load up a van and head out to a state park on a Thursday or Friday, and he would join us later. We would place "bets" as to when he would arrive. These trips were very valuable and important to us. Everybody needs a vacation once in a while. It was inexpensive and a much-needed change from the stresses of work, family, and responsibilities at home. We had no cares except taking care of ourselves.

The children all enjoyed it, as did I. The boys especially, young teenagers by then, matured somewhat because of their responsibility of being the "men" in the family in their father's absence. They learned to put up the tent, chop wood, build a fire, secure the site from rain and wind, and to be sure the tent wasn't under dangerous overhead branches. Lawrence had shown us how to wrap a rock in the corners of a big sheet of plastic to provide something to tie ropes to, which we would then fasten to nearby trees. This was our canopy. He then would put a paper cup over the top of a pole found on the forest floor, and prop up that sheet of plastic over the center of the table. The cup prevented the stick from poking a hole in the plastic. When it rained, water would run off, but also gather in the depressions and slack areas of the sheet, and startle us by suddenly pouring off in astounding quantities onto the ground. Plastic (usually available when you have greenhouses) also came in handy to put under the tent, to keep moisture from seeping up through. It also was used to cover the campfire stack of wood, in case of rain.

We were able to stay at our camp through many a shower—or even a rainy day—because we came prepared. The children read or played cards or other games, while I might be washing (cloth) diapers and hoping the weather would clear enough to dry them. One time, the kids and I even stayed through the edge of a hurricane, which we hadn't known was coming when we left home. When the campers began leaving the park, the rangers told us what was going on. We inquired as to the expected severity and duration of the storm, and decided to stay, with their permission. We had the place pretty much to ourselves! It wasn't a very bad storm, but we probably should have gone home. We really wanted that trip, though, and couldn't willingly give it up.

We bought a tent through our friend Clyde Morgan. It was perfect for our family. We got it in 1965. It had been used all one summer by a family who lived in it while building their house. It was a "Ted Williams" tent, blue canvas, separated by curtains into two (actually three) rooms. The space between the two rooms was wide enough for Lawrence's and my sleeping bags. One room was for the three boys and the other for the three girls. Five cots came with the tent. Dan, the youngest, did without. They all decided eventually that sleeping on the tent floor was better anyway!

I took good care of that tent, keeping it clean and sweeping it out carefully before packing it away. It was a symbol of our getaway life. No shoes and no foods were allowed inside. After a few years of our loving care, we loaned it to someone with children. When they returned it, one curtain was ripped, and the curtains were both covered with chocolate where the children had wiped their hands. Anna and I set it up out back to work on it. We took soap and warm water and tried to wash the sewed-in curtains in place. We were partially successful, but the tent never was the same for me again.

I was well aware of the factors that caused us (or at least me) to enjoy camping so very much that we went five times one summer. First was the carefree getaway aspect. Second was probably the beach, swimming and boating, and water fun. Next would be the campfire, the serenity and warmth that it provided, and the food cooked over it. We always brought special treats, too. There were many other enjoyable aspects. I didn't worry that the children would misbehave, or get lost, or anything. They got along peacefully and safely for the most part. Then there would be the call of loons, the sound of birds in the campsite in the morning, and the little chipmunks and squirrels to watch. The togetherness and the outdoor experiences were wholesome. We became very familiar with Mt. Blue State Park in Weld, and it felt like home. We also went to Rangeley, Lily Bay, Mt. Katahdin, and Peaks Kenny. Lawrence built many a memorable fire. We usually brought wood from home, but he would find a log in the woods, build his fire, and then put the log in lengthwise, one end first. As it burned he would keep pushing it further into the fire. Some of his fires were memorable for a different reason—their size!

Bears were around sometimes, and when Lawrence wasn't with us, it was up to me to shoo them away. I did it several times. Then there was the time at Mt. Katahdin that Dan growled as a joke as we went by some bushes, where we thought there could actually be a bear. As we came back by there, the bear was at our campsite, where a petrified Alice was waiting in the tent, alone. Rangers were coming into our site to shoo him away, but we saw him around the campground all the next day. Another time, a guest slept on the ground outside our tent, and the next night there was a smelly old bear walking all around in our site, right where the young man had slept the night before.

Once, on our way to Mt. Blue, we stopped and bought a bicycle inner tube for a flat tire on Wayne's bicycle, which had balloon tires. He and Scott wanted to ride their bikes while there. Wayne carefully fixed the tire after we got to camp. When he tried it out, the tube was pinched and blew out again! There was no place to get yet another tube. We did call Lawrence from the ranger's station, though, and he brought another one up when he came.

Every two or three years we would make the longer trip to Mt. Katahdin in Baxter State Park. Lawrence and the children climbed the mountain numerous times. I actually made the climb five times (twice on the Katahdin Stream Trail, twice on Abol Trail, and the last time on Cathedral Trail and down the Knife Edge. I made that descent with a twisted ankle.) The youngest were left with my folks or other relatives on those trips; many other times I stayed at the camp with the youngest children while the rest of the family made the ascent.

Age eight was about old enough to attempt that ordeal. I remember the first time we had Wayne climb with us. He had new jeans, and the seat was worn through by the time he got back down the mountain. (I wonder why it was the seat that wore out!) Dan was younger than that, and we were on the Knife Edge trail that time. It was too dangerous for him, and I thought we shouldn't risk it, but we made it.

Sometimes we took some of the cousins with us; other times other whole families were there. One such time, we had a big windstorm that collapsed some tents and broke the front pole on our tent.

On our very first trip up the mountain, we didn't realize the magnitude of what we were undertaking. Some cousins were with us that time. When we got to the top, the youngsters were already there. Lo and behold, there sat Nancy on the edge of a cliff, with a huge drop-off down to the valley below, her legs dangling over the edge! Talk about danger...

One memorable trip, when Lawrence was taking his early morning paper route, he was up at three a.m., took his routes, then drove to our camp (a three-hour trip), climbed the mountain with the kids, drove back home for a short night's sleep, and had to get up again the next morning at three. That was a long day! The rest of us always stayed at camp the night after hiking all day, and enjoyed a night's rest in the tent.

There was another time that Lawrence was too tired to drive home from Katahdin, but wouldn't let me drive while he slept. Instead he had me sit close, hold the steering wheel with him, and keep him awake. That was one wicked long drive! I remember there were cousins with us on that ride home, too.

One other trip to Katahdin comes to mind that really wasn't much fun, but was certainly memorable. We pulled into Katahdin Stream Campground just before it started raining. We did, for the first and only time, ask for a shelter, which was a three-sided wooden affair facing the stream. We got the tent up, moved our gear into the shelter, and went to bed in the tent. It rained all night, and certain areas of the tent began to leak. It was torture to have to get out and run down to the toilet. Next morning we dashed into the shelter.

111

Lawrence kept telling us to be cheerful, that this was only a little dew off the mountain! Well, the "dew" continued in the form of pouring rain, and we stayed in the shelter all day! We finally left about four o'clock. Driving out through the park, we found that our road was not far from being impassable due to the rain. We soon learned that it had been the edge of a hurricane that we had experienced. Some dew!

We made another once-in-a-lifetime trip in 1963. The older Longfellows had friends, Earl and Myrtle Kierstead, whom they had known since their days of keeping bees in Aroostook County, circa 1920. The Kiersteads had moved to Gardiner to be near their son, so we got to know them also. In fact, we were good friends, and Myrtle worked for us for a few weeks during our busiest time in the spring for a couple of years, preparing supper and doing other household chores. Earl and Myrtle had spent many years working at sporting camps, she cooking and he guiding. They suggested that we might like to take the older children and go to remote Chandler Pond (in the Moosehead-Katahdin part of the state). Earl would be our guide, and we would go fishing. We took him up on it.

Anna, Scott, and Wayne went with us, and Alice and Dee stayed with my folks, who came down and got them the night before we left. I wanted to call off the trip when Alice cried and protested that she wanted to go with us. I could hear her crying as they left, and it pretty much spoiled the whole thing for me. Of course, I put it behind me the best I could, enough to enjoy our adventure. She wasn't even five yet, and the north woods was no place for her.

First off, Earl said I needed pants that would cover me, and long sleeves, because of black flies and mosquitoes. I had my own slacks, but he said for me to buy a pair of men's pants in Lawrence's size, and Lawrence could wear them later. I did what he wanted me to do, and you can imagine how I looked! Earl went grocery shopping with me, as he was going to do the cooking, but I didn't know what he expected—was I supposed to plan the menu? Yes, it turned out. We were to get along without refrigeration (or maybe we had ice for as long as it lasted), so it wasn't easy.

We had to fly in, as there were no roads. Ray Porter was our pilot, and Earl knew him. Earl, Scott, and I went on the first flight. Scott and I had never flown, and in that little plane it was truly a great first experience! Earl had Ray set the plane down in the middle of the trip because he wanted to see friends at Millinocket Lake. Once we were at the camp on Chandler Pond there was no contact with the outside world until Ray came back to get us. It was scary, with kids. If necessary, Earl could have hiked several miles to a ranger station, but it would have been slow going. The camp was nice, with heavy doors in case of bears, and bedding supplied. My pillow smelled of booze and sweat (or worse), though, and the weather was unusually hot all week. Each morning, Earl brought us warm water to wash in and cooked us a hearty breakfast. There were several buildings there, and our cottage was just for sleeping. Earl had his own cabin, and we ate in the one with the kitchen. We were right on the lake. Earl took Anna and me fishing, and directed Lawrence and the boys to another place. I had never learned to cast a line, and he tried to show me how. Suddenly we saw a whole school of brook trout jumping, and Earl got all excited. He wanted me to catch the fish, but I continually snagged the bushes behind me and he had to go back and unhook my line. He fell down, hurrying on rough ground. Finally he took the pole and caught two before they disappeared. I think those were the only fish any of us caught all week. It was too hot for them. Earl cooked them; they were tasty!

There were huge bullfrogs there, and Anna named one Charlie and brought him home. He didn't much like the flight. She let him go in the brook by Alden's, or across the road. We didn't notice any difference in the frogs over the next years, so he didn't start a new crossbred species or anything!

We had another camping trip a couple of years later with Earl and Myrtle and their grandson, Timmy. We didn't yet have our big blue tent, but we got it later that summer. We may have borrowed a smaller one for this weekend. We went to Baxter State Park, but not just to the mountain (Katahdin) as we usually did. We went to enjoy the whole wonderful area, camping the first night at South Branch Pond. I remember Dan was less than a year old, and I put him to bed on the floor of the front seat of the passenger side of the carry-all. Either there wasn't room in our tent, or we didn't have a tent. I know that Scott and Wayne slept outside on the ground. They had sleeping bags. I remember that because sometime in the night we heard frustrated sounds coming from the direction where the boys were sleeping. Finally getting a flashlight on, we found out that Wayne had got turned around in his sleeping bag somehow and couldn't find his way out! He was quite disturbed about his predicament.

While the children were growing up, we went swimming fairly often in hot weather. There was a good place in West Gardiner on Cobbossee Stream. That's where we often took along a bar of ivory soap for a bath and shampoo. The water was sometimes a bit swift, but we had many hours of family fun there.

Gone Camping with My Kids

I'm just a young mother out camping with my kids,
Running down the trail to the beach at Mt. Blue State Park,
Family favorite through the years.
What's this? Having to rest? A slow walk, not a run?
That hill never seemed so steep!
There are some of my children up ahead.
Should her laugh be so hearty, his voice so deep?
Where is the request for Band-Aids? The shrill "Mom,
    watch me!"
Are there no grubby fists offering dandelion bouquets?
There's a little one now, blond curls and blue eyes,
And another, hair short, straight, and black.
"Hi, Grammie!" they greet me. "Grammie!"
Yes, I'm Grammie, and I'm not running down the trail today,
And I have to stop to rest.
But when I go with my family to Mt. Blue,
I'll always be a young mother, gone camping with her kids!

The Alaska Trip, 1969

I must tell you about our biggest and best family trip ever. All of our children were old enough to go, and young enough to go, still at home but not burdened with jobs they couldn't leave. They ranged in age from 17 down to 4. We took Lawrence's sister, Ruth, and her three children with us. Steve must have been 18, Nancy around 16, and Carol 13. There were twelve of us, and we went in two vehicles, the green van and the green carry-all. We had five drivers—Steve, Anna, Lawrence, Ruth, and yours truly.

We almost didn't get going that first day at all. One thing after another presented a problem. Ruth was a teacher, and we had waited for her school to close for the summer until almost the end of June. Being farther north by the longest day of the year would have been nice, but we didn't make that. Finally the date of departure had been set, and Ruth and the children arrived, ready to go. However, Lawrence had to spend several hours getting the vans ready—tires, I think, for one thing. It was four o'clock in the afternoon when we got packed, drivers and seating were assigned, and we were driving over to the brick house to say goodbye. Suddenly I noticed a stream and puddles of a red liquid spreading out over the floor of the carry-all, which I was driving. I knew it had to be from the big punch container packed next to the back door. It had a spigot that, when pushed in, allowed the punch to pour into your cup. It had been placed where the rear door of the truck when it was closed pressed against that spigot, and out ran the punch! We finally got it mopped up and got on the road.

Right away we got separated because Lawrence drove his vehicle off ahead of me, out of my sight, and I wasn't sure which route we were following. I decided to go via Readfield from something I had heard him say earlier. We couldn't catch up to him there, so we finally decided he hadn't gone that way. We turned around and headed back. Thankfully, we met him looking for us. He had decided correctly that I must have taken the other road. So we got started yet again! Remember, we had no means of communication. We vowed to make sure from then on that everyone knew where we were headed, and that if we got separated again our meeting place would be the post office of that city. If we were near our destination, we would keep going and meet there instead.

We stopped for our supper at a picnic area in western Maine, and then went on. We got into Vermont and had not seen any campground. I was still driving and was ahead of the other vehicle. I finally saw a sign that said there was a campground nine miles down a side road, so I headed for it. After a while, Lawrence stopped us and asked where we thought we were going. I convinced him that it could possibly be our best bet for a place to get some sleep. We stayed there, finally, after a frustrating day.

We developed a signal to let the other driver know that we wanted to stop for some reason. If the headlights were on, we turned them off. If they were off, we turned them on. It worked pretty well.

Lawrence was the "wagon master" and made the decisions. First off, since there were so many of us, luggage had to be minimal. He limited us to half a suitcase (or three outfits) each, besides jackets, etc. We were camping, and there was no need to dress up. We did get tired of wearing the same three outfits for over a month, and we did wear our clothes a few more times between washings than we would have at home, but we stopped every few days at a laundromat. We camped every single night and cooked almost all of our meals ourselves. We actually ate four times most days, the extra time being late in the afternoon, usually sandwiches on the road. We would try to locate picnic areas or campgrounds whenever we ate, in order to have a table, but one wasn't always available. We carried a plastic tablecloth, and always folded it after use with the clean side in, always ready for the next table.

Toilets were usually outhouses, or sometimes at gas stations. Pit toilets were disgusting, but were more commonly available than flush toilets! One reason we remained healthy was that after every bathroom stop we poured water from a jug over everyone's hands. We usually found good campgrounds, but they sometimes were very primitive. The kids liked it when we could find one with a pool and running water for flush toilets. I remember one place where we had cold showers. Yes, I took one! We had to grab showers when we could. A lake was next best.

At one laundromat we visited, Ruth and I were surprised to see a customer take off all of her clothes and put them in the washing machine. There were showers there, too, and she proceeded to take a shower while her clothes got clean! There were no men there at the time, but it was a bit startling nevertheless! We left before she came out to put the clothes into the dryer. I wonder if she went back into the shower while they dried. I don't even know whether she had a towel.

I did almost all of the cooking, and Ruth did the dishes. I brought my pressure cooker on the trip, which came in handy. I served vegetable beef soup, salmon chowder, smothered beef, potato and canned vegetables, canned meats and tuna—a pretty good variety. We often ate late when we traveled all day and then had to locate a campground. For breakfast we might have pancakes, the batter for which I mixed up, and then everyone cooked for himself. We had two double-burner camp stoves, with room for four things cooking at a time, when needed. In Whitehorse, Yukon, Ruth bought Kentucky Fried Chicken for us, and we ate it for the first time ever. We didn't have the convenience of a table. The hood of the carry-all served adequately, as it did many times on that trip.

Another time we searched an area—in Alaska, I think—for a picnic area with tables, without any luck. We did come across a field where the power company had been stringing wire, and several of the big empty wooden spools were left around. We turned one so that one of its flat sides was up, and it was just like a big round table, only tall. Funny, the things you remember. I recall that we had canned carrots there, something we don't buy ordinarily. Lawrence thought we should try them, for convenience.

The kids, especially, loved it when we stopped at a store or a village. Everybody piled out and went in and likely purchased some little thing—usually a snack or a memento. If there were brochures, they had to pick some up to add to their collection. Postcard displays told the story of what was worth seeing in the area. Visitor Centers were very valuable for collecting knowledge, especially when there were films, which there usually were. We took good advantage of that means of learning about wherever we were.

We had to arrange to keep water on hand every day, especially drinking water. Campgrounds usually had it available, and the service places along the Alaska Highway did, also. I think it was Watson Lake where Ruth waded out in the water and scooped up a jug or two from around her feet! We may have had a little left over from the day before, for drinking.

We put up two tents every single night, a small one for the three older boys and our big one with the three "rooms" for the rest of us. Ruth chose to sleep in the carry-all. The weather cooperated. Sometimes it rained in the night, or soon after we got the tents pitched. Sometimes we hurried to get them packed away before it showered in the morning. Usually we let them dry out while we got breakfast and everyone got ready to leave. If they were wet, it took extra time either morning or night.

We had some very clean and lovely, scenic campgrounds with mountains, lakes, or rivers, and beautiful tall trees. They were just wonderful! Then there were times that we didn't have a real campground. One night I guess it was really a campground, but we had to pitch our tent on a wooden platform. How were we supposed to drive tent pegs into that? Another night we pitched the tent over bushes about two or three feet tall, or taller. We put the tent right down on top, bending the bushes over.

All along the Alaska Highway, 1200 miles of gravel roads, there were a few "stations" for buying gas and necessities. They had generators for their power. At some there was no real campground, but people were invited to find a spot in the field to set up camp, which we only had to do once. *The Milepost*, a book which described where the stations would be found, was our bible. The road was marked by numbers so we could tell where we were. (More about that highway later.)

Our route began with the Trans-Canada Highway, or Route 1,

across all of southern Canada. Our first big stop had been in Massena, New York, where we crossed the border into Canada. There we watched ships in the locks, being moved from one level to another, at the Eisenhower Locks on the St. Lawrence River. This was an educational opportunity to start us off.

Through beautiful Canada we drove to the Canadian Rockies. We were thrilled with all the sights. We walked on a glacier there. We drove along the Icefields Parkway and saw other glaciers. Lake Louise was gorgeous. There were so many wonderful sights, one right after another. We enjoyed them so much that we could scarcely tear ourselves away to strike out for the Yukon and Alaska.

We saw lots of wild animals, as you would expect. Several of us had cameras, some people kept diaries, but there was only one person who had binoculars—Scott. We would see some cars pulled over, and perhaps people milling around. We would stop to see what they were looking at. Once we saw two young "cinnamon" bears rolling around and playing with a stick. We saw moose, elk, buffalo, mountain goats, and numerous bighorn sheep. Scott got to use his binoculars first, and then passed them around to the rest of us.

There was so much beauty, so much enjoyment! There is no way my writing could ever do it justice. It was just spectacular. In Alaska, as well as in the Rockies, every turn in the road brought into view a new scene, sometimes even more beautiful than the last.

The "Land of the Midnight Sun" was fascinating! Some of the young folks claimed to have noticed that it never got completely dark all night long, even in the Yukon, before we reached Alaska. I know that they played softball one night near Fairbanks, Alaska, until eleven forty-five, when we got them to turn in. It was still light enough to see the ball, light enough to read. The plants and flowers grow huge and beautiful under those conditions of long hours of sunshine. It was cool but not cold; we wore shorts and short sleeves most of the time. Cabbages grow to huge sizes, and people have contests to see who can grow the largest ones. Flowers are often larger and nicer than the same kinds are here.

We were near Palmer, Alaska, the agricultural section, on that historic day when Neil Armstrong walked on the moon and uttered the famous words, "That's one small step for a man; one giant leap for mankind." We listened on the radio to the whole unbelievable feat as it unfolded, and we marveled at what our species has accomplished. Lawrence's father, like so many others, had said years earlier that people would never be able to go to the moon, and would never sit in their homes and watch dancers in another state via television. "Pictures flying through the air? No way! My stars!" I'm happy to say that he lived to see both things before he died.

We saw bears catching salmon in a river, and we bought an Alaskan salmon after the fascinating experience of watching them swim upstream in a couple of places. We bought our salmon from a fish shack, and I cooked it that night in a beautiful campground by a river. (Try cooking salmon for twelve people in a couple of frying pans on a camp stove!) It was memorable, and good.

Twice on the trip we had the chance to swim in hot springs, a novelty for us who live in the Northeast. One was at Kootenay Provincial Park in British Columbia—Radium Hot Springs. The other place we encountered a swimming hole fed by hot springs was in what is now Liard Hot Springs Provincial Park in British Columbia. I hope it has been fixed up to be more inviting than it was in 1969. It was not a provincial park then, I believe. There were bathhouses, so it was supposed to be okay to swim there. We had to walk quite a way to reach it, and the stench, like that of rotten eggs, got stronger as we got nearer. Only one, Ruth's daughter Nancy, actually went in the "quite hot" water.

The Alaska Highway was a marvelous accomplishment during World War II—putting any road through there at all. There is year-round permafrost a little way underground, and as a result, numerous small bodies of water lie on the surface everywhere. It can only seep so far into the ground.

When we took this trip, the experience of traveling that road required stamina. In our later trips, portions of the road had been paved, and the entire process was much less stressful. In 1969 the gravel roads meant flying rocks when meeting a car or truck, so most vehicles had cracked windshields, lights, and/or radiators. Many had shields erected in front of the radiators. Yes, we got big cracks in both windshields and had to replace them when we got back to Maine. Punctures in the tires were to be expected, and we had at least one flat tire there. We had been warned to carry extra parts that might be needed for the vehicles. Lawrence had the foresight to put all of our boxes and luggage into plastic garbage bags to protect them from the unbelievable dust. It took a few days to drive the 1200 miles on that highway, days without showers or laundromats.

One section of the road was especially dusty—with coal dust! It was an experiment to see how coal dust would act as a road surface. It was horrible! That night we couldn't get to any station to find a camping spot, so we drove off the road into a field where other vehicles had been. The grass outside the trodden-down area was a foot or two tall and absolutely loaded with black dust. We couldn't seem to avoid getting into it. It was impossible to move around without getting covered, clothes and body. Next day it was raining, and the coal dust made the road slippery! I'm sure their experiment was abandoned as a failure. I sure hope so!

A loud cheer went up when we came to the sign that announced our arrival in Alaska—and the end of the gravel road! As soon as we could, we found a stream where we removed our gear from the dusty plastic garbage bags and washed two very dirty vehicles inside and out!

The high point of the Alaskan experience for me was the long trip into Denali National Park to see Mt. McKinley, now called Denali, the highest mountain in North America. It is usually surrounded by clouds and thus is not visible much of the time. Back then, cars were allowed to travel in the park to the end of the road, at Wonder Lake. A few years later that changed, and tourists had to use the tour buses, except for those who had secured campsites, which are very limited in number. It is an all-day trip, and we camped overnight near Wonder Lake. It was beautiful!

It is a long way through Denali National Park, and the road is dirt or gravel all the way, with razor-sharp rocks protruding through the surface. Tires can't stand up to such punishment, and sure enough, we did have to change a tire that couldn't take it. The road is narrow, with very sharp curves and switchbacks, and places where the road has been stuck onto the side of a mountain. There are steep drop-offs, one after another. Traffic is two-way, so one keeps meeting cars.

The park belongs to the animals, and cars or buses must give them the right-of-way. That provides opportunity for close observation, of course, and photography. We were exposed to one of Nature's dramas in the case of a wolf and a moose who were each at the point of exhaustion, waiting for the other to succumb. The rangers had told us what was going on, and sure enough, they were to be seen down over a bank in a riverbed, facing off with each other.

After camping at Wonder Lake that night, we woke up at sunrise when other campers were heard exclaiming. We came out of the tent and saw Mt. McKinley's top and base, with its middle hidden by clouds. The top was bathed in early-morning sunshine, bright in a rosy hue. It was spectacular, and so near! The view didn't last for long, as clouds closed in. It was the only glimpse we got of Denali on that trip. (On our later trips, we didn't see it at all the first time, but on the second trip we saw it for three or four days in a row, from a distance.) It is so majestic!

We were well prepared, and hardy, capable people. Spirits remained high, among the children, too. The cousins enjoyed being together. Even siblings got along very well (at least in my memory). One night when the two tents were pitched fairly close together, we heard the boys in their tent laughing. It seems that they had had to wear their socks too many days without putting on clean ones, and the aroma was strong in the tent. Something was said about putting all socks and shoes outside the tent until morning! Problem solved— if it didn't rain!

Then there was the evening that the young people sat around our campfire. We didn't often have time for a campfire. That was one complaint we had about the trip—not enough time to enjoy the camping experience. On this night, the fireplace had a rim around it, and the kids put their feet up as they talked and joked. When it was time to stand up to leave, they found that the soles of their shoes had become very hot—too hot to stand in! Steve, especially, had a real hotfoot. Didn't they laugh as they shed their shoes! That's the way our days went.

We enjoyed having Ruth along. She was apt to be outspoken and quite frank, especially with her brother. She did not challenge his position as wagon master, though. Lawrence respected her and her knowledge and experience, and it was great! We learned quite a few things from her.

Ruth was nervous riding in some of the situations we got into. She particularly wished Lawrence would not look around and point out the scenery quite so much, but pay more attention to the road!

Ruth asked a young girl, who was holding the stop signs on a highway repair project, where she went to school, since we were many miles from any town. Her answer was, "We don't need no schoolin'."

Another young person was talking with some of us at one of the stations on the Alaska Highway. We asked to buy some mosquito repellent. Our request was met with derisive laughter, to think that we were not the hardy souls that *they* were, and would bother to use repellent!

Yet another time, someone with whom we were talking mentioned that two years before she had gone on a trip south during the winter. Wondering if it might have been to Texas or Arizona, or maybe California, we asked. It was a bit of a jolt when she answered, "To Vancouver!"

There were more mosquitoes in some areas than we would have liked, but not everywhere. On our two later trips to Alaska, we found the problem to be much worse. I remember putting on long pants, pulling a sweatshirt on and tightening it around my face, spraying with Off, and getting by nicely all evening. (I was usually too hot, though.) It was imperative to keep the tents closed and to kill off any buzzing varmints as soon after retiring as possible, and then we were able to sleep.

As we left Alaska and headed south, Nature bid us a fitting goodbye, with a beautiful rainbow in the sky. We considered it a special farewell from a very special land. "Dark and true and tender is the North."

We headed for the coast and visited Victoria and Vancouver. Butchart Gardens was well worth the time we took, as were the other places in southwestern Canada, Washington, Oregon, and northern

California. We visited Yellowstone National Park, where we waited for Old Faithful to do its thing. We traveled in Glacier National Park with its beautiful wildflowers, saw Mt. Rainier, passed the Tetons on their "back side," and went on to Jackson Hole. We really liked Jackson Hole; it has character! Each of those areas is absolutely wonderful to visit. We enjoyed them greatly, and had some beautiful campsites.

On the way east, we camped one night at Makoshika in the Badlands of eastern Montana, near Glendive. The camping area of what is now (and may have been then) a state park, was on a hilly plateau ending in a bluff high above the surrounding countryside. We camped near the edge of the bluff, and could see miles of lowland spread out below us. It was relatively early when we pulled in, and we had time to watch as night came on slowly, with ominous clouds in the distance bearing active lightning. The storm was coming our way. We pitched the tents, had supper, and tidied up for the night. We all went to bed, very aware of the storm's approach. After a few minutes, most everyone had gone to sleep, but the wind had become frighteningly strong. Lawrence asked me, and I remember he spoke out loud over the sound of the wind, not in a whisper, "Do you think we need to leave?" With no hesitation I answered, "Yes, I do!" We hastily woke the others in both tents and told them we needed to get out of there quickly and down to lower land. We packed a few "valuables" and gear we could grab easily, especially things that would blow away, and drove through the wild storm down, down, down off the high ground to wait out the big blow. Then we drove back, wondering what had survived. The boys' tent was completely collapsed, and our big one was mostly blown down. I'm glad we were not in them! They were not damaged, really. Things were blown around. One casualty: Our smaller camp stove had been left under the van in our haste, and we had run over it and flattened it beyond further use!

There are many other things that I could have written about, like the time we got separated in the city, and Lawrence put Scott out on a sidewalk at a street corner to wait for the other vehicle to come along and pick him up, and drive to where we would be waiting. Or the night we camped by a lake and when the sun came up there were zillions of flies everywhere! We packed out and ate later on! Or the

Pacific beach where we looked for and found those agates. Or the pumice we collected samples of, and obsidian on the one-way road that goes around Crater Lake. We visited giant springs. We bought prints at the Charles M. Russell museum. That 35-day trip was educational, amusing, fun, and unifying to the family. It was the first big trip, and the last one in which all of our family could participate together. For us, it was truly a trip of a lifetime.

Big Changes

I do not often boast. In fact, I am much more likely to be apologetic. But there are three accomplishments that I have the right to be proud of, as well as several more, I'm sure, of a lesser nature, like being a good student, making good bread and stuffing, and potato salad. I feel that I can take some credit also—in fact, quite a bit of credit—for helping to build our business up to the successful company it became on our watch.

Those three things are: giving birth to and raising our six children, thereby making the world a better place; mastering the method of natural childbirth and using it successfully without assistance, in a time before it became common; and starting college at age 39, with six kids and a husband at home, and finishing "with highest distinction" only five years later. I guess getting a teaching position and staying with it for five years goes along with that; but I don't have as good feelings about that. It was an accomplishment, though, and an important phase of my life.

During the sixties, for something interesting and stimulating to do, I had taken a few night classes, a couple of them with Lawrence. The University of Maine had come to Augusta. A man at church, Fred Downing, suggested that if I was going to take courses now and then, I should get into a program and work toward a degree. My degree would be from the University of Maine at Orono, but my classes were all available at the new Augusta campus. They were afternoon and evening classes, held mostly once per week. That meant, for me, classes four times per week.

Meanwhile, having married at the age of 19, having had babies about every two years from age 22 to age 34, having lived my adult life pretty much with my nose to the grindstone, having lived in a rural setting, and having the desire to help my husband, all took their toll. I didn't grow and develop and mature as a person in their twenties and thirties should. I was stagnant. I was uninteresting. I was uninterested and depressed, by spells.

Lawrence suggested that I take courses and become a teacher. Beginning teachers at that time earned about $18,000 a year, and that looked awfully good to me then. I knew things would have to change, as going to school would take a great deal of time and effort. I didn't know if I could do it, or should do it. I wouldn't have as much time for my family duties, and some of the work and babysitting would fall on the older children. I told Lawrence I could not do it just because he wanted me to, that I wouldn't be able to do it for someone else. It would have to be my own desire, my own goals, that would carry me through. I talked it over with the family and told them I wouldn't be able to manage everything without their help. Together we decided I would go for it. It was the support of my husband and family that enabled me to be successful.

So in the fall of 1969, after the wonderful Alaska trip that summer, I signed up for four courses. I was embarking on a life-changing journey which very soon began to improve my feelings about myself and my world. My successes, my challenges, my fellow students, my new life all began to build the foundation I had been lacking. I needed this so much!

Does a mother have the right to do something like this? Dan was not yet in school during my whole first year, and he needed more stimulation and company. I had to stay home and study when I wanted to go with the family to a school concert, for instance, or be included when my family was doing anything together. I couldn't continue to cook something every day for a treat when they got home from school. When they needed something from Mother, they very often had to ask their father or a sibling, because Mother was writing a paper. Of course, I could not do as much work for the greenhouse business, but I did continue keeping the records and working as much as I could.

The way I have rationalized my decision is that the improvement in quality hopefully made up for the lack in quantity of my nurturing. I grew so much, I blossomed so noticeably, I was so much happier, and I learned so much, that hopefully it made me a better wife and mother in the larger scheme of things. Anyway, I am proud that I was able, with the help and support of my husband and children, to accomplish this. I don't know what would have happened to me if I had decided not to do it.

In 1973 we took another major family camping trip, to Oregon and the Rockies. My father had just died of cancer. I needed that trip. Lawrence's sister, Arlene, had lost her husband, Roy, the year before. Shirley, their daughter, was 12, a little younger than Dee. The two of them and five of our children went with us on what we refer to as the "Oregon Trip." Anna was married, and she and Jeff were in Morocco. There were nine of us, in two vehicles with five drivers. As we had on the Alaska trip, we camped all the way, using two tents. Our route was somewhat different this time, yet we visited many of the same places we had enjoyed so much in 1969.

One of our adventures took place in one of the parks out in the Rockies. Once the tents were pitched, we ate supper and did the dishes. Arlene and the girls and I were in the tent, about to get ready for bed. Lawrence and the boys were clearing the area, putting any food back in the carry-all, which happened to be backed up fairly close to the door of our tent. We hadn't closed the tent yet, having just gone in. The men were making trips back and forth to the rear of the truck, putting things away for the night. When they were all away from the truck for a minute, a big black bear decided he would like some of what was in there and walked right up to the open back door and began nosing around. We all hollered at him and he ambled off a little way, where he stood for a moment, looking at us. Then he started to come back! We were feeling very vulnerable! Scott picked up a good-sized chunk of wood and heaved it in the bear's direction, which did stop him, but only after he made a final lunge toward us. Then he disappeared! We spent an uneasy night, having only a canvas tent between us and possible danger. However, we saw no more of him.

My teaching career began right after I finished college. My first year was in middle school, teaching reading and the weekly art courses. I found it very difficult even though I had six children of my own. I have great respect for teachers who are truly successful dealing with kids of that age. I was moved to third grade after that and found it much easier.

The new greenhouses were up and running and doing well, and I really wanted to be able to work there more. Although our accountant didn't think I should quit my teaching job, which had kept us in groceries for a couple of years when it was about all the money we had coming in, I decided that, after five years of teaching, since I had a choice, I would seek peace and happiness instead of the constant stress of teaching school. (What a difference in my life when I came to work full-time in our new business! I even looked younger, and rested! We had to work very hard, of course, but there's nothing like being your own boss!)

Was I a good teacher? Most of the kids loved me, and I them. One little girl cried when I left. She was really upset that I was leaving. She even called me at home once later on. I believe my students learned. At that age, they sit quietly and listen when you get serious! I cared about them and gave my all. As one teacher said, you have to wonder how some of these kids are able to get themselves to school each day, their lives are so difficult! I had some very dear children who loved me and were a pleasure. I also got along well with the parents. In general, I enjoyed certain aspects of teaching a lot.

It takes a special person to be a really good teacher these days, one who is an entertainer and who also must possess all the other time-honored qualities. Since TV became a fixture in every home, in the early sixties maybe, many children have sat passively for hours at a time receiving stimuli from the "idiot box" without any effort or interaction on their part. That changes the expectations of youngsters, along with their attention span and willingness and ability to apply effort. Dad and Mom are both working, so the daycare worker is with them more than their parents. Some of them do a good job of "bringing up" the children; some don't.

Even back in the seventies, when I was teaching, many children had no respect for the authority of their teacher—or for *any* adults, for that matter. Of course, many did. The numerous social changes that began in the sixties, the exodus of mothers from their homes into the workplace, and the lack of teaching children manners, all played a part in the change. The average student in the first half of the century was a respectful, hardworking young person. Too many of them now are brash, disrespectful, lazy youngsters who stand up to their teachers and threaten to have them sued! It wasn't (and isn't) easy; my hat is off to truly successful teachers!

A very sad thing happened during my first year of teaching. One of my homeroom students, one of those a teacher loves having in her class, was riding her bicycle one evening in the village. She had a brother about her same size, and it so happened that he was out biking, too. Their parents were both home when a drunk driver hit a bicyclist right in front of their driveway. The child was mangled and bloody. The only way the parents could tell whether it was their son or daughter was by seeing her bra strap! The father was a doctor and tried every way he knew to save her life, but she died. My student! I was really fond of her.

I became rather close to her mother, as she came in to see me a few times and we cried together. After a year or so, I had moved to the other school, and she volunteered to help with some special ed students of mine at a table in the hallway outside my third grade classroom door each day, as I really didn't have the time to give them the extra help they needed.

She and her husband eventually adopted a little girl. She told me she still had love to give to someone.

The Really Big Change

When both of Lawrence's parents had passed away, we decided the time had come to expand our business. Since he had been in partnership with his folks, he had erected new greenhouses over the years on their property. That, of course, left him in an awkward position when they died. He had wanted for a while to expand the business anyway, but required more space to do it right. He needed to be in a better area to reach a larger customer clientele, and to have a good flat area of land. We would need to live near the business, so that meant moving away from our home.

This was a definite turning point in our lives. It was major. However, once the changes were made we felt that we were better off than we had ever been. But getting there certainly took a big toll—so much work, stress, and heartache. It was very discouraging. The process took months. It was a hard, depressing time.

We bought thirteen and a half acres of flat, low land on Puddledock Road in Manchester, Maine, procured an accountant, Bob Jackson, and got our loans. Before the financing was final, we stuck our necks out and had the platform under-drained and graded to the proper slant. We put in a wide driveway with posts and a gate and put up a mailbox. We finally got the loans to pay for all this and to go ahead with building the range—(the array of greenhouses)—on the last day of 1976, after this much work had been completed on faith.

In order to get the loans, we had to have all of our property changed from Lawrence's name as sole owner to both of ours as joint owners. The new land for the greenhouses had to be in both our names jointly, also, and the loans. I felt as though I had gained quite a bit in stature and importance! I don't know what Lawrence felt. I didn't ask.

Concerning the purchase of land for the new greenhouses, it was a good location, not on a busy highway, but not far out, either. Maine's major highways brought people close from all over the state. Augusta, Lewiston, Waterville, and Winthrop all were nearby cities. We were able to open on time for the 1977 spring season, and through our care, good employees, and hard work, we were successful from the start. I used to say that my work at home was my vacation from teaching, and my work at school was my vacation from my work at home.

We planned to build a house on one parcel of the property. It was very difficult for me to leave our home, which my father had built over to suit us. It was the home we had come to as newlyweds, and we'd brought six new babies home to this house. It was where we brought up our family. I eased my sorrow by purchasing house plans for our new home and looking forward rather than back. We even dug the cellar hole.

Our new house never was built, since a different path opened up for us.

There was a pretty three-year-old cape about a quarter mile from the greenhouses. The house and property came up for sale at just the right time for us. Bob Jackson didn't think we were well enough established yet in our new business to dare to take on the expense, but we didn't think we would find anything better than this deal that had opened up. Building a new house would have cost a lot, too. We got a mortgage from the bank, and the owner provided a second mortgage for the balance, so all we had to come up with was $1,000 for closing costs! We moved late in September of 1977. We filled in the now-useless cellar hole.

Now we had to deal with the worry of owing a lot of money: the loan that paid for the land the greenhouses were on; the Farmers' Home and Canal Bank loans that the greenhouses were built and the business started with; two mortgages on the house and property; insurances and taxes; another loan to cover costs of new supplies to continue running the business; expenses of two children in college; and of course our own living expenses, with two children at home. I don't wonder Bob feared for us! We had to generate a lot of cash to cover it all, to augment my meager teacher's pay. Thank goodness, we made it! We had to be very careful with our spending and go without any extras for a long time.

Our new house was very pretty and only three years old. With our kids all growing up and moving away, we had plenty of room. In the old house, we had brought up six children with only one bathroom; now we had only two kids still at home and two bathrooms!

Of course, life was going on for our children and the rest of the world during this tumultuous period for us, from 1975 through the first spring season at the new greenhouse in 1977.

I remember one quite difficult trip, in 1976, when we all drove to Pennsylvania for a nephew's wedding. We drove all night, after work, because it was in June and we were still very busy. We got to the town in the morning and had only two or three hours before the ceremony. Lawrence got a motel room and we all just stretched out on the two beds, the chairs, and probably the floor, and got just a few winks before getting our clothes changed, ready for the merry day. Wayne was working at his summer job in Leroy, New York, and he came in his Fiat to join us. After the wedding, we drove west and camped out overnight. It was a nice extra to have that time with Wayne.

While Wayne was at Cornell University, we had a family camping trip each year in order to get together with him. When he didn't have a car, Lawrence drove to Ithaca to pick him up and take him back. When Dee was at Cornell, she didn't have a car, and we did the same for her.

Those were some days! That was some decade!

We chose for a business logo "Large enough to help, small enough to care." (Can you find it in the poem which follows?)

I wrote the greenhouse ads for the newspaper, and this one is really different. The creative juices must have been running wild! Once the spring rush in the greenhouse was over in 1978, Lawrence and I took a day off every two or three weeks. Riding through the countryside one Sunday, I was composing the next ad for the paper. Rhyming phrases kept coming into my head, and I decided to go with a poem for an ad, and came up with this. I even got one request from an employee for an autograph on the clipping!

The Garden of '78

The snows had gone for '78,
The time for gardening near.
But you couldn't plow or till anyhow—
The puddles were up to here!
      And when at last it finally dried,
      You eagerly called the man,
      Only to learn (in no uncertain term)
      "I'll do it when I can!"
When everyone else had planted theirs,
And picked a radish or two,
When all your weeds had gone to seed,
Your turn to till came due.
      The good brown earth sat ready and bare.
      You bought seeds and plants and the rest.
      'Twas Longfellow's, of course, you chose;
      Their product and service are best.
You planted them and all was fine,
And then the weather changed.
The rains came down, the plants all drowned,
Your plans were rearranged.
      Back to Longfellow's, still well stocked,
      To try again this year.
      Your tale of woe you murmured low
      To sympathetic ear.
That time the sun shone bright enough,
Too hot and dry the air.
"What's this?? The tops are half cut off!
And bugs are everywhere!!"
      Longfellow's Ortho products shelf
      To the rescue—one more chance!
      They helped you choose the spray to use,
      And of course, replacement plants.

Now here you stand—it's July 1.
The calendar's cold stare
Reminds by date it's getting late
But still—two months and to spare.

> Two months is time enough to grow
> Longfellow's plants, you bet!
> Time for Nature's scheme and your
> summer's dream
> To get together yet.

Just look ahead a few short weeks
For your work you take a bow!
The foods you've grown are all your own—
You can almost taste them now!

> Longfellow's plants have had a good start;
> They're sure to make you a winner.
> So put them in place and fill in that space
> Where the bugs enjoyed their dinner!

Longfellow's service is courteous,
Their quality fine, prices fair.
To carry good "stuff" they are large enough—
But still small enough to care!

I wrote the following for the greenhouse to use in their advertising:

History of Longfellow's Greenhouses

The winter of 1976–1977 was an especially cold one. Nevertheless, hard work and determination turned a hopeful vision into reality, as Lawrence and Mavis Longfellow and their oldest son, Scott, with the help of their other children whenever schoolwork allowed, began construction on what would be (and still is) the largest greenhouse range in Maine. In the snow and the cold, they put up twelve large greenhouses and a sales building on an empty meadow lot in Manchester, on a country road with a funny name.

Scott, as grower and general manager during the first ten years, brought to the business the benefits of his University of Maine education in Plants and Soils to complement his parents' experience. (Scott's is the third generation of the Longfellow family to grow plants as a business.) Loyal employees felt like family, and they gave their best. At first the work was done largely without labor-saving equipment.

It would be an understatement to say that the spring of 1977 found them barely ready to grow a spring crop and to find customers to buy their plants. Actually, in several of the new houses, the transplanting crew was filling the benches as fast as the carpenters could build them! But the healthy young plants were as full of promise as the new range itself.

Word spread, and the customers came, charmed by the size of the operation and the sight of so many healthy and beautiful flowers and plants. They enjoyed the experience of walking through all the greenhouses, where they were made to feel welcome. From the beginning, the philosophy at Longfellow's has been to treat the customer fairly and honestly, to offer expert service and assistance, and to stand behind their product. It has always been a goal to see that every customer leaves happy.

Mechanization gradually eased labor-intensive production. More greenhouses were added, and also an employee lounge and conference room. The space between the two rows of greenhouses, which faced each other, was covered over, creating a "mall," and protection from the weather made walking through the extensive range even more enjoyable.

In 1987 the senior Longfellows retired. Scott and his wife, Sandy, as the new owners, brought in fresh and creative ideas and innovations, as expansion of facilities continued with the addition of more growing space, a display building, and new lines of merchandise. Recognizing the need for larger and more efficient sales areas and parking space, and envisioning an even more aesthetic presentation of their products, they made a major commitment in 1995. They erected three connected modern structures for a new and much larger salesroom and foliage plant display area, leaving the former sales building available for classes and workshops, thus expanding service to the community.

From the twelve original greenhouses, welcomed as they were those many years ago, Longfellow's has grown and matured to the much larger, state-of-the-art, twenty-one-greenhouse range it now is. The hard work and dedication of the Longfellows, and of their willing and capable employees, and of course the many happy customers, have in combination built a business which has brought beauty and pleasure to people from all over the state and beyond, as they enjoy a visit to Longfellow's in Manchester, on the road with the funny name—Puddledock Road!

The employees at the greenhouse formed some friendly bonds. On birthdays, we ordered bagels for everyone. One woman anonymously presented small gifts, too. We had our suspicions about who she was. I wrote this poem and posted it on the fridge, where everyone enjoyed it.

Our Own Birthday Fairy

Our own birthday fairy was at it again!
She watched for the bagels, just before 10:00.
When she saw them, she hastened; her purpose was clear.
Was anyone watching? Was anyone near?
  So quickly her magic she deftly applied.
  She fingered the package, and slipped it inside,
  Atop all the bagels and cream cheese, with care.
  She chuckled and gloated at how it sat there.
Then swiftly she turned and went straight back to work,
Placed hand over mouth to hide her broad smirk.
"Happy birthday!" she chortled, and watched with delight
As the present was opened, no giver in sight.
  Her secret she cherished, for nobody knew;
  Suspicions aplenty, but no one knew who!
  We'll find her, that sly one with such a big heart!
  Good deeds will be found out, who's playing the part.
Just a question of time 'til we know who's the culprit,
We'll show her no mercy, even though she deserves it!
And when we find out who is playing these pranks,
We'll show her! We'll get her! We'll give her—our thanks!

Our Special Birch Tree

It stood on the corner, where field met woods. Woods cleared, the
field sprouted greenhouses.
—Our new garden center! We left it there, the birch, for shade,
beauty, and comfort.
It was the pivot between old and new; Phoenix for the old, rising
star for the new.
It grew tall and lovely, center of the range. We saw more than its
beauty, with flowers at its base.
We saw a hard winter when the project began, without money, with
little but hope and strength.
We saw success from our labors and dreams,
as the World found our greenhouses,
Our Better Mousetrap, and beat a path to our door.
Onward through the rigors of life.
We saw success in abundance in a new generation, as we passed the
reins to our son.
Watching the changes, we knew they were for the better. It was hard,
but had to be done.
The birch was still there, taller now. Then came the ice storm of '98—
cruel without conscience!
Trees left bent and broken, everywhere we looked. The birch—the
beautiful birch—also!
A full year it stood there, in half of its splendor, trying but failing to
recover.
Then expansion of the range (called progress) denied it even that life.
There was no room. It had to go.
Its lumber saved, it will live on in its memorial:
a table, cupboard, or chest;
And we will remember, the only way now to say—"Thanks!"

Horse Sense Learned from the Old Folks

"How come you have never been overweight, Myrtle? You've always cooked, a lot of good food."

"Well," she answered me in her brisk and direct way, "I've always said that it's easier to say no to the first piece of candy than to the second or third!"

The lady with whom I was talking was Myrtle Keirstead, a family friend for many years. She was past the age of 90 at the time of this conversation.

Several years earlier, she had been earning a little extra money by working for us, cooking our evening meal during the busiest times of our greenhouse operation, mostly in the springtime. It was that period in our lives when I was teaching school and working in the greenhouse as much as possible.

On this particular night, I was boasting about how well I was watching my diet by eating only a sandwich for lunch. In her direct way of getting to the heart of a matter, she quickly put me in my place, saying with a laugh, but without skipping a beat, "Yes, and then come home and eat twice as much for supper!"

Myrtle was like that—no nonsense. She had worked hard all her life, and she knew how to keep house and cook a meal "correctly." She was a storehouse of down-to-earth information and common sense.

One time I came home from work tired and feeling swamped (which was not unusual). No one was home. In my sink was a pan of bleach and water, with my dishcloth soaking in it. I knew Myrtle had been there, helping a little without pay. She had seen a need and filled it. Yes, it is true that her action was saying that my dishcloth was dirty, but she wasn't saying it unkindly. I understood; and I probably kept my sink and dishcloths a little cleaner from then on.

Her life was far from easy. Still, she seldom referred to hardship. Living in Aroostook County, she and her husband had raised a big family. She had cooked for them, for crews, and later for sporting camps. She worked hard on their farm, as women did and still do.

After her husband died and she had lived with her son and his wife for a while, her doctor told her to prepare to go to a nursing home, as her heart was failing. She was not about to accept this verdict. She told us that she had to fight to convince her doctor, but she had won. She was given a pacemaker and lived independently for many more years.

When she finally did go to a home, she made the best of it, stressing the positive aspects, like having people around for company. When I visited her there, she and a couple of other residents were playing a board game.

Finally, Myrtle had to deal with something that was too much for her. Her husband's death had been a terrible blow, but she had her son to depend on. Now frail, she could scarcely hold up when her son died. For a while, she did fairly well, but it was all downhill from there. She died a short time later. A good friend, a good woman, who had lived her life well and victoriously, was now gone. Yet, having been a source of so much strength and inspiration, her influence lives on.

Me First?

While we in America have much to be thankful for, we have a lot to worry about these days. It seems that almost every day there are killings and heinous crimes. There are people born and raised in this country who are rejecting our value system and joining the terrorists. Standards for moral behavior are lower than in the past, which can cause an increase in criminal activity. For years now, we have been a "me first" society, a long distance from "love thy neighbor." Crime, killing, and acts of terrorism have become far too common. While some of it is due to mental illness, we do need to do a better job of bringing up our children to be law-abiding citizens. Many animals keep their young with them long enough to teach them how to fight enemies, get food, and whatever else they need in order to survive on their own. Humans keep their young in their care for twenty years or more, to socialize them and prepare them to be self-sufficient. Most parents have a desire to see their children become productive citizens with good character. Many of them do succeed in instilling good values. Most teachers and daycare workers do their best. We all know many young people of good character, children brought up well, youngsters to be proud of.

That said, too many children are adopting the "me first" values from movies, television, popular music, and even from some of their mothers and fathers. The people who are their heroes and heroines are a far cry from the good examples they need. The difference between right and wrong has become "It is right if you want it, and it is wrong only if you get caught." If not trained otherwise, each person looks out for getting what he wants, with no regard for others.

We need a modern-day Dr. Spock, someone who could initiate effective child training methods as broadly as Dr. Benjamin Spock did in the mid twentieth century. Until one appears, I urge all parents to spend as much time with their children as possible, to talk with them about values they want to instill, to discuss and try to counteract the wrong values that constantly bombard them from movies, TV, their music, and the musicians and superstars, and to teach them the difference between right and wrong. Try to help them to develop a good conscience and to let their conscience guide them in their behavior. Teach them respect and regard for others. Watch for teaching moments, and take advantage of them.

The problem with constantly teaching is that the child could interpret it as criticism, and that could make him feel inferior. You must remember to praise him, and give praise every time he is on the right track, and he will see that praise as reward. Much can be accomplished with a reward system.

We have countless organizations, for everything imaginable. We need one devoted to raising the character and behavior of human beings. Actually, we already do have one. Whether or not you attend church, you should be grateful that there is one very huge organization on the right side of improving human behavior, one which is dedicated to teaching people to respect and love others and follow the Golden Rule. Those so inclined can get a tremendous boost in raising their children successfully if they will take them to church and Sunday school.

Children learn best from their parents. They need good examples to follow, and their parents need to set that example. Doing so may be the most difficult part of raising your children. Don't be part of the "me first" philosophy!

Sweet Springtime

Springtime in Maine is especially welcome after a long cold winter. As is the case with many country people whose lives are tied to the seasons, spring found us every year so busy that we could scarcely enjoy it. Being in the greenhouse business, preparing young flower and vegetable seedlings for people to plant, demanded all of the time and attention we could manage. I remember more than one year, looking around one day to find that the new leaves were already out on most of the trees, and I had missed their arrival.

It is different since we retired. On a warm sunny day, I notice that the snow is mostly gone, except for a few leftover snowbanks, which were built over the winter by the snowplows. Numerous birds add their joyful songs to the springtime medley. Soon there will be baby birds, and their parents will be swooping to their nests with a bug or crumb to feed them.

There are many specifically springtime sounds. Crows complain of real or imagined injustices or disturbances. Canada geese are honking their V-flights northward. I step outside in the evening and recognize the signature sound of a familiar springtime chorus—spring peepers in their nearby mud-bottomed ponds, their winter sleeping quarters. Theirs is such a welcome song, coming as it does with soft, warm air and the annual stirring of life after a long cold winter. At last we have the promise of flowers, long summer days, and the freedoms that come with spring and summer.

How sweet it is to be here in the country, in Maine, when it is waking from the bonds of winter.

Empty Nest, but a Full Life

By the time the 1980s rolled in, Longfellow's Greenhouses was getting to be well known, with customers coming from all over the state, with wholesale deliveries ordered from distant counties, with our garden center becoming a showplace where people came to entertain their visitors, and with people hungry for green growing plants and cheerful blossoms coming to get their "fix." They had seen our booths at the summer fairs and flower shows. I was writing ads regularly. Word of mouth is the best advertisement, and people were responding with enthusiasm.

Lawrence and I began taking winter trips. The first ones were very short, only a few days. We had purchased a Volkswagen Rabbit, and we drove that to Florida the first time. Twice we flew down. What a shock to the sensibilities to board the plane in our Northeast winter weather and get off into Southern summertime! Of course the reverse, coming home to the cold weather, was less pleasant. Aunt Hazel and Uncle Paul had moved to Florida to be near their grandchildren, and we had a nice visit with them each year lasting a couple of days, and saw the biggest and best of the many sights in Florida. I delighted in collecting seashells. I loved the Gulf of Mexico waters and enjoyed watching the pelicans.

I remember one year when we flew down that we hadn't had time to think about the trip or where we'd go first. It seemed so good just to not have to answer the phone! We rented a car and sat in the yard deciding which direction to go. We drove to the Bok Tower in all its pink stone grandeur, listened to the wonderful music from the tower, walked the grounds and drank in the solitude and beauty. By then we had recuperated enough to enjoy the rest of the vacation.

Vacations are so very sweet when they are so badly needed!

I think it was in 1989 that Guy flew down to Florida while we were there, and we drove him around, even to Key West. It was a great trip, and fun having so many of us visiting together at Aunt Hazel's. Over a nine-year span, we visited Florida each winter. Around 1987 we began visiting Alice in Missouri on the way home.

We met for a family camping trip each year for a while. I have mentioned the one night of camping after Steve Bruce's wedding, at Pickett's Glen in Pennsylvania, in 1976. It must have been before that year that we camped at Blue Mountain in New York State. I remember that Wayne was at Cornell and chose the location. I remember that it was very cold! In September of 1977, the year we moved and started the greenhouse operation on Puddledock Road, we managed a camping excursion to Branbury State Park in Vermont. The next year it was a Labor Day trip to Pawtuckaway State Park in New Hampshire. The next couple of years it was in Maine—Mt. Blue and Peaks Kenny. In 1981 we went to Wells State Park in Sturbridge, Massachusetts, near where Guy lived. He joined us there for daytime visiting. Dan and I had driven down and set up camp the evening of the appointed date, as the others were not yet free to leave.

There was a time, a night, when I did my part so granddaughter Kristin's parents, Anna and Jeff, could attend to her very urgent need. She was just learning to walk, a healthy and normal baby. She became sick and Anna took her to the doctor. He (or she) sent them home with the diagnosis that it probably was just a virus, like kids are always having. In the night she became much worse—so bad that Anna feared for her and realized that they needed to take her right away to the emergency room.

Anna called me and debated waiting for me to get there to stay with son Seth, who was sleeping. I could tell that Kristin needed medical help immediately. That proved to be the case. I told her to go and not wait, to leave Seth alone and I would come right away. I suggested that she call me there later to put her mind to rest that I had arrived, which she did. Seth was still asleep when I got there. I brought him to our house the next morning.

Kristin had meningitis, and she was one sick child! We knew of other local cases about that time, and some of them didn't fare as well as she did. She had no lasting effects. I visited the hospital to give

Anna some support. She grabbed the chance to take a shower. She had spent every minute right with Kristin. A few days later, Kristin was much better, but she was still in the hospital. Lawrence and I went up and stayed with her so Anna and Jeff could leave the hospital together for a couple of hours off.

On their first or second day at the hospital, Jeff came to our house, where we were caring for Seth, and said he had been told to take Seth's temperature to be sure he was not coming down with the illness. Back then, thermometers still were breakable, and they were quite delicate. I think he had bought three, anticipating breakage! Sure enough, he put the first thermometer under Seth's arm, but Seth wouldn't hold still. It dropped out and broke. The same thing happened again. I remember we were down in our cozy basement by the wood fire. I had Seth sit beside me on the sofa; I put the third and last thermometer under his arm, and I read a story to him while we took his temperature. I had my hand and arm firmly around his shoulder in a hug, and I held his arm in place. Success! And no fever!

This was the big decade for weddings among our children. Anna and Jeff had been married for some time. At Scott and Sandy's wedding, Wayne and Carol were taking note of some of the fine points. It soon got out that they were planning their own wedding and were waiting to tell us until Scott and Sandy had enjoyed their time in the limelight, and had received their well-deserved special attention for a good length of time.

In June of the next year, we all gathered in Rockaway, New Jersey, for Wayne and Carol's wedding. I remember that Guy came with his children and a lady friend. (He and Lucille had divorced, and his second marriage, to Dixie, had also ended.) I remember that I wasn't feeling very keen about myself. I hadn't had time to shop for a dress and went into Sears at the last minute and bought a dress that I didn't really like, that wasn't flattering, but for which I had to settle due to time restrictions. Oh, well! I was happy for the wedded couple, and after all, that day was not about me. We rejoiced for our son and were pleased to accept our new "daughter."

Alice was next in line. After college, she had worked for us for a while. She had her own apartment in Monmouth and bought herself a new Nissan car.

She and Lawrence went to a greenhouse conference in Grand Rapids in the early eighties. She met a man at the conference who was from Missouri. After that week, there followed phone calls, a visit in Missouri, a visit in Maine—you get the idea. She moved to Missouri in 1984.

In Missouri, Alice worked for a while for a florist, but she developed a landscaping business out of her car. She and Bob were soon married, in Maine. As the business grew, she eventually bought land with a building, which she turned into a prosperous garden center. Once they felt sure the garden center was likely to be a success, Bob left his job at another greenhouse and joined her in her endeavor.

During the summer of 1984, Alice and Lawrence and I went on a greenhouse tour through Scandinavia. We met her at the airport in New York. It was my first trip overseas and my second flight in a plane, not counting the little plane that took us to Chandler Pond in 1963.

Dee, like Wayne, chose Cornell for college. She enjoyed some good friendships at Cornell, some girls and some boys. She and Andy Sosa hit it off pretty well from early on. He was from Texas and was an ROTC student. Their wedding was August 15, 1987, at a scenic place on the coast of Maine—Southport, near Boothbay Harbor. It was outdoors with a close-up view of the water, a lovely spot! When they departed, they left by boat. What a picturesque touch! At the reception (same location) we had lobster. They had seated me beside Andy's father and step-mother, so I could show them how to eat a Maine lobster!

That's five out of six children married. Dan's wedding wasn't until 1991. He and Tammy opted not to have a big wedding or reception. They had been living in the Bangor area for a long time, in fact, ever since he was going to college at Orono. He was working as an engineer for Bangor Hydro, the electric company. He called us one night to tell us that they were going to be married the next day, with only another couple in attendance. They had been engaged for a while, so we were not surprised.

When I turned fifty, in 1980, my arthritis and similar body problems began in earnest. I had a ruptured disk in my lower spine, and sciatica. I spent a week in the hospital in traction, with no improvement. I realized that I had a serious condition. I decided to take charge, since what the doctor had done for me was not enough. Jeff brought me a book from the library, the name of which I have forgotten, but which said as its thesis, "Get off your duff!" There were exercises described, which I undertook, adding a new one every few days. Walking was part of the treatment. I spent the time necessary to do these exercises and take my walks for years as a priority and it was successful, to a degree. Three miles was my usual distance to walk.

During the '80s, Lawrence and I took time occasionally to get away for a couple of days, to drive over to New Hampshire for an overnight stay. Sometimes we called Scott on that second day to say that we were going to stay another night. When we left on the trip, we agreed not to talk about the business, which was what we needed the vacation *from*, or about the children, which are what parents always need a vacation from. That left very little to talk about! Usually we wound up discussing those subjects anyway, regardless of good intentions. The trips were pleasant, though. They helped ease the stress under which we lived. They also helped keep our marriage fresh.

Another one-day jaunt for which we signed up turned out to be very pleasant. It was in September and was called a fall foliage trip by rail. It began in Portland and ended at Island Falls, Vermont. Actually, there was practically no colored foliage at all, as it was too early. Nevertheless, it is beautiful country anyway. One happening marred the beauty of the day and the trip. When we pulled into the Portland railroad station at dusk, a group of young punks threw rocks at the train, breaking some of the windows! That really made us furious! We had fond memories of the day as a whole, regardless.

In 1982 our electric company, Central Maine Power Company, conducted an ad campaign to get people to buy their stock. They selected a half dozen or so men and women who owned stock and featured them in TV ads, and even in a full-page newspaper portrait. The people chosen were from different walks of life and were presented one at a time. Lawrence was one of those chosen. Jack Havey, a local artist, did Lawrence's portrait—a large one—with a secondary smaller insert of another pose of him wheeling a wheelbarrow loaded with African violets. It was very good! I have a copy framed and on our living room wall. When Alice started up her garden center in Missouri, she put a copy on her wall, also, for inspiration.

I can't say which year, but it was while Dan had his motorcycle, we had a serious break-in at the greenhouse. When you have a business as open as a greenhouse necessarily is, it is hard to protect it. We had had plants stolen in the past, and minimal damage. This time when we went to work one morning, we found every exposed bag of fertilizer, peat moss, soil, or other such bagged products in the salesroom, and some outside, slashed or stabbed with a knife! They could not be sold. We could use some of it ourselves, of course. Worse, every tire on the delivery trucks, tractor, and Dan's motorcycle was slashed! Now that was bad! Wasn't Dan angry! We felt quite violated, and it was a big loss.

We set up a night watch to guard against a repeat. We had called the police that first day, and they eventually found out who did it. The police wanted to know if we wanted one of the boys responsible to work for us to help pay off some of the damage, but we really didn't want him around.

In the mid-eighties, there was a development in our lives that could have come straight from a novel or a movie. It began with a long-distance telephone call to Alden and Esther late one evening, from Madison, Wisconsin. The woman calling was trying to find Esther Longfellow. Alden's wife was named Esther, and the sister who had died was Esther Marie Longfellow. It was Esther Marie who was wanted. At the end of that call, Alden phoned us, even though it was late. The story was bizarre!

The caller identified herself as Margaret. She had been raised from infancy in a black family's foster home, along with other children (at least one brother). Her foster parents knew her mother's name and home address (or else she found those two pieces of information when she went looking for records of her birth and her birth parents). She had been born in Milwaukee in 1949, and she was black.

Of course, we thought back to 1949 and determined that her

claim could be legitimate. Esther had worked for some time in Milwaukee during that time frame. Esther's superior had called her parents then, saying she hadn't come to work for a while and couldn't be located. Lawrence, as older brother, and being able to leave to investigate and find her, went to Milwaukee and spoke with her boss. It seems Esther had been very upset emotionally but had not told her boss the reason. Lawrence then found Esther in a hospital (or at her home when she left the hospital) and talked with her. She told him that she had had an operation but was now okay. He came home, and she never referred to it again.

We thought of the possibility that she had had a baby, of course, but never had reason to believe that she had. Looking back, we remembered how desperately she wanted after that to find a husband, and how acutely she reacted to young children. I also remembered years later, after our last baby, Dan, was born, chatting with her about naming him. I said that, if he had been a girl, we would have named him Susan Margaret. She reacted very strongly to that comment, and I asked why. Her answer was, "I once knew a baby named Margaret." Those were hints, but we didn't realize it at the time. We remembered also that she had mentioned while she was in Milwaukee that she was dating a black man.

After Margaret's call, Alden made arrangements for her to pay us a visit. Even though she was black (actually mulatto), there were similarities between her and Esther. Their voices were very much alike, and her laugh was similar to Esther's. She had a stocky build. She had gone into the same line of work Esther had been in, although she lacked the training, and had an office job at a mental health clinic. Esther had been a therapist. Skipping ahead a few years, another similarity was that Margaret died very young, as Esther had, of reproductive organ cancer.

It was an interesting visit, and she had myriad questions about what her mother was like. She needed particularly to know of genetic particulars and diseases, and said that was why she had started her search. I gave her the Betty Crocker cookbook that had been her mother's, which had been given to me after Esther died. We found a few snapshots to share. I think there was a sweater that had been

Esther's. She was, of course, very sad that her mother had given her up instead of keeping her and raising her. We knew that would have been unthinkable in Maine in those days, since her baby had colored skin. There were many reasons that Esther really did the only thing she could.

Emma and Lester, Lawrence's mother and father, had both died intestate. Their estates had not yet been settled, and now there was a new heir. As Esther's daughter, Margaret was entitled to what would have been Esther's share of the estates. Lawrence and Alden hired someone to investigate her claim, to be sure that this was not a case of stolen identity. It also made a difference whether she had been adopted or was a foster child, as to determining if she was a "rightful" heir. The investigation found her to be a legitimate heir. We were not surprised.

In August of 1989, she brought her two young sons for a visit; an older son was unable to come. Lawrence went all out to entertain them. We took them on a camping trip. We thought city boys would like a camping trip in Maine. We bought a new tent and everything for them to use, and it went quite well.

Anna kept up a correspondence with Margaret, and Arlene's daughter, Marion, did also. They accepted her as a cousin.

I don't remember how long it had been when Anna told us that Margaret had called to say that she had terminal cancer, and to say goodbye. We sent flowers, and were soon called by someone among her friends or family who thanked us and told us that the flowers arrived on the morning of the day Margaret died.

It is sad that Esther couldn't have had a normal married life, and children to enjoy. These were Esther's daughter and grandsons. We would have liked to be able to embrace them as family, and as a part of Esther given back to us, after our grief in losing her to an early death. Esther obviously intended that we never would find out that her child existed, and that knowledge helps a little.

Another note from the eighties: Our little town of Manchester, Maine, was famous briefly because of a little girl named Samantha Smith. She went to school locally. You may remember that she wrote to Soviet President Yuri Andropov many years ago, when she was

12 years old, urging peace. Andropov responded, inviting her and her family to visit the Soviet Union. The visit was made, and Samantha became quite a celebrity. Some say that she contributed to the process that eventually ended the Cold War, or perhaps even *started* that process. The sad thing is that she and her father were both killed in a plane crash a few months later, in 1985. Manchester has put in a little park where the old fire station used to be, dedicated to Samantha's memory.

Nineteen eighty-seven finally came, and we officially retired and sold out to Scott and Sandy. We had hired a bookkeeper, Donna Baker, to learn the ropes and take my place. Bob Jackson had recommended her. The lawyer and accountant worked up an equitable plan for the sale, which took many factors into consideration.

The greenhouse crew gave us a nice retirement party. They gave us a camera, which we used a lot. Dennis Monroe was master of ceremonies. We sat at the head table with Whit and Bee Hodgkins and Joe and Jean Scott, our best friends. It was held at our favorite restaurant, the Steer House in Winthrop.

To us the sale was somewhat like handing over your baby for someone else to bring up, and continuing to live next door! I adjusted soon, but I'm not really sure that Lawrence ever did! Before retirement, he used to say that we would move away if we sold the greenhouses, but we never seriously considered doing so once the deed was done. I didn't want to move, anyway.

I was only 57—really too young to retire. I did stay retired for ten years, though, quite contentedly. I don't intend to give advice often, but one thing I do tell people who are thinking about retiring is that one needs to retire *to* something rather than *from* something. I had lots I wanted to do.

I found quilts interesting and decided to walk in my mother's and grandmothers' footsteps, and the footsteps of countless generations of great-grandmothers before that, to learn the art of choosing patterns and fabrics and sewing quilts—an art form I felt I could master and enjoy. I knew so little about quilting that I wasn't acquainted with "quilting stitches," which hold together the three layers of a quilt—top, batting, and backing. I had always seen quilts "tied off" with little knots of yarn or heavy thread every few inches all over the quilt, holding it together. There is a world of difference between the two kinds of quilt in value—work involved, skill needed, and time required. I began by taking a class, and it was very helpful. I learned a lot! And I enjoyed it. That Christmas I made quilted bags for each of the women in my family, all different. I was very proud! I also made sofa pillows with quilted tops. That is the kind of present I would like to be able to give every year.

I made a big decision along the way: to undertake to make a quilt for each of my six children. They would be made with hand quilting, although I would piece the tops on my sewing machine for strength. Each child in turn would choose the pattern he or she would like me to use, and the colors (although I would usually choose the actual fabrics). I had always thought I probably wouldn't live to be much older than my parents had been, so I wondered if I would live long enough to finish all six. I knew it would likely take me a couple of years for each, and that turned out to be a very conservative estimate!

I lacked confidence in how well my first quilts would turn out, and Dan was the only son not yet married. If I didn't do very well, I didn't want a daughter-in-law to know about it! More important than that, the youngest child is seldom the first in anything, so I happily chose Dan to receive my very first quilt. I did manage to get it done in a couple of years, and proudly presented it to him for his twenty-fifth birthday.

All kinds of things over the next several years prevented my attention to my retirement project. Think about that as you read the next few chapters here. Hopefully you will understand why it took so long.

Twenty-two years later I finished the sixth one. It was Scott and Sandy's, and I gave it to them on June 15, 2011. Two of six were full-bed size, two were queen-size, and two were kings. None of the quilts is perfect by any stretch of the word. I chose to do lap quilting, which means cutting the fabric into blocks or squares and working on one block at a time. The blocks are sewn together after all the quilting is finished. That way I was able to take a square or two with me when we traveled, and work on it in spare moments. At home I worked mostly in the evening, with the television on. Since I am including here some of the poems I wrote to present with the finished quilts, that statement of fact may help you to understand some of the references in them.

Brown Is for Fall

"Brown," you said.
"A quilt ought to be brown.
Because when I think of quilts I think of Fall,
And the color of Fall is brown."

Brown? Of course. The color of acorns, chestnuts, cones,
Mums and late-Fall grasses, frost-wilted vines,
Leaves composting on the ground,
And brown-crusted loaves, fresh from the oven.

There ought to be birds—partridge or pheasant,
And blue—you need blue,
The color of the sky on a crisp, bright Fall day—
You need blue to bring out the beauty of brown.

What about orange? Now that's a Fall color! And white for contrast.
And what design would you like? What size?
And so your quilt plan was conceived,
Bringing warmth already!

Like the wood that warms your stove,
Your home, your heart,
Wood warms when you cut it, haul it, split it, pile it,
And again as it burns.

So quilts warm the quilter with the process of conception,
Refinement of details, selection of fabrics, planning with you,
Cutting, piecing on the sewing machine
(Notwithstanding the frustration of making the points meet!)

Then the hard part, the long part, the quilting part,
Cut short or avoided by busy modern quilters—the quilting itself,
Hand-quilting (heart-warming) with the tiniest stitches and straightest,
Shapes of leaves and vines, to look like Fall.

This quilt went to England with me, and gained a few stitches
In the Orkney Islands, ancestral home, itself like autumn;
It went to Bermuda, and Florida a couple of times,
Because quilters don't need vacations from quilting.

Quilters enjoy the warmth. This quilt saw episodes
Of "Cosby," "Cheers," and "Golden Girls," week after week.
It sat with company, and endured humiliation (possibly admiration?)
At the class where others were making a "Quilt-in-a-day."

Those quilts will never know the warmth of yours.
Why, they may never have drawn blood on a needle even once!
But yours—the love and dreams stitched into its future,
The gift of part of oneself, almost, to live on through the quilt.

An heirloom, to bring warmth again and again, and comfort,
A token of love, to a son,
And remembrance of a mother/son bond—
Love beyond measure.

Quilts can talk, if you can hear them.
They say things like "pinwheel design," "four-patch,"
"Full or queen size," "partridges and blue sky."
They also say "love and warmth" from quilter to son.

They also say "Fall."

Dee's Quilt

With all of life's interruptions, like going back to work for eight years, I didn't find much time for quilting. I wrote a poem to present with each one, but this one may express my feelings the best. These sentiments could apply to each of them. The reference in the poem to the quilt growing—it actually happened. I was making Dee a queen-size quilt when she and Andy got a new bed, king size. She humbly asked if I could enlarge the quilt. I had to search nationwide for more of one fabric, but I did it! I think Dee's was fourth out of the six. Hers was finished on April 12, 2006.

To Dee, 2006:

To My Dear Daughter, Dee

The quilt is not perfect, you'll have to agree,
But it's pretty and cozy, as a quilt should be.

Is it warm? Just right! Is it light? Quite!
Is it sturdy? I think so! And the colors, bright.

The scheme is not perfect, but most carefully built.
My goal is your pleasure in this heirloom quilt.

It took far too long, but not as long as it might.
Plans grew from queen-size to king overnight!

After all, I had cataracts, arthritis, and more,
And when I was working, finding time was a chore.

Hand-quilting is slower, but nicer, you know;
Hand-quilting adds value, with each stitch "just so."

The hours I spent were well-spent for you.
My love is sewn in with each color and hue.

I enjoyed all those hours, and thinking of you,
For this symbolizes mothers' love, ever true.

Part of me is sewn in here—the essence of "me,"
My everlasting love for my dear daughter, Dee.

If you need a hug sometime down the road,
And I am not there, let this be our code:

Just look at your quilt, with all my love there,
And you'll have my "hug," for I'll always care!

To Wayne, with Love from Mother

The hour is late. My eyes are blurred.
Been working on your quilt, you see.
Your Dad's asleep, the phones don't ring,
And nothing good is on TV.

> I like to "multi-task" and sew.
> It helps me chase my quilting dream.
> But not tonight; it's time to quit.
> But first I'll stitch just one more seam!

And on I go—it's been so long!
Two years, eight months, and counting.
I want so much to get it right.
The task was truly daunting!

> This heirloom quilt brings love to you
> And to your good wife, Carol, dear.
> Whenever thoughts of me grow dim,
> This quilt that brings my love is here.

You are my son, and loved so dear;
Your wife is so beloved, too.
This quilt, my fifth, is meant to show
The love I truly hold for you!

> So look beyond its faults and ills
> To all its comforts, warm and true.
> That's where you'll find my warmest love
> Sewn in this quilt I made for you

To Scott, June 15, 2011:

The Sixth Quilt

At last I've finished all six quilts,
My goal for retirement,
A gift of love to bind us close;
Now I can rest, content.

In '87 I started this;
Who's last? Who's first? No plan!
"Will I live long enough?" I asked.
I told myself, "I can!"

I'm now eighty-one, a good long life.
There are six bright stars in my crown.
Yes, they are my children, these six whom I love,
And their families, too, gathered 'round.

I sewed in the evenings while watching TV;
Success in my project I've won.
After twenty-four years, (long rests in between)
I've lived to say, "They're done!"

Now who was the last (but surely not least!)
Waiting twenty-four years of his life?
It turned out to be you, my oldest son,
And Sandy, your beautiful wife.

You're last, my dear Scott, to get my gift,
But yours is a special one,
An heirloom for you, and your family, too,
My wonderful first-born son!

Now this quilt is different, as each one has been,
The pattern and colors, your choice.
We don't know its name, but we know how it came
To be "Sally's Quilt" with one voice.

You saw Sally's; you liked it; took pictures and such;
And I said I'd do what it takes.
Not exactly the same, but it's close you'll agree.
(I wish I had made no mistakes!)

My stitches, not finest, are somewhat too long.
What if the quilt won't hang true?
My seams, not all straight, some bulges remain—
Surely pattern and colors please you!

With tired, old eyes and arthritic hands,
Some problems I could not fix.
Through all these years I've sewed, to leave
A remembrance for each of you six.

A year and a half I've devoted to yours,
(Least time of any I've made)
With love and great pleasure I've taken each stitch;
With enjoyment I've been richly paid.

I hope you know how much of my love
I've sewn into all the seams.
Enjoy your quilt's warmth—and my motherly love—
And I hope that it brings you sweet dreams!

Quilts for the Grandchildren

In the years since finishing this project, I decided to make as many quilts for my grandchildren as I could. I made them a generous size for twin beds, whereas those for my children were all larger. Also— and this is a huge difference concerning the time it took to make their quilts—those for my children were quilted with little stitches all over them. For the grandchildren, I "tied off" the quilts, making spaced knots.

I have fourteen grandchildren, and have made five quilts for them. Six of them can inherit their parents' heirloom quilts; I have a couple that I made for myself that will someday be for them, as well.

The first quilt for the grandchildren went to Will, the "boy next door," who had been away, working out of state. The second went to Amy, Wayne and Carol's daughter. She works in New York City, having grown up in New Jersey. Amy has a good head on her shoulders. We see her at all the family gatherings, and we visited her family and our other out-of-state families when on our trips, while the children were growing up. The third quilt was for Rachel, Alice and Bob's daughter. She is my youngest grandchild and is a "go-getter." Rachel owns several horses and is a prize-winning rider. She and Ryan expect their first child in October. The fourth quilt went to Stephanie, who lives with her husband, Curtis, in Texas. She is Dee and Andy's oldest daughter and grew up in Virginia, just outside Washington, D.C. Stephanie is a hairdresser. The last quilt I made, with hands partially disabled and eyesight dimming, was for Cassie, Dan and Tammy's daughter. She is doing well as a single mom and lives in Hampden, near Bangor, with her little boy, Benny. She is finishing her college education part time while working.

Making Amends

Once upon a time, more than twenty years ago, there was a very young girl named Cassie. She lived with her dad, Dan, and her mom, Tammy, and her brother, Mitch. The children had a Grammie and a Grampa, their dad's parents, who lived about an hour's drive down the road.

Now Grammie and Grampa loved their grandchildren very much. Every now and then, the children came down to visit for a weekend. They would sleep over, upstairs, and have a chance to play with their cousins, Will, Evan, and Ellie, who lived nearby. (Those cousins were Scott and Sandy's children, our grandchildren, to whom we were privileged to live next door as they grew up.) Everyone enjoyed those visits a lot.

Now I have to tell you that I am that Grammie. I had a big idea. I don't know what put the idea in my head, and I am so sorry that I ever thought of it because it "upset the applecart" and made a little girl very sad. The idea was that everyone might enjoy the visits more if Mitch came alone one weekend, and Cassie came by herself another weekend. Someone should have stopped me and told me that it was a bad idea.

I drove up on the appointed day to pick up Mitch and bring him home with me. Now, Cassie was very young, and she didn't understand why Mitch could go down to Grammie and Grampa's but she couldn't. I noticed that she was sidling over toward the car as he got in, her eyes big and begging. Why, oh why, didn't I change the plan then and there? Why didn't someone veto my plan?

So I have always wanted to apologize to her, for hurting the feelings of a little one whom I loved so much. I never knowingly hurt feelings of anyone, anyway, and I feel bad if it happens.

So how could I apologize?

Well, I thought of another episode from the time of those visits. Cassie, still a very little girl, was in the bathroom at our house. I saw that her face looked guilty as sin, and she was scared. (She needn't have been scared—I never punished her, or even scolded her.) On the shelf was a jar of my face cream—opened. It was so beautiful—pink, and so inviting. It was expensive, and I didn't exactly want children using it like finger paints, but I understood. I simply put it up out of reach. I hope I put a little on her hands or face.

So now, these many years later, I am giving Cassie her own jar of beautiful pink face cream, along with a very sincere personal message: "I am sorry that I hurt you, and I never meant to. I love you just so very much!"

One Busy Year—and Then Another

The year we retired from the greenhouse—1987—was a very active one for us. I kept a record of the various activities and trips that year, and some of the family activity. (See list below.) It seems to me that we made good use of that first year of retirement. We did fairly well the second year, too!

Retirement party
Winter trip to Florida, including Longwood Gardens—
   visited both Alice and Wayne
Alice and Bob built their house
Dan's first car
New building at greenhouse (Lawrence's idea);
   employee lounge, conference room, restrooms
In May, overnight trip aboard the *Scotia Prince*, from Portland
   to Nova Scotia
Alaska trip, with Arlene and Allie
Day trip to Wyman Lake, north of Bingham
Dee and Andy's wedding
Camping trip at Mt. Blue right after the wedding
Tozier family reunion at Mt. Blue (the Toziers were my
   relatives on my mother's side)
Week at Harrison Lake, the week bought on PBS auction
Eastern States Expo at Springfield, Massachusetts
Visit to Gary Olsen's new house, just built in Jefferson
My cousin Carolyn and Steve Pelehach visited us from
   Florida—took some day trips with them
Took quilting class

Made six quilted bags as Christmas presents for my six
    daughters and daughters-in-law
Made several quilted sofa pillows for presents
Started Dan's quilt, my first

In 1988 we were pretty busy, too. We went to Florida, then the
Portland Flower Show. I went alone on a special bus to the Boston
flower show. We had a wonderful trip to the British Isles. Later we
enjoyed a day trip to Pemaquid. The extended family got together
and camped at North Conway, New Hampshire. In early October, we
visited Wayne and family in New Jersey. Lawrence went trekking in
Nepal, and I went to Bermuda.

Traveling

After retirement we traveled more than we had ever been able to before. We had the health, the desire, the time, and the money, thanks to the sale of the business. A lot of people do not have the blessings that we had.

Lawrence's sister, Arlene, was eager to have us go with her and her husband, Alvin Jordan (called Allie), to Alaska. She was determined we should go that first summer of retirement. Allie was not a traveler, and so was not confident about finding his way around, so we led the way for 56 days on a wonderful trip.

We left on June 14th and spent the first night at one of the prettiest camping areas of the entire trip. We were on the west side of Lake Champlain, which we crossed by ferry. It was a great beginning.

In the van, we had a mattress which we left spread out in the back. Between that and the back doors, there was plenty of room for our boxes of supplies, cooking equipment, and suitcases. We knew how to travel light from our prior experiences. I made curtains for the van windows, which were needed for privacy. They stayed on the curtain rods, which were easily taken down each morning. I also made a removable cloth screen, which I fitted tight over one front window with Velcro, so we could have fresh air when sleeping in the van and still keep the mosquitoes out. That, too, came down for driving each day. Arlene and Allie had a somewhat smaller van, but got by nicely. We camped a lot, but stayed in motels whenever there was a reason—like needing a shower, or battling mosquitoes, or just because we wanted to!

We visited Alice's new garden center, staying overnight in a motel in Jefferson City, or Jeff City, as the locals call it. Still in Missouri, we went to the Harry S. Truman Library and to the Dwight D. Eisenhower home and library.

In Colorado, we had to get accustomed to higher elevation. We camped one night at 9000 feet, and the next day drove up Pike's Peak, which is over 14,000 feet high. That was an experience. Arlene and I were both affected by the elevation, but we both managed to get by. The funny thing about driving up to such high elevation was that their air mattress got bigger and bigger as we drove into thinner air, and stretched all out of shape. They eventually threw it away!

At Salt Lake City, we didn't go into the Mormon Tabernacle, but the public was allowed to attend one of the choir rehearsals at another church next door. That was beautiful. We also visited the International Peace Gardens there, and of course, Great Salt Lake.

Wyoming was next. We watched rafting, boating, or floating on the Snake River and saw white pelicans at a distance, which we didn't know came that far north. We visited Yellowstone and Glacier National Parks, and Logan Pass. From there we went north into Canada, with its beautiful provincial parks. We enjoyed Banff and Lake Louise once again, and marveled once more at the beauty of the Canadian Rockies.

In Edmondton, Alberta, there is a huge mall, the largest on this continent at that time, I believe. They had a lot more than stores there. There was a swimming area with manmade waves. We watched bungee jumping. Noticing the sign with the cost of jumping printed on it, Allie said, "What? Pay money to do that? They'd have to pay *me*!"

Kluane is, in my estimation, about the prettiest lake in the world. Part of its beauty is the color of the water, which is a bright aqua, and part is the scenic surrounding land. I would love to be able to gaze upon it once again.

Steese Highway is a dirt road going north to the Arctic Circle. The Yukon River was a pleasant sight once again, way up there. There is a community called Circle, and another one called Circle Hot Springs. At Circle Hot Springs, there is an old hotel which I found to be very charming. It is full of old-fashioned furnishings and decorations. It has the feel of the gold rush days. The hot springs are enclosed as a swimming pool, just outside of the hotel, and we were told that the locals use it even in the winter. We did go swimming that evening, and found that we couldn't stay in the water very long. It was too hot. What I found most unusual, though, was that all of the hot water in the hotel comes from the springs. Also, for a very unusual experience, the toilets are flushed with that hot water, too! It keeps the toilet seat nice and warm.

I just loved that old hotel! Of course, we had the "midnight sun" experience there, too. It didn't get really dark all night. I wish I could be there on the longest day of the year.

Mt. McKinley is now called Denali, which means "great one." We took the bus tour into Denali National Park, as cars were not allowed except for those who had campsites in the park. The road is twisting and narrow and two-way. It seems most of the road is stuck onto the side of the steep mountains, and there is one sharp curve after another! Going by bus was easier, though, than driving our own vehicles was, on our first trip in 1969. It was cloudy around the mountain, as it was sixty percent of the time according to the information given us.

Next we were headed for Portage, where the glacier is near the road, and chunks of its ice are sometimes available. In 1969 we had gathered one for our cooler. It was blue in color, and lasted much longer than an equivalent piece of ordinary ice would have.

Homer Spit is an interesting place. Wikipedia says it is the longest piece of land jutting out into water in the world. This spit is 4½ miles long, and narrow, and it takes fifteen minutes to drive the length! Docks on either side, some in deep water, some in shallow, accommodate boats. Campers line the road. There are a couple of Porta-Potties. Allie and Arlene chose one side of the Spit for their camp for the night, while we liked the view on the other side. Allie, being a fisherman/farmer, struck up conversations with one or more fishermen. He brought me a live crab that someone had given to him. (I don't know the name, but it wasn't like our Maine variety, and it was not a big so-called Alaskan crab.) This was late at night, and I cooked it and ate it at eleven p.m.! Yes, it was still light out!

We enjoyed our time there and in the town of Homer. We drove along the Skyline Drive. It is so beautiful and so quaint. Arlene and Allie elected not to go, but Lawrence and I signed on for a boat trip on Halibut Cove aboard the *Danny J.* ferry. It took several hours and was great.

I have a word for you to learn—*solifluction*. As you know, Alaskan soil is frozen year round, down a few inches. This is permafrost. In the summer, the sun melts the surface soil, and solifluction happens on the steep slopes of the hills and mountains. It is the melted surface soil "dripping" down the slope over the stationary frozen ground. Wikipedia says it is water-soaked soil, and that it may move downward by gravity at the rate of a few inches a day. It is visible at a distance, once you know what to look for.

We had another unusual experience taking a "shortcut" to Valdez. In Portage, we drove our vans onto railroad cars which transported us to Whittier like a ferry. We remained in our vans, and it was a very wild 12-mile ride! Allie and Arlene were next behind us, so they could watch as we swayed and leaned. Allie said he was sure a couple of times that we were going right off the edge! It was quite scary! Along the way there were two long tunnels. The darkness in those tunnels didn't help any!

This was before the horrible oil spill in Valdez, which happened on March 24, 1989. We were there July 18, 1987. Valdez was beautiful, with a lot to see and do.

We enjoyed more of the beautiful parks and campgrounds as we returned to Canada. Arlene and I went swimming at Fraser Lake, Beaumont Park, British Columbia. We had left Alaska, but the trip was far from over. I'll hurry through a few of the highlights.

Hope, British Columbia, is another very pleasant little town or city. We visited Minter Gardens there, and then Queen Elizabeth Gardens and Van Dusen Gardens in Vancouver. We enjoyed Victoria, with its hanging baskets of beautiful flowers along the streets. We had a scenic ferry ride from Vancouver to Nanaimo, with unbelievable scenery everywhere in this part of the world. The famous Butchart Gardens lived up to expectations. The Coho ferry took us from Victoria to Port Angeles.

Back in the United States, we went to Olympia National Park, and then to the rain forest. It seemed odd to find such tropical conditions. We explored Mount St. Helens. The volcano had begun its activity there on April 1, 2, and 3, 1980. A few weeks later, on May 18th, there was an earthquake which caused it to erupt and wreak havoc with its massive power. We were there more than seven years later, and the area still showed complete destruction, with trees lying about everywhere, knocked flat by the explosive eruption, but with some vegetation beginning to come back.

Mt. Rainier National Park was splendid. We spent some time at Grand Coulee Dam. We learned about the town of Frank, Alberta, after going back into Canada and heading east. Frank had once been buried by a rockslide, its story interesting and tragic.

Near Winnipeg, we stopped at Egli Sheep Farm for a short tour. I bought myself a woolen knit hat and mittens, pink in color, which I still have, and which I wore a lot over the years.

We stayed at St. Johnsbury, Vermont, on our last night of the trip. We got home on August 9th.

Ah! 1988! That was a year for major trips! In late May, Lawrence and I went to England, Scotland, and Wales, and the Orkney Islands, getting over there in time for the Chelsea Flower Show. Later that same year, he and nephew Peter Maxwell traveled on a once-in-a-lifetime trip to Nepal, while I went to Bermuda with Bee Hodgkins. We were making the most of retirement while we were still young.

We made good use of the AAA Travel Agency for those trips. Traveling in the UK is simple if you get a railroad pass here before going over. You pay the one fee, and all train rides over there are free for the length of time stated. Just show your pass.

Typically we would come into a town by train, carrying our luggage—one good-sized suitcase on wheels with the handle extended, two umbrellas, maybe two jackets, and another bag on top of the big one, for Lawrence to maneuver; and another canvas or quilted bag for me, with my purse across my body from right shoulder to left side. We certainly looked like American tourists, right down to the camera on a strap hanging from my neck! From the train we would walk to the visitor center or information booth, or sometimes I went and he stayed with the luggage. We would get a bed and breakfast room for the night. Often we booked for the next town on our list, also, if it was not far away. In Scotland they have a well-organized plan called "Book a Bed Ahead." Usually we could walk to our B & B, but sometimes we went by taxi. A few times, our host or hostess picked us up at the station.

These people wanted us to visit with them. The room was typically just a bedroom in their home, without lock and key. The "loo" was usually down the hall; you paid extra to stay in a place that had a private bathroom. They would find out what time we wanted breakfast, and what we wanted to eat. I had begun to watch my cholesterol, but breakfasts were invariably greasy. We needed more than a bowl of cereal for the day ahead, and what we ate for breakfast was part of the paid deal anyway, so it saved money to make breakfast a big meal. A dish of baked beans over fried buttered bread was usually offered, as well as the usual eggs and meats. We got broiled tomato slices and cold toast. They even have serving "racks" that separate the toast slices and keep them standing and cooling off!

There were many times that we got a sandwich at the train station for lunch. Mine was often tuna and cucumber. We found bar meals to be affordable and good. Sometimes Sundays were a problem, with some eating places closed, but we never went hungry!

We went sightseeing every day. We visited a lot of gardens. The rhododendrons and azaleas are spectacular—and big! They have chestnut trees with pink blossoms. When visiting the ancient ruins, I felt close to my ancestors who had come from there. The 500-year-old churches, or the old stone cottages, sometimes just ruins, spoke to me of their lives—perhaps right there—so very long ago! We know the towns where some of them lived, and we even did a little exploring. That was fascinating!

We learned to use the underground (subway) and the trains pretty efficiently. They have a great deal more active train service than we have in this country. Over there, if you miss a train, no problem; there will be another one along soon.

Once, getting on the train or subway, Lawrence got on in the crowd, but the door closed before I could board! Through the closed window, he was saying he would get off at the next stop and come back to get me on the next train, but I was telling him to go to our destination and wait for me there, that I would take the next train. The train pulled out before we settled it, but it turned out all right. We both did as I said, and we got back together. Without cell phones, we could have gone back and forth all day looking for each other.

Before going over, we had booked a package including dinner, room, and a Shakespeare play. For that reason, I had packed one dressy outfit, heels, and nylons. Once that night was over we realized we were carrying around stuff we wouldn't need again on the trip, so we put together a box which we shipped back to the States, to lighten our load.

It was a memorable trip, a truly and remarkably great trip, not easy but we managed. We would say to each other, as we hauled our baggage around, how much easier a tour would be, with someone making the arrangements and handling the luggage. Lawrence would always say that doing it our way, we can go where we want, when we want, and do our own thing. He said when we got old would be the time to take tours. We never got "old" enough that we did that, though!

That trip to the UK was in 1988 and lasted several weeks. In the fall of that same year, Lawrence (age 66) and Arlene's son, Peter, went trekking in Nepal. I was glad Peter was going, too. It was a wonderful trip. They had Sherpa guides who cooked their meals, set up tents, and provided all their needs. They didn't even have to carry their own backpacks! They didn't climb mountains as such, but did go up to some very high elevations—14,000 feet, I believe. As I remember, he was gone about a month.

Since he was going on a trip without me, I decided I would have a trip of my own! We left at about the same time, but mine only lasted a week! I debated going by cruise ship, but decided on flying—to Bermuda! As I made my plans, I thought I was going alone. However, I realized that our good friends, Whit and Bee Hodgkins, were going through some tough times with his illness, and she was having a lot of stress. I asked her if she would like to go with me. She did want very much to go, and I knew it would be good for her. Also, I would have a companion. We loved the hotel, dressing for dinner, swimming in the ocean and pool, and walking or taking the bus everywhere. The pink sand and pastel-colored houses added to the beauty and charm of the island. We really had a relaxing and fun time.

There was still one more trip that decade. It was in 1989 and was the reunion for that summer, even though Alice, Bob, Dee, Lawrence, and I were the only ones who went. We traveled to Colorado and tented together in a favorite area of Bob's, after picking Dee up at the airport. Bob had hunted there over the years and was a good guide. The elevation was very high, and it really bothered me so much that I got up during the night and slept sitting up in the car. I had trouble breathing when lying down.

We rode around enjoying the beautiful scenery, John Denver's outdoor concert "auditorium" in the red rocks, and Estes Park. It was so charming and endearing at bedtime to hear Alice, who was alone in their tent, singing to her unborn child. She was expecting her baby early in October. What a good mother-to-be!

That was a good year for welcoming grandsons! How quickly they grow up! Alice's baby hearing the lullaby in the tent was Eric Call, now owner of his own business, and married to Carrie, with a youngster of their own, Toby, and another on the way. They are very active in their church. Two other boys joined our family that same year. First was Wayne and Carol's son, Steve, now living in Pennsylvania with Nicole and their son, Hunter. We used to play board games with him when we visited. The other boy was Will, general manager at Longfellow's Greenhouses in Manchester, and a very capable young man. He and Michelle were married nearly a year ago.

The 1990s—More Travel and a Big Worry

At the beginning of the decade, in 1990, we took an extended second trip to the British Isles. We were away a couple of months this time, and I think it was the most interesting and gratifying journey we ever made. We were on our own, on the same type of trip we had made over there two years earlier. We went to the Chelsea Flower Show again. Flowers everywhere were absolutely the most lush and prolific imaginable. We visited the outer islands, whereas in 1988 the only peripheral sites visited were the Orkney Islands and the Isle of Skye.

This time it was the Orkneys, Skye, the Shetlands, and the Western Isles, or Hebrides. We spent a lot of time traveling in England, Scotland, and Wales, too. We thoroughly enjoyed the landscape, the weather, the people, the countryside's rural beauty, and the occasional absolute and utter silence except for the muted bleat of a sheep, hum of a bee, or song of a bird.

We live our lives these days mostly in competition with noise pollution, such as traffic and heavy equipment, lawn mowers and snow blowers, televisions and radios, air-conditioners and refrigerators, and ever-ringing telephones. Some places we visited on that trip seemed more like the town where, and the time when, I grew up.

The silence that is rejuvenating is the absence of noise that results from the activities or inventions of humans. In the moments when we come closest to that state of affairs we ordinarily call silence, there is usually some intruding sound still—at least the tick-tock of a clock! I sat reading in a sheep pasture on the Isle of Harris, in the Hebrides, while Lawrence hiked up a small mountain one pleasantly warm and sunny afternoon. The sheep didn't seem to mind my presence, and I didn't mind theirs. There was complete silence all the time I sat there, except for sounds of the sheep and birds.

I believe our nerves would calm down, along with our blood pressure, and our lives would seem less hectic, if we could have a dose of such tranquility once in a while—maybe even on a regular basis.

On our first couple of days in England, we stayed at a B & B south of London. On the second night a burglar made a late-night visit to the house! We were very tired, so tired that Lawrence slept through it all, and I thought, in my state of half-sleep, that it was Lawrence up and walking around in our room. The next morning, our hostess asked if we had heard anything suspicious in the night. I had seen our bedroom door opening and had pushed it shut, early on. Immediately, I had heard footsteps hurrying down the stairs. I woke Lawrence, and he said it was probably just someone looking for the loo. I told her about that. Her handbag had been stolen from beside her bed.

Police were called, and they came and questioned us. Nothing was stolen from us, and I couldn't remember much of what had happened in our room. I still thought I had been talking with my husband in the night, when it was actually the burglar! We stayed around an extra day and night in case the police needed anything more from us. They did fingerprint us.

Wisps of memory kept coming back to me over time as the weeks went by; I remembered a few words here and there of our conversation, and how I felt about it at the time. For instance, I asked the burglar if he needed my flashlight, thinking it was Lawrence I was talking to. When he said he had a light, I wondered where he'd gotten it, since we had packed only one flashlight. I said things to him that I would only say to my husband! He kept looking for money, even around me in my bed. I think he was amused by my thinking he was Lawrence, and he left without taking anything from our room. Many people would say I dreamed half of it, or had false memories of things that didn't really happen. I don't agree.

When we went to the Western Isles, we met a very interesting Scotsman. (We went by ferry, but had to wait for hours because it was broken down and had to be repaired.) Michael Robson was his name, and he was traveling on the ferry, too. He loved the islands and wanted to move there and open a bed and breakfast. He was retiring as an archivist at the university at Edinburgh. He had written a historical book (which I later bought) about happenings at an obscure small island north of the Hebrides. We got well enough acquainted that day that we exchanged letters for a few years, until he got tired of it. I found his stories fascinating. He probably hoped that we were prospective future paying guests at his B & B. He did move there and follow his plan during the time we were writing. It was interesting having a pen pal for a while, and learning about a land where some of my ancestors had lived and died.

We took a nice trip in June of 1991 to the Provinces—New Brunswick, Nova Scotia, Newfoundland, and Prince Edward Island. I recommend that trip to anyone who enjoys nature, the coast, quaint villages, and remote areas. Going to Newfoundland was very interesting. We took the "short ferry" over and the "long ferry" (overnight) from St. John's coming back. That was a rough trip with severe weather. They lashed the cars down in the ferry to keep them in place! I couldn't walk without hanging onto something, we were tipping and bucking so much.

At Gros Morne National Park in Newfoundland, we walked quite a distance through woods to take a boat tour of the Western Brook Pond Fjord. While admiring the scenery, we learned about the geology, a very interesting study. That was great.

It had been our intention to go by mail boat/ferry to Labrador from Newfoundland. It is a trip that we had read about and really wanted to take. Mind you, this was June 26th or thereabouts, and there were still too many ice floes in the seas and the boat was not running yet. Too bad!

On that trip, we went by ferry to Prince Edward Island, but later in that decade a long bridge was built from New Brunswick to the island. In 1999 we celebrated our fiftieth anniversary by going to just the island, and we were able to go by the toll bridge. Toll is charged going to the island, but not when leaving. I guess they'd rather have you leave than arrive!

We enjoyed the play *Anne of Green Gables* while we were there in 1991. We ran into friends Russ and Nancy Jack and his parents at the theater. We also paid to tour the house where the author had lived.

Another local performance was very interesting one evening—a musical concert of local talent. It included young girls doing Scottish dances. There is heavy Scottish influence in the Provinces. That is one reason why I enjoy going there, I guess.

1992 was the year of our third trip to Alaska, our second with Arlene and Allie. We did a few things that were different from the trip five years earlier. First we had the long ride across southern Canada, always beautiful. Then we went by ferry to Alaska, from Prince Rupert to Haines, following the route taken by the cruise ships, but with less luxury. There was a short stop at Juneau, which is separated from the rest of Alaska and not accessible by car. I'm glad we did it that way, taking the ferry. It was an interesting way to get there—a good trip in itself.

On this trip, we were able to see Mt. McKinley about three days in a row, from great distances, and we took the bus trip into Denali National Park all the way to Wonder Lake again. What a magnificent ride!

The next day I was very sick with my inner ear vertigo. Arlene took pity on me and urged Lawrence to have us shut down early and find a place to stay the night. The only place available was over a dance hall, and we had loud music into the wee hours! I was much better the next day and able to function, but some dizziness always lingers for a few days.

We went to California at the end of this Alaska trip, and Arlene and Allie drove home on their own. Our mission was to be with Dee when her baby was born.

Now for the worry: The list I have of family reunions each year notes that the Browns (Anna and Jeff) visited Dee and Andy in California in 1992. Their son, Seth, was 14 the year of that visit. While there, he developed a severe stiff neck, which didn't go away. Their medical doctor at home provided pain pills, with no further investigation.

Anna and Jeff finally took him to a chiropractor, who was unsuccessful in treating the pain. Next he saw an orthopedic surgeon, who diagnosed a tumor of the spine. It was not treatable anywhere in the state, so Seth was sent to Boston, where some of the best doctors in the world took charge of his case.

The diagnosis was "cancer of the blood vessels of the bone" (epithelioid hemangioendothelioma) located on the second vertebra from the top. The condition was so rare that there was very little literature for the doctors to consult. Seth's case was followed by three different hospitals in Boston. The doctors didn't agree on whether it was a true cancer; they did agree that if it was cancer, it still would probably not metastasize. They all knew that it was a very serious condition, even if only because of the location. The situation caused an emotional roller coaster for months, with cause first for optimism, then disappointment, over and over again.

The tumor was biopsied at Boston Children's Hospital, and that itself was a risky procedure. The cells were sent to five centers on the East Coast. Only one, Mass. General, identified it as a benign form, epithelioid hemangioma. They still had no idea how to treat it.

We were impressed by Anna and Jeff's aggressiveness in seeking answers for their child. Anna was like a mother bear when her cubs are threatened. (They now have grandchildren, the local ones being Kristin's boys, Aidan, Tanner, and Heath. They show the same kind of deep nurturing care for them, traveling often to Winslow.) We felt their pain and stress, not only Seth's but also his parents'. Anna is our daughter. When your child suffers, you suffer. Anna and Jeff suffered for him; we also suffered for them.

Seth made medical history that year: The oncologist stated that no one else in the world had his situation.

Anna and Jeff took him to the National Institutes of Health in Bethesda, Maryland, for evaluation.

At both Boston and Bethesda, Nobel Prize winners in medicine were on the boards reviewing his case. Each group recommended contrary treatment and gave dire warnings about what would happen if the other treatments were implemented. In Bethesda, they were told that nothing could be done, and they were sent home. They had come up against the proverbial brick wall. Then they received a call about a new procedure.

Seth had angiograms of the area, before and after the treatment. Those were very uncomfortable for him. They were made via an artery, starting in the groin, the way a cardiologist views the heart. The new treatment was to inject ethanol (the product from corn that is added to fuel) directly into the tumor, a procedure which they viewed by repeated CT scans. He had to be awake for this long, excruciatingly painful treatment. The purpose was to "starve" the cells of nourishment to make them die.

It took some time, but seemed to be working except for one area. So, he went back to have the procedure repeated, which was understandably difficult for him, and that is a huge understatement. Bad news again—they were sent home with the devastating news that the procedure had not worked and they could not do it again. There was nothing left to do but wait and see.

Over time, the tumor did shrink! The procedures had worked after all! He had to have checkups for a few years, of course, by CT scan, and he was left with limited mobility and chronic pain in his neck.

About three years earlier, when Seth was 11 years old, he broke his arm for no apparent reason. An X-ray revealed a large tumor that took up most of his right radius. When he developed this new tumor on the spine, it was assumed that both tumors were the same type. After his first ethanol treatment, the arm tumor was biopsied and found to be a different very rare type! At that time the cancer diagnosis was discarded.

So the record was finalized without the designation of cancer. I wonder if there have been more cases in the years since that have helped medical science to decide what to call it!

Early on, before the ethanol treatment, I got the bright idea of organizing a Sunshine Box for Seth. You know how that works—presents are placed in a big box, and he opens one each day. I contacted many friends and relatives and organized it. I wrote a poem for him to go with it, which I have copied below. One of my presents for the box was a list of the gift-givers and thank-you cards. I addressed and stamped the envelopes and wrote his return address on them. He wrote the notes. People were impressed with his creative expressions of thanks and appreciation. I think he enjoyed the project, and I felt better doing something.

I composed this poem in my head as I went for my daily walk and included it with the Sunshine Box:

To Seth

Of friends and relations you do have a ton!
They're wishing you <u>good health</u>, and soon—every one!
It's been a long summer, not much you could do.
We hope this brings <u>Sunshine</u> and big <u>Smiles</u> to you!
Though our gifts may be small ones, they're packed with our <u>Love</u>.
That's something you know that you have plenty of!
You'll open just one—choose with care—each day,
You'll spread out the <u>Sunshine</u> and <u>Smiles</u> that way.
We hope we've packed <u>Courage</u> with each gift in here,
And <u>Hope</u>, for the taking, to help vanquish fear.
Here's <u>Strength</u>, though you've lots, we'd add to your powers,
And <u>Faith</u>—here, there's plenty, please share some of ours!

Many of the people I contacted were church people. Seth had a lot of individuals and two or three church congregations praying for him. Guy's was one of them. I sent a donation to his church.

During the worst or most worrisome time during all of this, we made a trip to Missouri in October 1993. We traveled to other states, also, and made a longer trip out of it. In Sedona, Arizona, in red rock countryside, there is built into the rocks and hills a small chapel made to fit naturally into the landscape. We drove up the winding road and joined the quiet group as we went inside the chapel. The view is magnificent! Once inside, the view is enjoyed through the glass windows which form the whole wall. It is quiet. There is music, and candles. Sedona is known for its spiritual qualities, supposedly coming from the vortex of the rocks. I find that hard to believe, but I do know there is an aura there, felt by many people. I felt it within that little chapel. My oldest grandson was in need of a miracle, it seemed, while I had just learned of my dear Uncle Paul's death. As I sat there in a state of deep emotion, I prayed fervently. I prayed that Seth would be granted a cure soon, and I said a prayerful goodbye to Uncle Paul. I felt better when we finally left the chapel—more optimistic and emotionally cleansed. I had achieved a degree of peace. We very soon got word that Seth was going to have the new procedure, which was eventually successful. In spite of some residual pain and stiffness, and some loss of mobility, he now lives a good life in Indiana with his wife, Sarah, and their son, Alex.

Go to Sedona if you ever can. Find that chapel. It will be worth your time, whether you are religious or not. I believe all people have a spiritual side and need to nourish it. Each person will have his own way of doing that and may have to search out the process and/or places that work best. If not prayer, then meditation or directed thought may suffice for some. That would be "thought" of the kind that will cleanse the mind and bring hope and peace to the spirit. For emotional health, everyone should find ways to use, nourish, and improve access to that part of the self. I promise it can improve life if you give it a chance.

Later on in this book, I have some original Christmas poems. I would call your attention to the one I called "The Peace of Christmas."

I received a lot of positive feedback from people to whom I sent copies along with our Christmas card. I mention it here to conclude my above words urging everyone to nourish their minds and spirits. Surely, seeking peace in one's life is part of that endeavor.

Now back to the '90's!

Elderhostel had always seemed to me to offer opportunities to get to know interesting places at reasonable prices. They offer hundreds of locations all over the world. People have to be 55 or older, or be the guest of someone in that age group. Depending on the location, living arrangements may be offered in dormitories, motels, or whatever they have found there and made available for groups. The usual procedure includes study, lectures, field trips, etc., about the area for four, five, or six days. Meals are eaten together where there is a dining hall.

Even if you are confined to a wheelchair, you can find courses that you will be able to attend; but you would need to be careful not to sign up for one that would require hiking.

In mid-decade, I asked Arlene if she would like to go on one of these trips with me, since Lawrence wasn't interested. She would, especially when I mentioned one at Churchill, Manitoba, which is on Hudson Bay. The focus would be on the autumn color of trees and flora (the fall color there is mostly in bushes and plants, as their trees are boreal forests, mostly evergreens), and birds and animals. The latter was mostly polar bears, which were encroaching on Churchill and the bay before winter ice came. The other point of interest was the northern lights. The building is Northern Studies, and astronomers and scientists from all over the world seek opportunities to study or teach there.

We went in September 1995. Churchill is very remote, and our trip was long. We could have gone into Churchill by train instead of plane, but there were no highways in. We were not exactly seasoned air travelers, although I had flown more than she had. We made it, though. She used a cane, and that prompted our inclusion among the pre-boarders.

We shared a room with two other women. There were two sets of bunk beds. I got a bottom bunk, but Arlene took the other top one.

The meals were plain but hearty, and there were snacks available.

The windows all had very heavy iron bars across them for protection against the bears. Also, we were not allowed outside without a guide who carried a rifle. When we traveled in a small bus on our field trips, a guide with a gun looked the area over first before we were allowed to disembark. As it turned out, we didn't get to see even one bear. It was a few weeks early for them, although some had arrived. We could have taken the course in October instead, but it was already fully booked. The weather would have been much colder then. There would have been a lot of bears by that time, though.

The weather was cloudy the whole week, so we didn't get to see the aurora borealis, either! We didn't feel badly gypped because the whole experience was so enjoyable and interesting. We talked for a couple of years of going back and possibly getting our husbands to go with us, but we never did it.

Lawrence met us in Montreal, and we stayed overnight and did some sightseeing the next day. We visited gardens there. I had accomplished one more great trip, one to remember!

It must have been in the fall of 1992 that Lawrence left an important decision up to me, and I went ahead with a project that has served us well over the years since. But first, we needed new vinyl linoleum on the kitchen floor. I had a ball choosing the pattern, and decided to replace all of the old linoleum, in the bathroom and hallways, too. The big decision was to knock out the wall between the breezeway and dining room to make one big room. It needed to be done before the flooring was put down. If we were ever going to do it, that was the time. We have never been a bit sorry.

The big room has provided extra space for our growing extended family, as each of our children married and gave us grandchildren. We have nearly forty in the family now, and during our Christmas celebration, the room is really packed!

I have forgotten the year, but it was while we were still going to Florida each winter, that we were invited by Whit and Bee Hodgkins to stay a few days in their mobile home in Zephyrhills, Florida, since they were not currently using it. They were so generous!

Years before that, they had let us use their little camp on Pocasset

Lake in North Wayne, Maine. Being an apple grower, Whit was too busy from early September on to use it, and we enjoyed it so much! It began around 1980, and most every fall for a while we would go out after work, eat a quick supper, and get out on the lake in Scott's canoe (the safest canoe we ever saw). It was not a busy lake, and we would have a flashlight with us in case we met other boats, which was highly unlikely. We would listen to the loons, watch the planes and satellites overhead, and enjoy the stars and the quiet. We often stayed overnight, even when we had to get up early and get to work at the greenhouse. It was just so nice to look out at that lake in the morning, and eat breakfast out on the porch! Sometimes we would get a chance to be there in the daytime and explore the whole area. The weather got cold fast, and then we would reluctantly return their key and stay at home. The opportunity Whit and Bee gave us for rest and recreation meant a great deal to us.

Getting back to that year in Florida, Lawrence got the bright idea of having Arlene and Allie come down and spend a week with us there. It took a couple of phone calls to get Whit's permission and to make arrangements with Arlene. There was only one bedroom in the house, but at one end of the screened-in porch there was a room they called the bunkhouse. It had two cots and was a tight and secure structure. In a day or two, we were picking them up at the airport. I bought new sheets and towels and a few groceries, and we were all set! Lawrence and I took the bunkhouse, and it was really quite cozy. We set about showing them Florida—the places we liked most. We did a lot in one week's time.

Skip ahead now to the winter of 1999. Lawrence and I had been going to the Southwest on winter trips ever since Aunt Hazel and Uncle Paul had died. We had gone to Florida nine years in a row in order to visit them. The first few years, I didn't care much for those southwestern states because I love Maine's green grass and flowers, trees and lakes. Over time, though, I realized that those states have their own charm. We don't need to compare the attributes of different places, but just enjoy each for what it is.

That winter we were able to introduce Arlene and Allie to that area of our beautiful and diverse country. Arlene and Allie took their vehicle and we drove our car for yet another trip together. We didn't take camping equipment this time, but stayed exclusively in motels, as Lawrence and I always did when going south. We followed our usual route south as far as Florida, but then headed west along the Gulf Coast to Texas. There we always enjoyed the Big Bend country and Chisos Mountains before heading north to my all-time favorite place to stay, Indian Lodge in Fort Davis State Park. As usual, we visited McDonald Observatory, and then in New Mexico we saw the sandhill cranes and other fowl at their wintering grounds at Bosque del Apache. Arlene enjoyed Sedona, as I always have, and even asked for a slightly longer visit at the little cathedral in the rocks and hills near there, which I described earlier. Next, we took the long drive down to Organpipe Cactus Park in Arizona.

Lawrence was glad, as am I, that we helped Arlene to see some areas that she might never have seen otherwise. She had an interest in traveling that neither of her two husbands shared. Allie did enjoy our trips, though, with Lawrence leading the way.

In Maine we are no strangers to ice and snow, but there was a very unusual storm in 1998, an Ice Storm with capital letters! That morning before we got up we could hear loud cracking noises all around outside, which we finally determined to be tree limbs breaking. The weight of the ice had become too much. That meant broken electric lines, too, of course. We were without power for seven days, and we were among the lucky ones.

The smart thing to do would have been to go to a motel, but we didn't. After all, we were campers, and we had grown up in homes without electric power! Scott offered us one of the greenhouse generators, but we declined. It was not terribly cold those first few days, so we set up the camp stove on the porch, wore coats all day, and got by. We saved water that drained off the roof for washing and flushing.

But then it turned colder, making our situation worse. We had recently discovered that we couldn't use our woodstove in the basement anymore because the chimney had a crack or hole, and the liner would need to be replaced. I tried out our one kerosene lamp, but the fumes were bad, much worse than I remember from childhood. I was using colored, perfumed kerosene that I had bought earlier for the lamp, and I really think it was not like what we used to use when I was a child.

The stress of living that way began to take its toll. We made it through, of course. It was only a week, but Anna and Jeff were without power much longer. A lot of people had many more days than we did, to do without heat and electricity. Loss of freezer contents was widespread.

We lost trees. The pretty birch tree that we had saved when we cleared the land where we built the greenhouses was badly damaged. It had been my request to save it then, and I always thought of it as mine, and as a sort of symbol of our venture. My poem about the birch appears earlier in this book. The maple on our front lawn was completely down, and lots of other trees lost limbs. That storm was one for the history books!

The next phase of my life actually began in 1997. I was only 57 when Lawrence and I retired, but I stayed quite happy with my situation for the ten years after we sold the corporation to Scott and Sandy. I began to think seriously about the possibility of helping out at the greenhouse again, on my own terms, and only part-time. I talked to Scott about it, and I soon began counting down the registers at night, taking out the day's receipts and getting deposits ready. Scott got me a desk and chair and a computer, and I came to work for a few hours daily in the office.

It was wonderful working beside Scott again, even though he was so busy. He always took time to greet me, and he showed appreciation for having me on board. Anna was working there, too, and I saw her often. It was a wonderful eight years.

Whenever it worked out for Scott's and Anna's families, I put on a weekend supper for all of us. I don't remember when that began. It seems as if I have always done it. Sometimes Saturday worked best and sometimes Sunday. Dan and family would come down every few weeks. I made the effort because I do so enjoy visiting with my family, but also to give them a chance to visit with each other and remain close. Those parents who complain that their children never come to see them should try inviting them to supper once in a while.

Those were the high points of the 1990s. We were doing fairly well health-wise, but we both had issues. My arthritis was constantly getting more troublesome. But we were still able to do most everything for ourselves, and travel, and enjoy life.

What wonderful scenic journeys we have made! I am so glad that Lawrence wanted to travel and that we have done so. I am also glad that he was interested in seeing the same things that I am, wonders of nature at the top of the list.

What beauty there is in this old world! So many people are denied the long years of retirement that we enjoyed, and some could not travel because of poor health or lack of money. For some it is lack of interest. How wonderful that we were able to enjoy as much of it as we did!

The Sovereign Sea

I stand at the edge of the ocean, the cool water swirling around my feet. As the wave recedes, the sand on which I stand tries to go with it, gently threatening my equilibrium. Conforming to the rhythm of Nature, the waves keep coming—one after another, after another, after another.

Overhead, pelicans circle gracefully, then swoop and rise triumphantly from brief contact with the water. Each bird's skill yields yet another fish, ready for his lunch. Raucous gulls call belligerently as they dive for their own share. Some are resting on the more gentle waves. Along the shore, sandpipers dart this way and that, with their impossibly quick little steps, tending to their own business.

The hot sun beats down on this semitropical coast of our country, where I stand. Sunshine gleams off the water here and there, decorating the turquoise waves.

A few mostly broken shells wash ashore, adding to a high tide line, accumulated by the steady action of the constant waves. I carry a bag to collect those that suit my fancy. Maybe I will use them to decorate a unique jewelry box or something. Their shapes and colors are so pleasing—pink, white, gray, olive. My hobby yields more than my trophies; the frequent bending can result in a lame back.

I gaze across the great expanse of water, and I contemplate its magnitude. I think about the land on the other side, seemingly half a world away. I think of my ancestors, who ventured to cross the unknown ocean at a time when the journey was vastly more formidable.

I notice a ship nearly against the horizon and, as at other times in the past, I think I can see the curvature of the earth at such a distance. I marvel at the magnitude of the scene before me. The power and strength, constancy and fidelity, beauty and timelessness of the ocean bring to mind a picture on the wall of my home while I was growing up. It was a picture of the sea, of water only, and at the bottom of the picture was the caption, "Roll on in silent majesty." Amen to that!

Call of the Wild

"My heart knows what the wild goose knows, and I must go where the wild goose goes…" There is something about wild geese flying that calls us seductively. Our senses on this February day are filled, and the old song repeats in my head as we stand filled with wonder at the scene before us.

The word *cacophony* springs to mind. Many species of migratory birds are chattering together—honking, quacking, trilling, rumbling, bugling, trumpeting, prating, cackling—the sound is overwhelming.

All our care is pushed aside, replaced for this hour before sunset with a quiet sense of joy that we are privileged to witness this show by Mother Nature.

We are at the Bosque del Apache in New Mexico, where these birds spend the winter. The preserve is large. We watched the sandhill cranes at their cornfield feeding grounds, and now they are flying into the wetlands and lake, where they will be safer during the night. We wait, almost with disbelief, as group after group, couple after couple, family after family appear in the sky and approach the wetlands. The air is full. They look like cobwebs on the horizon, then take form as they get nearer. Their necks are outstretched, their long legs are extended behind, and their powerful wings beat slowly. They come in for a landing and seem to step down gracefully as they come to a stop. Here and there in the crowd, two of them will face each other, chest to chest, and rise off the ground in the dance for which they are known.

Back at the cornfield, we saw three of the endangered whooping cranes feeding with the sandhills, their brilliant white standing out through the binoculars. We keep watching to see if they fly in here, but they don't appear. They could be way over on the other side.

Two or three large areas of the lake are white with hundreds of snow geese. As the cranes come in, these snow geese are leaving for the same cornfields where the cranes have been feeding. One flock after another takes off, rising with a clamor and maneuvering to form their V shapes in flight. They honk their way overhead, to feed for an hour or two before dark. As we watch, all but fourteen leave. We learn from the ranger that the geese are agitated now, due to the need to begin their flight north. Some have left already. They may have altered schedules for eating and resting. The cranes will be leaving soon, too.

Like you, beautiful birds, we too are travelers. We humans say to one another, after a chance meeting along the way, "Goodbye, and have a safe trip." Magnificent wild things, thank you for letting us stand among you for a brief hour, feeling your call to know what you know, and to go where you go.

"Goodbye, and have a safe journey!"

Better Than Opals and Pearls

It happened one summer night some years ago. After work, my husband and I hastily got ready to attend a recital in the early evening. We left the house in a hurry, not wanting to be late.

It was still early, just getting dark, when we returned home. The house smelled warmly of the pie I had made earlier in the day. We didn't notice anything unusual until I went upstairs to get ready for bed. I noted that our bedroom door was open, but I was sure we had left it closed. Next I noticed my top bureau drawer was pulled out! Some clothes had obviously been handled and thrown back in a heap. I saw that my jewelry box and a music box were missing, and the top of the bureau was swept clean of other such treasures. The bed was turned down roughly, and my pillowcase was missing.

It became obvious to me that a thief had been in our house and had used the pillowcase, right off the bed where we slept, to carry the bounty he was stealing.

We went into other rooms and found a broken upstairs window. A piece of brick lay on the floor among the glass shards. Downstairs, two closets had been ransacked. With dread, I looked at the so-called safe, a small insulated box, where I kept my two most precious pieces of jewelry. Sure enough, the hinge on the box was broken, papers were strewn around, and the jewelry was gone.

We called the police and waited for a while, still finding out that more items were missing. We wondered if the perpetrator was still somewhere in our home and wished we could put this behind us and get some sleep. It had been a long enough day without this disturbing climax!

Finally the sheriff came. He noticed the aroma of the pie, and seeing it, he commented, "The thief wasn't a teenager or young guy, because he would not have passed up that pie!"

He took down our story and looked for fingerprints, but found no good ones. He said when a burglar intends to break into a house, it is not an uncommon practice to break a window to see if there is any response—human or dog. Hearing none in this case, so assuming correctly that no one was at home, the thief quickly found that in our haste we had neglected to lock the back door. To use a pillowcase is fairly common. He went to closets and opened bureau drawers. The sheriff said top bureau drawers are where people often keep valuables. It might be wise to change that habit.

Folks feel extremely violated when a thief enters their home. Home is our trusted place of peace and safety, and our haven for privacy. If he paws through our clothes and handles the pillow on which we rest our heads, his hands have defiled our most personal belongings, and he has taken precious items.

Our monetary losses were not great, and we did have insurance. But the emotional or sentimental toll was huge. One piece of jewelry was a string of real pearls that my brother had brought back from Japan, where he had been stationed in the late 1940s. It had been a beautiful gift for me, and I loved it. Each of my three daughters had worn the pearls at their weddings.

The other piece seemed irreplaceable. My mother's engagement ring was an opal, with a small pearl on either side of the unique stone. Opal varies a lot in color. This one had a beautiful blue side. On her deathbed she had given me the ring—one of her most precious possessions—and now I had lost it!

Several weeks later, I received a phone call from someone in the court system saying they had caught the thief, who had admitted our house was one of those he burgled. I asked if anything of mine had been found. The answer was no, as expected.

I love happy endings! While nothing can truly compensate for a sentimental loss such as mine, my six children put their heads together, and their money, and figured out a way to make it up to me. My daughters had worn not only the pearls, but also the ring at their weddings. One of the wedding photos showed the ring very clearly. They took the photo to a jeweler and had a ring almost identical created for me! They gave it to me for Christmas. That may have been the first time my children saw me cry!

Fast-forward now to my 80th birthday. They joked that I'd need a box of tissues handy when I opened my present from them. You guessed it—it was a beautiful pearl necklace! (No tissues needed this time!)

This experience had a devastating down side, and brought sadness, but there was definitely a happy side, too. I learned a lesson about top bureau drawers, and also closet "safes"! (Take a short hike to your friendly neighborhood bank and rent a really safe box!) More importantly, I realized that thoughtful and loving people are more valuable than any jewels, and the love of my children is more precious than opals or pearls!

To a Wonderful Daughter

One day in 1952, a little girl was born.
She brought her parents pride and joy! She came home in a storm.

Our first night home, at two a.m., proud Daddy braved the snow,
Crossed the road to his parents' house, and rapped on their window.

He was young, excited, and proud as well, in spite of the snowy clime,
And as a joke called out to them, "It's two a.m. feeding time!"

The roads were closed, the wind blew wild, but Grampa made it down
To help, and keep his family safe, but found us safe and sound.

Grammie was there to help us, too, to cook and clean with smiles.
We all smiled at that cute little girl, with all her baby wiles!

At two she started drawing, and soon showed talent great!
(Just one of many talents that soon showed up on her plate.)

She was a little "princess," and she was loved by all.
As oldest girl she helped me much—my "right arm" by my call.

With her good mate she had two babes, faced trials, joy, and such
With strength and love; and now the grands, also loved so much.

Now she goes to work each day, doing her life's plan—
Helping others find their way, or to the greenhouse when she can.

Happy birthday, Anna dear, our exceptional, wonderful daughter.
You've made our world a better place, as a strong and capable anchor.

To Scott, My Son, on His Birthday

A wonderful man is my eldest son, Scott. He's truly my
    pride and joy!
His father and I enjoyed him so much as a baby and growing boy.
He loved to be out with his Dad on the farm, and, yes, in a
    greenhouse, too.
In Nature and soil he formed character strong, and got training in
    what to do.

He planted snapdragons (he much preferred red) and cabbages
    down in the field.
He helped plant the glad bulbs, and dug them come Fall,
    and helped all the crops with their yield.
He helped nail up boxes for seedlings each year, dug pansies
    he planted in advance,
He watered and weeded, de-budded and spaced, found room
    for when Norman brought plants.

Now skip to the present, fifty years—even more—to see why I'm
    proud of him now.
Good husband, great father, hikes, skis—he excels! Woodworking?
    He loves it, and how!
He and Sandy are owners of the biggest (and best) of
    greenhouses found in Maine!
Well-known 'cross the country, frequent speaker and host, he
    works where pleasure is gain.

Growing up he had learned from his elders the truth: he should
   treat people right (Golden Rule).
His business has prospered because of his way; good treatment has
   been a cool tool.
"The customer's right, make her happy somehow" goes for customers,
   also some other!
The mark of a good man forever has been, "He always was
   good to his mother!"

Happy birthday Scott! With love, from your mother

My Son, Dan

My son is strength, when I'm in need,
A help to me in word and deed.
My son knows how a hand to lend;
I count on him to fix and mend.

My son brings joy when I have none.
My son brings courage when mine's gone.
My son brings love and honor too;
I love to hear his "I love you!"

So, Son, this birthday should be great,
For you deserve joy on this date!
Be happy then in all you do;
And please know this: I love you, too!

Happy birthday, Dan

To Evan

He likes to cut wood;
He likes to plant seeds;
He likes to run races;
Has few money needs.

He helps out Maine farmers
Where trouble may be,
He's in Agriculture,
The Department, you see.

He grows a mean garden,
Spends hours on end,
Growing veggies for dinner.
Ticks and "skeeters" he'll fend.

So Evan, my grandson,
What fun to employ?
Spend the day in your garden—
That's what you'll enjoy!

You're a wonderful grandson,
You're great every way!
My love and best wishes
For a HAPPY BIRTHDAY!

Happy Birthday, Ellie

Oh, happy day! Its Ellie's birthday!
She shines in the latest style!
From the bun in her hair to her twinkling toes,
A source of pride all the while.
    Don't settle for less, don't do half the job,
    Keep trying until you succeed.
    "If things are worth doing, they're worth doing well,"
    Is a saying that she seems to heed.
She's getting her master's, a degree super high,
Soaking up all the prep that she can,
Since life, for adults, calls for effort and strength,
You will see she prepared, then began!
    At such a young age, prepared so well,
    She's got the world on a string!
    She's very well set to begin the next stage,
    With the happiness it can bring.
And so, Ellie dear, have a splendid birthday!
You're at a wonderful age.
In the book of life (as a metaphor)
You're ready to turn the page!

Looking Back from Age 90

My brother has known me longer than anyone else on earth.
He probably knows me better, then, whatever that is worth.

I also know him pretty well. From childhood through our teens
We shared the same Depression life, and Grammie's pork and beans.

No plumbing, no power, an unfinished house; with wood, Dad kept
    us warm.
They kept us fed, clothed, loved; Mom's prayers kept us from harm.

We had our chores, like haying, and bringing in firewood.
Guy dug a trench, and cared for cows, helped garden for our food.

I ironed clothes, washed dishes, cleaned, rode rack and rake—so hot!
I learned to sew, and cook, wash clothes, and also emptied pots!

Then "life" rolled in; we went our two ways—Korea, and family.
He spent life pointing out the road to Heaven, verily.

I tried my best to do likewise, tried "preaching" by example,
I sang in choir, taught Sunday school; six kids an ample sample!

We lived our lives for our families, no stone was left unturned.
Though many things got in the way, our kids have love and concern.

So, Guy, take pride on this birthday, at 90 years and counting.
Yes, you deserve to celebrate, and there should be no doubting!

Happy Birthday!! Written for you for your 90th birthday, by your sister

Aging in Place—and Not Too Gracefully!

"And what is so fair as a day in June? Then, if ever, come perfect days..." James Russell Lowell had it right! Every year I think of this quotation on such perfect days. Those are the days when I enjoy life the most, and hate to think about being old.

Why do you suppose time flies faster the older one gets? It has something to do with the amount of accumulated experience, knowledge, and memories in the brain, so I hear. Being at that advanced age, I find it scary that time goes by so fast. I cannot pretend that I look at things quite as I did throughout my more carefree younger years, when it seemed as if time was unlimited. Anyone who is elderly has to know that life cannot go on indefinitely. Things are certainly going to change. That knowledge looms ever present, and is in turn frightening, depressing, and pertinent to our lives. I try not to think about death very much, but an old person really has to.

When I was in the sixth grade in South Portland, Miss Crandall, the teacher, made a statement that I took to heart and remembered all these years. She said that by the time old people die they don't mind dying, as younger people would. Thinking that to be a true fact has been comforting to me ever since. Now that I have lived about ten years longer than I ever expected to, I see better what her meaning was.

No such feelings of welcoming death have overtaken me yet! I have, however, been forced to acknowledge that aging is a process of loss of one pleasure, sense, health condition, or ability after another. It is quite possible that a person eventually reaches the place where death is preferable to what his life has become. That wasn't quite what I thought Miss Crandall meant!

My mother used to sit at her beloved piano and play and sing, "Will there be any stars, any stars in my crown?" and other hymns like

"When the Roll Is Called Up Yonder I'll Be There," and "I look away across the sea, where mansions are prepared for me; I view the shining glory shore, my Heaven, my home forever more!" To most people, death is the great unknown, and always will be, except to people of faith. People have always clung fervently to their faith when facing death. Often it serves them well.

I have been fortunate to have had a good life, and a long one. I have tried to be a good person, and to make the world a better place. Times that I have fallen short, I have suffered for it. I have a very well-developed conscience! I have tried to help others, especially my loved ones. I have even tried to save them some problems and keep them from making certain mistakes with some tactful advice, imparting knowledge that I have gained over my many years. I really don't want my life to end, but that's the way it works. I have had my turn. The world will go on. My family will miss me, but the sun will still rise and set, new babies will be born and grow up. It will be their turn; I had mine. I have not been shortchanged. I only hope that I will find the courage to face whatever comes my way. When you are young, you think you've got forever; but you turn around a few times and you find you are old.

Maybe you will pick up this book, my gesture toward immortality (along with the quilts I made) and realize how much I have put into the writing of it. It has been a valuable project for me, and my hope is that it will be a positive addition to the lives of others, even though on a small scale.

I try not to spend much time thinking negative thoughts. Instead, I try to remember when I get up in the morning, "This is the day that the Lord hath made! Let us rejoice and be glad in it!" (from the Bible). I say to myself, or I assume, that I will have this day to do my usual things, and to add to those I have already lived. I think and plan my twenty-four hours ahead and take pleasure from that process. Most days are good days. "One day at a time" is easier said than done, though.

On the positive side of old age and my present situation, there are many good and happy factors, and I need to dwell on those! I can sleep as late or get up as early in the morning as I want. I can stay up at night when I want to watch some television show or work on my writing or sewing. I can take naps, and I do so daily. Seniors get discounts. People hold the door for you and ask if you need help if you carry a cane, walk bent over, and are obviously old (although I hate that I look as if I need help!). Modern medicines have probably been keeping me alive now for some time, longer than I would have lived without them. Keeping house isn't a fraction of the job it was when the family was growing up, because some chores have become too difficult, or have shrunk in importance—or both. Forget about planning meals; it usually requires only opening the fridge and picking out a few items. I have a handicapped parking card which gives me the right to arrive close to my destination. My small pensions come in regularly in the same amount every month, regardless of any recession, and I don't have to go to work to make that happen. (Some people would not find that to be enough, but I am frugal, and I don't require a lot of "things.") I can take care of myself, and see and hear (though not as well as in my youth). I keep track of what is happening in the world and do not have dementia—yet. I have a family that cares, and on whom I can count.

In these, my elderly years, I am blessed not only with a close family, but also with a best friend, Eva Smith. We are about the same age. She is Sandy's mother, so we share those three grandchildren, Scott and Sandy's children, Will, Evan, and Ellie. Eva and I have a great deal in common from our early days on, and we enjoy reminiscing. She is a most thoughtful and generous person.

In spite of old age necessitating a dent in our activities, we did quite well making the best of things.

My brother, Guy, has kept in touch pretty well over the last few years. When we were traveling, we usually stopped to visit him in Massachusetts on our way home. He drives up here three or four times a year. Usually his visits are about three days long. When he comes he likes to have lobster. A few times we bought the lobster on the wharf and had our picnic at Muscongus Bay, right on the ocean. Other times we had it here at our house. Our cousin, Arlene, was an especially good cook and brought lots of food. We always had a ton of goodies to eat!

I am so glad Lawrence and I learned to use the computer. We each took a class. Mine was when I was working at the greenhouse. Whit Hodgkins got Lawrence to go with him to an adult ed class. I write letters, poems, my book, etc., in Word, and use the e-mail a lot daily. I search for information often.

Our house on the Litchfield Road had stayed empty for quite a while after we moved. Walter, Alden's son, and his wife, Pam, asked to rent our house. Later they asked to buy it. We agreed, and the deal was on.

In the year 2000 we all went to Missouri for our summer re-union. Alice had made arrangements for us to stay at memorable plac-es. After a couple of days in Jefferson City, we moved on to Branson. We two were already acquainted with Branson and its shows, and it was great having everyone gathered there.

It must have been on this trip to Missouri that we had the de-lightful float trip on the Buffalo River. It was truly lovely—the scen-ery, the day, the company—except for one little thing. Lawrence and I tipped our canoe over and we got dumped into the river! I take a lot—but not all—of the blame. I am really not an accomplished ca-noe paddler! However, what happened was that the side of the ca-noe came up against a submerged tree limb and tipped sharply to one side, catching us off balance. We couldn't counterbalance quick-ly enough, and over we went! The water was shallow, but surprisingly swift. Seeing that we were okay, everyone laughed as our plastic bags of lunch leftovers and such floated off downstream. They all piled out and retrieved our stuff and we never heard the last of it! Alice even gave me a pin for Christmas for my blouse or dress—a pewter mod-el of a canoe!

In 2001 Dee made the arrangements, and we stayed at the Residence Inn in Washington, DC, and toured the capitol. This was just before the terrorism of 9/11/01. It was much easier then to cir-culate freely there; after that date security tightened a lot. Dee pro-cured matching T-shirts for everyone in the family, printed appropri-ately. We also spent a few days at Gettysburg. There is so much to see and learn there! It is a favorite family destination.

The next year it was our turn to choose. They came to Maine, and we were happy. They got cabins at Echo Lake in Fayette. We stayed at our house and visited days. I worked at least part of the time.

In 2003 we went to Grand Lake Stream in Downeast Maine. We all got places to stay there, mostly cabins on the lake. It is such a beautiful area! Of course, there were no cities nearby, or amusement parks, but everyone enjoyed that vacation. Just being together, on the lake, was enough.

That same year, some of them hiked on the Appalachian Trail in New Hampshire and stayed at Zealand Hut. There is a series of "huts" in New Hampshire along the Trail, about a day's hike apart. Hikers, having made their reservation and paid ahead, can bunk (co-ed) and have a hot supper and breakfast. Lawrence went many times over the years and got to visit most all of the huts. He loved it! I went about three times, and found that amount of hiking to be too much. I also didn't like the sleeping arrangements, and I was cold and wet even on a day in June. There was snow and hoarfrost on Mt. Washington that day! I was wet because my water bottle had leaked down my leg! I needed a warm fire, dry blankets, and a hot shower and comfortable bathroom! I'm no city slicker, and I did enjoy the beautiful scenery and being close to nature, but this was not my cup of tea!

In 2005 it was Dan's turn to choose, and we met at Bar Harbor again. That is another family favorite, with so much to do. Dan and Tammy visit Bar Harbor and Acadia National Park on weekends when they can, just because they love the area. So do Scott and Sandy and their family. They take their bikes and ride on the carriage trails in adjacent Acadia National Park.

I don't know how many winter trips we made to the Southwest, or just which year was our last. We had difficult trips the last two or three times we went, with illness mostly (which is not fun when you are away from home). Also we found the hassle of travel tiring—living out of suitcases, hauling luggage in and out of motels, etc. Our diets had become restricted, so the enjoyment of eating out was greatly limited. Most of our favorite places in that part of the country are at rather high elevations—over 5000 feet. It bothered me a lot, and finally did Lawrence, also. It is hard to enjoy travel under such circumstances.

In 2006 we stayed at home all winter, but in April we drove part of the Skyline Drive and the Blue Ridge Parkway in the Shenandoah Valley. That year we began the Drive at Asheville and drove north. We toured the Biltmore Estate in Ashville while there. We had visited Dee and family on the way down (at which time I gave Dee her quilt) and Longwood Gardens, where Alice had worked one summer while in college. The Shady Maple restaurant in the Amish area of Pennsylvania was always a favorite. On the way home, we visited Wayne's family in New Jersey.

Many of the southern states in the East have resorts at some of their state parks. They are great, and off-season rates are not bad. Our intent was to visit as many of those as we could. We stayed at eight or nine of them in West Virginia, Kentucky, Tennessee, Alabama, and North Carolina!

The first such resort that we ever stayed in was at Gulf Shores, Alabama. It had been a favorite for many years. A hurricane destroyed that several years ago, and it was never rebuilt. They do have cabins in the woods still, but our resort had been right on the beach.

Along the Drive are several of those National Park resorts. We stayed at three that year. We also found cabins at Roan Mountain State Park in Tennessee, near the North Carolina border. We fell in love with ours, and were fortunate to stay there twice the next year. The scenery that year was beautiful. The Blue Ridge Mountains were accented by the white blossoming dogwoods as we gazed out across every valley.

We went to the Shenandoah Valley again the next spring also, in 2007. The dogwoods were not as noticeable as they had been the previous spring. We were traveling two weeks later than in the year before, but also there had been a freeze earlier that spring, which may have killed the buds. It was still a scenic trip. This time we drove the Drive and the Parkway from north to south.

The third trip to the Shenandoah Valley was that fall. Lawrence had planned the trip for a long time, wanting to take Anna and Jeff with us, to share our enjoyment of the area. We left home October 2nd and picked them up at the Asheville airport a couple of days later. We reserved two of those much-loved cottages at Roan Mountain and stayed two nights. We hiked through the extensive rhododendrons; that area is the rhodie capital of the world. We didn't see them in bloom, unfortunately, but it still was an impressive sight. I believe their festival (when they are blooming) is in June.

We stopped to let Anna and Jeff hike in a few places. We took the Biltmore Estates tour, which they found interesting. We drove a section of the Skyline Drive and stayed at one of the resorts, at Pisgah Mountain Inn. We walked the high swinging bridge at Grandfather's Mountain. Being able to do that made me feel proud to be one of the brave!

Sunday afternoon we stopped at Alta at an apple orchard with a good-sized store where there was a concert going on, and a country dance. We stayed to watch couples dancing on a dance floor right in a corner of the store, and people clog dancing. It was really fun. It gave us a real taste of Appalachia!

That was rather a short trip, with no stops in Virginia to see Dee and family, or in New Jersey to see Wayne, Carol, and the youngsters. Anna and Jeff only had the long weekend with us, Friday to Tuesday.

There is an unhappy event that occurred but shouldn't have. We were at home in the late afternoon, and Gary Olsen, who has worked at the greenhouse for many years, was here visiting, as he occasionally does. There was some tool or item that he had been looking for at the greenhouse, without finding it, so I called Scott's cell phone to see if he could help. After a few rings Sandy answered. I asked her the question, and she answered that she didn't know, that they were at the hospital, and that Scott was having a heart attack! Their son, Will, took the phone to give me some more details.

It seems Scott and Sandy were out riding their bicycles, which they often do. They travel long distances and had done so that day. They were headed home, and Scott didn't feel well. He thought probably he was coming down with something. They rested at the Winthrop beach for a while, and Scott called Will at home to bring the van and come to get them and their bikes. Will wasn't sure where the beach was, so Scott said they would ride up to the top of the hill, next to Route 202, to the store parking lot, and meet him there.

Going up the hill, he had to stop, and he passed out on some-one's lawn. They got the ambulance in short order and were at the hospital when I called. The staff there was having trouble stabiliz-ing him, so they sent him to Portland, again by ambulance. The sur-geon there wanted to wait until morning to do the angioplasty, with a stent, which was needed. I guess it was the nurse in charge who told the doctor to come in right then and not wait until morning! He agreed, the procedure was done, and Scott was on the mend.

He was not really a typical candidate for a heart attack. His cholesterol was only slightly high, and his other numbers were not cause for much concern, either. He leads an active life, has nev-er smoked, and has never been overweight. It should not have hap-pened, but it did; and he has been diligent about diet, exercise, and taking his medicine ever since. He has been able to live a normal life.

Trouble seems determined to attack in bunches sometimes. Poor Kristin, Anna and Jeff's daughter, was suffering from appendi-citis that very same night and was at the hospital having an appen-dectomy while Scott was having his heart attended to! She came through it nicely, and so did he! It sure shatters a mother to have to recognize the uncertainty of this life, when it comes to one of her children—and a grandchild, too!

The next year was Anna and Jeff's turn to host the reunion, and we went to North Conway, New Hampshire. That was great. Some of us stayed at the Eastern Slopes Inn, and the rest were all in a big house with many rooms, some distance away. They enjoyed being to-gether there, and it was a nice place for all of us to get together eve-nings. There is a lot to do in a place like North Conway.

In 2012 it was Dan and Tammy's turn to choose the location and make the arrangements. They chose Bar Harbor again, a favor-ite for so many of us. They found us a place to stay that was fairly reasonable in price, which is hard to do in a place like Bar Harbor in the summertime. It was the Cromwell House. Lawrence and I didn't venture far from our room except to drive the Loop Road around Acadia National Park. Our room was the only one with kitchen facilities, and that brought us lots of company as family members dropped in to use our stove.

I always breathe a sigh of relief when everyone has reached home safely again. I truly feel thankful.

Another happy time: Everyone was home for our annual Christmas celebration for 2009. Before heading home, they gave me a party for my 2010 birthday—my 80th! It was just a couple of weeks early. You will remember that I told you about the burglar who stole my opal and pearl ring that had been my mother's engagement ring, and also my pearls that Guy had given to me when he came home from the service, and how badly I felt about losing them. My children had presented me with another opal and pearl ring, related earlier. For my 80th birthday, they gave me a string of real pearls, to replace those I'd lost. They gave me another gift also, which means a tremendous amount to me: They all went up to the greenhouse and took pictures of my six children together, framed one, and hung it on the wall where I enjoy it every day. It means so much to me! I have asked for another one, of the spouses as well as my children. I love them all. The grandchildren gave me a lovely amethyst brooch—so pretty!

Plans were laid for having the larger all-inclusive Longfellow family reunion every year, and Alden is setting the date this year (as I write this) for the Saturday we leave our rented cottages, August 3rd. Alice and family are planning to stay a few more days anyway, and Dee says she will stay, too. I expect both of them and their families will be at that Longfellow get-together. Wayne will have to head straight home from the Lakes, as they have a seven-hour trip, and reasons that they have to be home that night.

Lawrence's heart problem had become serious; it is not easy to write about. When a person reaches his nineties, it comes as no surprise that the body begins to break down. Lawrence had always been very healthy, very strong. When we went to the Weathervane restaurant to celebrate his 90th birthday, we knew he hadn't been as well for several months, but hoped it was just a natural slowing down. He was quite short of breath, but he thought the stent he had had in his heart for nine years was probably in need of adjustment. In short order, the diagnosis was decided to be heart failure.

Lawrence made his choice to go on as long as he could without a dangerous operation, and not take that chance. The doctor said that was what he would advise for his own father. He told him at every visit that if he began feeling that his quality of life had become so poor that he didn't want to go on that way—that he would rather die—he could choose to have the operation then, and take a chance on pulling through.

Occasionally Alden and Esther dropped in for a visit. There was always family news to share, old memories to review, and people from the past to refer to. The men tried to remember the family connections of people—who someone's mother and father were, or sister or brother, where they lived, who they married, what class in high school they were in, etc. They kept up to date on present-day news also.

Yes, we were aging, and were not too happy about it. We still enjoyed life, especially family, and did pretty well at taking one day at a time.

One Day at a Time

It's the fall of the year and the autumn of life;
The apples hang red on the bough.
Don't forget we had summer and springtime so nice;
Though winter is on the way now.

One day at a time in the fall of the year;
Today is a blessing indeed!
Soon "Old Man Winter" will be drawing near;
One day at a time fills the need!

Ev'ry step slow and weary, the back stiff and lame—
We recall the past youthful day.
But remember we had it, and won at life's game;
That never is taken away.

So enjoy each day's pleasure, each blessing, though small.
Be thankful for family and friend.
Crisp days can be lovely in colors of fall,
And love is what counts 'til the end!

Could This Be Me?

The end of the trail is in sight now; the race has been lost or won.
Goodbye to life's pain and sorrows, farewell to life's joy and fun.

Never to learn a new language? Never gain fortune or fame?
Never to write that novel, or mark history with my name?

Too late to make quilts or paint pictures. Too late to meet and
make friends.
Too late to correct my errors; too late to make amends.

So anchor the well-worn needle, dry the brushes and lay down
the pen.
Work's finished, so fasten the thread now, and close the door to
the den.

Someone else will sew with the needle, paint the pictures, watch TV
at night;
Someone else will write at the desk now, use computer, keep things
going right.

We've heard of the Straight and Narrow and how hard it is not
to stray.
Part of problem or part of solution—part of which have I been,
would you say?

When I look in the mirror I wonder—do others see whom I see?
This journey was so brief and rapid; I'm less than I hoped to be.

Lord knows I have aimed for perfection, and tried to be faithful
and true.
Lord knows how far from my vision I've fallen, as all humans do.

What makes us do things we know better? And hurt those we
truly love?
And say hurtful things or cause trouble? Sink below what we should
rise above?

Why didn't I tell them "I love you?" Give more of self once in a while?
Give praise, give of time, give of treasure; think of others and give
them a smile?

Is it me, in this picture, who lies there, my loved ones gathered
'round, in tears;
The ones whom I loved, who loved me, looking back through all
the years?

I'm thankful it's not come to pass yet, there's time yet for you and
for me
Before we cross that wide river, to whatever is going to be.

In the wilderness we're still wand'ring, in life with its struggles
and strife.
So begin anew on this day, the first day of the rest of your life.

Advice I would leave at my passing is not to have money, or fun;
But to have few regrets at the finish, and have hope that you'll hear
"Well done!"

The End of an Era

It was February 5, 2015. Lawrence had been in the hospital, yet again, for a couple of days. I was so exhausted from my duties as his caregiver that I had been resting, and had not visited him. Anna and Scott took turns staying with him around the clock.

I was going to leave in a few minutes to make an evening visit. Dan was already on his way down to Augusta from the Bangor area, to stay with his father on the night shift, and give Anna and Scott a break.

It was too late. Scott called me to say that Dad's struggle was over; he had died a few minutes before. The man to whom I was married for 65 years, and whom I loved, was dead. He would have been 93 years old in a few weeks.

The hospital policy allowed us all to gather in his room while his body was still there. I was like a zombie, knowing the facts but not yet comprehending them. Seeing his body was like seeing his coat, or something familiar that he had been using; but he, the person, was gone. I was able to function, but without much strong emotion. That would come later.

After the rest of the family arrived a few days later, we had a gathering at the greenhouse. Lawrence had specified that he didn't want a funeral, or any "fuss" made. That evening's gathering was in lieu of a funeral. Typically, he had earlier made the comment that we could put on a dinner if we wanted.

So that evening we did provide a meal right there, at the greenhouse. Alden's family provided a lot of the food. Quite a few people came, but many more would have if the weather hadn't been so fierce. We had a big snowstorm.

Burial was not until the week in July that the family always gets together. We didn't have a formal service, but we did have my eulogy read, and a few poems. We kept it private for family, including some of Alden's family.

Guy came from Massachusetts. I asked him to read my eulogy for me. I am including it here, so you can get to know what a special person my husband was. Keep in mind that I wrote it to include things about him that his grandchildren ought to know, as well as to emphasize the successes of his life, for all of us.

I miss him, a lot, but perhaps widowhood as a way of life has not been as hard for me as it is for some women, in spite of that. For one thing, we have a wonderful and close big family. Also, we introverts enjoy having time alone. I enjoy having things as I want them; I make all the decisions. I keep reminding myself of these positives. In an effort to preserve his memory, I fixed up a portion of a wall with his flag, and pictures from the main elements in his life—his military service, the greenhouse, our children, our wedding, and other memorable times. It helps me to feel closer to him.

The world is poorer because of the loss of a good man.

Eulogy

Lawrence Longfellow was my husband for more than 65 years. He was a good person, and was widely loved. We struggled to find the right phrases to have engraved on the marker for his grave, to capture the essence of the man we loved and lost, whose memory would be recorded in those few words. We could only touch on his interests and the qualities of character by which he lived. The phrases we chose were: "family man, life enthusiast, student of nature, man of vision."

His military gravestone shows that he was a soldier, an important part of his life. He was on front-line duty in Germany in WWII, then in the Reserves, for a total of twenty years. He retired with the rank of captain. The horrors of war that he experienced affected his character and outlook all of his long life. In later years, as you well know, he often shared his war stories. He had a lasting need to talk about it.

That he was a family man was very evident. That extended beyond our family to in-laws, grandchildren, his brother and sisters and their families, and to his parents. When caring for Sal, his handicapped sister, he showed a kind, nurturing, gentle nature. He often advised you young people to think big, to do the unusual, to establish your own business. To borrow from the lyrics of two beautiful songs, I'd like to remind you of those times when he tried to inspire you, "When I am on your shoulder, you raise me up to more than I can be." Some of us remember occasions when we could have truthfully admitted "You are the wind beneath my wings."

"Life enthusiast" was a way of saying that he had many strong interests. To name just two, I chose travel, and the financial world. Before we were married, he told me that he might never make a lot of money, but he knew that we would travel. He was right. We took a garden center tour to Scandinavia. We went twice to the UK, including the islands and a side trip to the Netherlands. We made three trips to Alaska. We drove nine times to Florida, and several winters to the Southwest. We visited Canada's Atlantic Provinces two or three times, once including Newfoundland. We enjoyed the Blue Ridge Mountains. Our family often went camping and climbed mountains in Maine. New Hampshire was a favorite "getaway" destination for the two of us. He loved hiking in the White Mountains, where he stayed overnight in the Appalachian Trail huts. He went trekking in Nepal, near Mt. Everest, at age 66.

This man studied financial publications and the stock market's gymnastics with zeal. We had many books and magazines, a lot of which were finance oriented. He bought a computer, and took a course to learn to use it. He marveled at this new world that computers and their progeny have created.

He was a student of nature, and really enjoyed flowers, trees, birds, rocks (which he collected), and all the wonders of outer space. He loved collecting seeds and growing plants. He knew where the marsh marigolds grow. The white-throated sparrow's song and the loon's call were his music. The gain in scientific knowledge since use of the Hubble telescope was to him a cause to rejoice. He could tell you how many galaxies there are in one section of the sky. He had his own theory about the Big Bang.

We hope that saying "man of vision" is broad enough to include the fact that the greenhouse range we built was the result of his vision. He chose the location, drew the plans, envisioned the market, and was successful in his endeavors, with our help. He thought big. He showed good vision also in other facets of our lives, such as buying both of our homes—the schoolhouse to make over into our first home, and then our second house near the new greenhouses. He enjoyed planning our trips. We were blessed with many years together after retirement in 1987. With the help of his vision and keen interests, we made good use of those years. He often had that ability to look ahead and make the right call.

I remember his mother saying to him many times, "Do your own thinking, Brother." He had no trouble following her advice. He was a true "rugged individualist" and he often seemed to "march to the beat of a different drummer." He was one who could triumphantly say, "I did it my way."

A big omission on his marker is that he was interested in people and treated them well. He followed the Golden Rule without even trying, although he wouldn't call it that. He rejoiced at the accomplishments of others, and he grieved their failures and mistakes. He wanted to know all about people—who their parents were, their siblings, and what they did. When you see a doctor you talk about your health. When he went to the doctor, he learned about the doctor's life, where he was from, if he had children, or if his father was in WWII. People loved him for remembering those details. He had a memory like that of no other person I ever met, another quality we did not include on his marker.

An example of his generosity: When Lawrence returned from the war, he was ready to settle down. After we had dated for quite a while, we both knew that we probably had found the person we wanted to marry. However, he had not yet met my brother, who had been overseas in the service. Family background was very important to him, and he wasn't going to propose until he was sure that this member of my family also passed the test. When Uncle Guy came home on leave, he had people to see and places to go, but he had no car. Lawrence gave him full use of his recently purchased car (his first ever) for the entire time Guy was home! An unusual generosity, his act was a perfect application of the Golden Rule—"Do unto others…"

For many years, he worked an exhausting schedule in order to better support our family. He left the house at three a.m. to deliver bundles of newspapers to stores that would sell them and paperboys who would deliver them. That route ended each day in time for him to drive a morning Star Route from Hallowell Post Office to Litchfield, delivering in mailboxes along part of the way. That contract also called for two more trips between the post offices, at two p.m. and five p.m. There were a few years that he picked up another mail route, from Gardiner post office to Richmond. On top of all of that, he was a substitute for Uncle Alden's mail route for a while, which thankfully didn't call him out very often. This was in addition to the greenhouse and farm work. Such a schedule impacted his life, and also his family's lives, because he had to go to bed early in the evening. That precluded evening activities of any social or professional nature, and required a quiet house, which was not always attainable with six children growing up.

As a businessman, Lawrence was always honorable and ethical. He was generous to a fault, if that is possible. He was always giving away, or giving extra, of his product. If a customer came in thinking he had a grievance, he walked away happy, and was astounded because Lawrence treated him so well. Lawrence never knowingly cheated anyone, and never was greedy or selfish in his dealings with others.

If he made a mistake, or if he upset someone, he always tried to make it right. An example: Once, when working with a group of men, he saw a scuffle break out. He physically restrained one angry man, roughing him up a bit. That man then became angry with him. The next day, L.B. sent the man flowers!

As a newly commissioned officer in Germany after the war ended, starting at the age of 23, he was in charge of three different prisoner of war camps. The prisoners could have been the same men who had been shooting at him earlier, yet he treated them well.

He told a humorous story from his youth, regarding one of the chores that a farm boy was often given—killing one of the hens or roosters for the family's dinner. He caught a hen, finally got it laid out on the chopping block, and raised the axe. The hen looked up at him with beady, helpless eyes, and that was the end of that attempt. He didn't have the heart to bring down the axe. Either someone else had to do it that day, or the family had just mashed potatoes and peas for dinner!

He was lucky and dodged a lot of bullets throughout his life, both literally and figuratively. In his last sickness, he did his best to help himself, and submitted to treatments and dreaded hospitalizations with emotional strength and acceptance of what he knew was coming. He was patient with the care I was able to give him at home, and Anna and/or Scott stayed by his side night and day in the hospital. Realizing that time was short, he wanted to get word out to everyone that he loved them.

We lost a good man, the patriarch of our family. His was a long, productive life, and the world was a better place because he lived. He lives on in our memories and in our everlasting love.

Without You

The wind still blows, the sun still shines. How can they, without you?
The world still turns, but since you left, how can it still be true?

Stiff upper lips, we carry on, repeating "Yes, we can."
Days all alike, nights lonely, long. "Keep busy" is the plan.

Why did you go? You had to go; you'd lived your life, and plus.
We miss you so! You had to go; accept your death we must.

"One day at a time" is easy to say, but not so easy to do.
If your light's gone out, you cannot see. One day is hard to
    get through.

As days go by we'll carry on, your memory always near.
We'll find our way; you guide us still. Our thoughts of you are dear.

You made a difference here on Earth. 'Twas a privilege to share
With you in your good-natured life, with mutual love and care.

You're still with us, we're still with you, in spirit anyway.
Your memory will be part of us until our dying day.

Some day if light shines bright again, to be happy again the goal,
With part of you still in our hearts, full circle, we'll be whole.

For all widows everywhere; especially for Esther:

Esther has been a singer. She is also the most dedicated Christian I have ever met. I have appealed to these important parts of her life and character, in writing this, to try to bring her hope, and perhaps help, during her time of deep grief. Although written for a widow, it would be equally valuable, hopefully, in other circumstances.

An old saying says that "God helps those who help themselves." I would change that to "who try *to help themselves."*

On Life and Death—Sing Me a Song

Oh, sing me a song of the meaning of life. Sing me a song about love.
Sing of your joy at the birth of each child. Sing of your gifts from above.

Cry for your loss and the end of a life; cry for the death of your mate.
Death yanks you around, and rips at your heart. It is cruel, and
    sneers with hate.

It pushes and pulls, and crushes your plans. His death nearly takes
    you, too.
You feel that half of you is gone, just ripped away from you.

But what will you sing, the meaning of life? About loves and
    blessings they give?
Is the purpose of life to glorify God, and enjoy life while we live?

There is much to enjoy about that gift—of life that is given to you.
To build your new life without your mate, think positive thoughts,
    ever new.

Be thankful for friends and family, do a good deed each day.
Your life must still count, and count it does, and you will be okay!

He'd be proud of the progress that you make, the example you try
   to set.
You soon will feel joy in the songs that you sing; your reward you
   will surely get.

Pitching for Posies—the Value of Flowers

For almost any circumstance in which we feel the need to express some emotion to another human being, flowers will say what we want to convey in a warm, sincere, and loving manner. If the message is one of congratulations for a birthday, anniversary, a new baby, marriage, promotion, graduation, etc., nothing says it better than flowers. A husband in the doghouse says "I'm sorry" with a lovely bouquet. A man gives his wife or girlfriend red roses to say "I love you." We bring them to a friend in the hospital to bring cheer, and to someone at home who is having a hard time. The message is "I care." The words are not even necessary; the flowers say it well.

Flowers will say for you what you wish to say; their message will be understood. There are other ways to help and to show support; perhaps your efforts shouldn't cease with a pretty bouquet. For many years now, the age-old custom of providing flowers at funerals has been largely replaced by charity donations. Of course, everyone should donate to charities if they can. I would hope that anyone who can afford it would do both—donate to a charity and send flowers. Both are going to help people.

The presence of tasteful floral arrangements at funerals is very valuable; flowers belong there. They are far warmer, more comforting, and vastly more personal than a belated acknowledgment of a gift to charity. Money spent for flowers to comfort the grieving is money well spent; it really helps.

Funeral flowers and wedding bouquets could do double duty, their value and beauty not wasted when the ceremony is over. They could be given to brighten a nursing home or church, taken to shut-ins, or taken home by family and friends. Maybe someday this idea will catch on and be more popular.

Wherever flowers are placed, they bring beauty and show caring, enriching our lives. Flowers speak a universal language.

This was written for Anna and Jeff on their 44th anniversary. The refer-
ence to their music is that they recorded a few songs, which were beautiful-
ly done. The last line here refers to one of their songs, "Turning Toward the
Morning," by Gordon Bok.

Happy Anniversary!

Two lives as one, through the good and the bad,
Two hearts full of love, and as Mother and Dad;
Two minds to build bridges when going gets rough;
Two wills to move mountains—wills need to be tough.

Four eyes to see beauty, and learn from good books;
Four legs to go hiking, to the gym, or new nooks;
Four arms for support—for more than you two;
The "Sandwich Generation" was named for you!

Twenty fingers for music—piano, guitar;
Two voices for singing—the sweetest by far!
Your day should be special, two hearts still warming,
Remember the world always turns toward the morning!

Grandma Muses—a Few Random Thoughts

We all need people. This is a cliché, but everyone needs companionship, needs to be liked and respected, needs to feel useful and valued, and needs to feel that others are interested in him or her. In the world's current agitation due to the worldwide pandemic, we are forced for the time being to give up most of our close contacts with other people. Some folks may have lasting ill effects from this deprivation. Let us hope that the upheaval in our lives will not last too long. Meanwhile, we can exchange letters and cards, enjoy e-mail and phone calls, and use the marvelous invention that allows us to see the person to whom we are talking on the phone. We can, and we should, make use of other social media to interact with other people.

Recently some of my loved ones have moved and are even farther away than before. Dee and Andy brought up their girls, Stephanie and Katie, in Virginia, in the Washington, D.C. suburbs. Stephanie was born in California, but Katie was born after they moved to Virginia. I spent time with them after both births. In California we had gone to stay with them at the end of our Alaska trip, and we experienced a pretty big earthquake while there. Lawrence and I were watching fireworks out their bedroom window at Fort MacArthur on July 4th, while Dee and Andy were having their own "fireworks" at the hospital—their first child's birth. After Katie was born, I again helped as much as I could. I was only three weeks recovered from surgery for a burst appendix. Katie was always a smart little tyke, earning "gifted and talented" treatment all the way through school. She now shares the family home in Virginia with her partner, Maurissa, since her folks have moved to England for a few years, for Andy's job. The pandemic has meant that Dee and Andy can't visit back in the U.S. as they had counted on doing. The daughters also are unable to travel to

England to visit their parents, depriving all of them of family support during difficult times.

Meanwhile, Wayne and Carol retired a couple of years ago, and moved from New Jersey to Missouri, where they live near Carol's twin sister, Cathy, and her husband, Dave Walter. Their son, Steve, is still in Pennsylvania for now, working for Brinks. Their daughter, Amy, works for a company in New York but during this pandemic has visited with her folks in Missouri and worked from "home" there. Seems like a lot of my family has moved to Missouri! Mitchell, Dan's and Tammy's son, has been working for his cousin Eric there for a couple of years. Beth moved to Missouri when her folks retired there. She is my other "horse-woman" granddaughter, owning horses and riding. (Rachel is the other one.) I sure wish I could see all of these grandchildren more often. I am proud of all of them, and keep up with any news through their parents. I talk regularly with Wayne and Carol, and with Dee and Andy, enjoying video chatting. Dan and Tammy, although living in Maine, have to settle for video visits mostly, too. The pandemic is taking its toll on all of us.

Clearly tied to the above: People have needs above and beyond the physical ones. Severe deprivation of physical needs has severe consequences, but so does failure of relationship needs. I would add to those the need for introspection, for quiet time, for inspirational nourishment, for personal improvement activities, for continued learning, for seeking satisfactions, for setting goals and working at reaching them, and for intellectual stimulation and growth.

Another random thought: There is nothing wrong with being different, being an individual. Most people seem to like to live in cities, close together. I like the country, and personal space and privacy. A person needs to be himself or herself. The less we jump aboard bandwagons that are not of our own choosing, the happier we can be. Contentment is the key to happiness; in fact, it is the same thing as happiness.

Also: Outcomes that bring the greatest reward and satisfaction usually have required the most work, effort, or time. We really do get out of something according to what we have put into it.

I found: Schedules and routine can be comforting. All people have to face difficult times. It may be grief, loss, extreme disappointment, or any bad news that has to be accepted and dealt with. Random activity can leave one feeling worse—at loose ends. Following a schedule, particularly a familiar one, can lead to a more orderly feeling, and a quicker acceptance or resolution of the problem. The routine feels like an old friend—something to hold onto, a constant amidst chaos.

Also true: Generalizing about things is usually not accurate, but especially so about people. I can tell when a generalization is not the truth by looking inside myself. If the assumption would not be true of me, it may well not be true of those people, either. I heard someone say that ministers are frauds. I know that is false, by looking at myself. If I were a minister or a priest, I would be completely sincere and honest. I'm sure most of them are, too. A few bad apples shouldn't spoil the whole barrel.

I tried to teach my children: We are what we eat/read/think. Feeding our minds is as important as feeding our bodies. Feeding the body a poor diet can result in poor health, obesity, even illness. Feeding the mind a poor diet affects mental health, character, and levels of what I call a successful life. People should practice controlling what they feed their minds, that is, what they read, watch, listen to, talk about, and think about. It can make a big difference in character and personality, and degree of happiness. (Yes, you can control your thoughts.)

Not easy: Children are like sponges, from birth on. Parents need to be very careful about what they say and do, knowing that their action is teaching their child. Books, movies, etc., reflect the current society to some extent, but they also have a strong effect and influence *on* society. Consider the change in morals and the perception of right and wrong over the past several years. If a child watches a lot of TV or movies, what he gleans as acceptable behavior may not be the same as what you want him to believe. What young children see and read should be guarded and guided by parents.

I always say: Once a mother, always a mother! As my children grew up and moved away, they continued to come to me for recipes, diagnoses, comfort, understanding, advice…and will do so as long as I live, I hope!

A difficult concept to understand: (Psychologists and other experts, with their knowledge of the "id" and the "ego," etc., probably have a name for this.) Inside each of us is our core being, the inner self, which cannot be touched by outside conditions or circumstances or hurts. Apparently perceived a little differently by different people, it is sometimes symbolized or aided by a more familiar, yet different, idea—going to our "happy place." It is the ability to say to oneself, "This does not change or affect the real me, the person that I truly am, my basic being, the person that only I know." We need to learn how to reach that inner "me," without going outside the bounds of reality, so we can use the method to provide strength and truth to ourselves, to keep from feeling destroyed. It must not prevent our advisable or necessary action; but it should be available to provide welcome and needed relief from the world's troubles and cares.

It had been more than four years since my husband's death. My grand-son was to be married in the fall, and I wanted to offer him and his bride our wedding rings, if they wanted them. They were proud to accept, and it made me very happy. I feel sure my husband would have approved.

Wedding Rings

Your rings are a symbol of your love and care,
      Two circles unbroken, a good matching pair.

A circle is endless, like infinity,
      It's whole and complete, for eternity.

These rings mean a promise, so binding and true:
      Commitment and loyalty, from both of you.

The gold stands for value, for purity—the best.
      Its strength will remind you, stand strong in each test.

Your rings, plain and simple, are basic for care,
      Like love, with care basic, they'll stand up to wear.

Sadly, life can be wearing, some things seem unfair.
      Your love is your strength—like your rings, will be there.

These rings have already stood strong tests of time,
      And served well two people, with lives long and fine.

For sixty-five years, through good times and bad,
      The rings were a symbol of the basis we had.

We always loved greatly our grandson so dear,
      And wanted the best for him throughout each year.

For you both, our dear grandson and the queen of your heart,
      These rings begin over and have a fresh start.

Their first life is finished, their next life is new,
      Symbolic, they start with the love of you two.

Their symbol of love now begins a new life,
      With marriage of you, Will, and Michelle, your dear wife.

With faith they'll live up to the love you profess,
      Your rings will remind you, your lives God will bless.

I have had two serious surgeries in the last couple of years, from which I re-covered with the help of my faith. I wasn't "hearing voices," but I did ex-perience what seemed like a silent message, which helped enormously, from October 10, 2018, date of the first surgery, to February 23, 2020, when I was home again after the second. It was a continuing work in progress during a painful and troublesome time.

"I Am with You"

"I will be with you!" Oh, precious promise!
"I will be true, through pain and fear."
Though silent the words, they were strong with comfort.
"I am with you." Oh, words most dear.

Through endless nights, You held my hand, Lord;
Through painful days, brought courage, too.
We won the prize; oh, blessed bonus
From your sweet words: "I will be with you."

And now again I need your comfort.
I need Your strength; I need Your hand.
Fear once again makes courage weaker.
Oh, be with me! "I understand."

"I am with you!" Oh, loving message!
"I promise you, I will be true."
Though silent the words, they bring me comfort.
"I will be with you; I am with you!"

SECTION 2

Letters

Over the years, for one reason or another, I have written a lot of letters, for a lot of different reasons. Sometimes people I know have faced occasions in their lives that caused me to respond. The stories that my letters uncover as you read them are usually evident. I will explain where needed. Wherever it is advisable, I use fictitious names in order to protect the privacy of the "innocent."

A Visitor

Hello Family,

We had a visitor last evening, for two or three hours. I was in the "den" watching TV, with the door closed. Grampa was sitting on the sofa in the living room. He came in to announce to me that a chipmunk had been running around the living room, seemingly without fear! You know how fast they scamper. The little guy went into the hall, maybe up the stairs, but was soon back. He came over toward the sofa and sized up his safety situation. He climbed right up beside Grampa and explained his predicament to deaf ears. Grampa couldn't quite make out what he was saying!

We opened the front door for a while, thinking the little critter might go out. No such luck.

I went back to my TV program, and Grampa settled down on the sofa again. Pretty soon he heard sounds in the kitchen/dining room area. He went to investigate. The chipmunk had run across the mantel over the fireplace, and knocked down a couple of playing cards from a deck Grampa had there without any rubber band around them. Later he did it again, sending another card or two flying. He then raced up the closet door on the further side of the room and knocked askew the picture that hangs over that door!

He was silent for a while again. Grampa came back into the kitchen and looked around, and there was the little creature sitting right on the near edge of the kitchen counter, looking at him! The little guy jumped down onto the floor then, as I came out of the den to see what was happening. We watched as he climbed right up the back side of the closed curtains that cover the sliding back doors. We could see the curtain move as he wriggled and ran up and down.

Then it was the cutest thing! He appeared at the top of the

curtain, peeking out through the little space at the top, where the two sides of the curtain don't quite come together—just an inch or so of space. He was perfectly framed, clearly watching us. We opened that back door to see if he would go out. Again we lost track of where he was. We hoped he had gone out, but no! He was still running around.

I gave up, but Grampa kept trying to get him to go out. He finally told me that he was 87% sure that the little busy-body had gone. I didn't quite trust that percentage of surety, and I thought I heard him again after we went to bed. I guess it was my imagination, because he hasn't shown himself again.

He probably was the same one that I had seen many times outdoors beside the garage, as I took my daily walks. He had become used to seeing me, and so was not very afraid of humans. He probably got in the house somehow, and didn't know how to get back out.

He couldn't quite get us to understand his predicament for a while, and must have been very relieved when he finally left. As a guest, he was one plucky chipmunk.

Just thought you would enjoy the story!

Love to all,
Grammie/Mother/Mavis

Maybe You'll Like Camping

Dear Grandchildren,

Do you think you don't like camping? I think you might find that you do!

Do you like to look at a rainbow?

How about a sunset?

Do you enjoy the autumn colors of the trees?

Is a field of wildflowers beautiful to you?

Do you enjoy hearing the birds sing?

Have you watched mother and daddy birds feeding their babies?

Do you enjoy seeing a brook, river, lake, or the ocean?

How about mountains, cliffs, buttes, rocks?

Do you think views of a wilderness setting can be beautiful and peaceful?

Does the fresh-air-and-warm-earth-smell after a rain shower please you?

Do you like to hear the wind in the treetops sighing when all else is quiet?

Surely you enjoy lying on blankets on a beach with your family, on a starry night, far away from city lights, when the stars look so bright and near that it seems as though you can almost touch them, especially when there are shooting stars, too.

I could go on, but you get my drift. If you appreciate the beauty of those things, then you do enjoy Nature. Such appreciation can add to your life, and broaden you as a person. I think all people feel their connection to Nature and the Earth at times, and are richer for the experience.

Don't you ever feel that you would have made a good pioneer? They were tough and resourceful. They had to be strong and rugged.

They had to be made of "steel." Square your shoulders and feel the power!

A few decades ago, some young couples (not always young and not always couples) made the choice to live away from the city, on back roads, a primitive life without electricity or running water. Some collected energy from the sun for power. Some built houses that were mostly underground. Why do you think anyone would choose to do that? They call it "back to the land," and some people are still choosing that way of life. Those people enjoy living close to Nature all the time. They feel a kinship with their ancestors and with the Earth. They have a pioneer spirit.

I have always enjoyed camping because it is a simple way of living outdoors for a few days, in touch with Nature and the Great Outdoors. Your fathers or mothers, who are my children, remember how much we enjoyed camping as a family activity while they were growing up. Sure there are inconveniences, and nobody enjoys using the pit toilets. (All of our favorite campgrounds now have flush toilets and hot showers.) Rain and cold weather can spoil a good time. If it rains briefly you can get under a canopy or shelter until it stops. That's a good time to read or play cards.

It is fun to have a campfire, fun to cook over it. It is pleasant to hear the birds in the early morning, and to see the stars at night. It is fun not to have chores in the same sense as chores at home. It is a happy walk (or jog, or bicycle ride) along the path through the woods to the beach. It's challenging to go swimming in the cold water, get accustomed to it, and find that it's not so bad. You feel invigorated afterward, as you walk back to the campsite and hear people splitting wood for the campfire, and smell onions that someone is cooking. You can hardly wait for your tasty supper to be cooked over your fire.

When you first arrive at the campground, it is interesting to choose the site, choose the best spot for the tent, clear away any rocks that you don't want to sleep on, and arrange your space to be convenient, comfortable, and yours! The "cook" will do the same with his or her gear and the table and camp stove and lantern. You can make a nameplate out of a decorated paper plate, and put it out by the road to tell the world whose little "home" this is.

You can swim, fish and boat on the lake, walk, jog, run, bicycle, or ride around the campground to see who is there and what sites you like. Maybe you will find your favorite campsite, for next trip. You can read, write, sew, do crafts, put together puzzles, draw, color, play cards or other games, blow bubbles, model with clay, nap, sunbathe, chop wood, cook over the fire, make s'mores and banana boats, roast hot dogs and marshmallows, tell stories, play music, or sing around the campfire.

Best of all, on a family camping trip you can visit all the other members of the family at their sites. That's what it's all about—being together. You don't need a lot to do.

We humans are capable of adapting to, and enjoying, many diverse activities. I hope you will give yourselves the chance to have a good time next summer on the family camping trip. If you can enjoy it even a little, I promise you will broaden your interests and experience. It's only three days and nights to be away from your usual way of life. I am looking forward to those days eagerly, and I hope you will, too!

Love,
Grammie

Time for Dialysis

Dear "Mel,"

I am very sorry that you have this condition. My reason for writing: Being told today that you are going to need dialysis is not a death sentence. Read that again. Just the opposite! It extends lives for many years. Yes, it takes up many hours every week. Yes, your life will change because this will take precedence over everything. Yes, you may not feel very well when it's time to go in again. (I don't know whether that's true.) But most of the time you should feel LOTS BETTER! Also, apparently it keeps people functional and reasonably well for a matter of YEARS!! (Computer said 20 to 30 years depending on one's health and condition, and probably age.)

Hospice typically gets involved when a patient has a terminal diagnosis and has only a few months left to live. If you accept the remedy the good Lord has allowed people to use when kidneys fail, that is dialysis, you should put off Hospice for quite a long time. Actually, you are addressing your other health issues, too, and should have them under control so that you can enjoy life somewhat again.

If your second and third opinion sources agree with today's advice, you may not have to begin just yet. It depends on how good or poor a job your kidneys are still doing. If doctors offer you tried-and-true medications to improve kidney function, TAKE THEM! But DO NOT fall for any snake-oil remedies.

Find out what your options are for doing this. I know there are choices. Find out what you need to get for support—a driver, a home visiting nurse, a homemaker—I don't know. I know every state has senior services available, and probably a person on dialysis would qualify. You need to learn what is available to make things easier and safer. Don't hesitate to use your long-term-care insurance when or if the time for that comes. Call on friends for help if you need to. Talk with your children sooner rather than later, and ask them for what you will need from them. Ask for their love and emotional support.

Think about what you would like to do during those hours while having dialysis. Write a book. Read. Have you ever read *Crime and Punishment* (Dostoyevsky)? Do puzzles. Learn to knit. Bring a friend to visit with. Sleep. Make phone calls.

You can ask how long you could expect to live if you didn't take the dialysis, but why refuse dialysis and allow yourself to die sooner, when the treatments might give you several years? You can always stop later if something happens so it seems like the best way out. Please give it a try.

Remember, think positive, trust the Lord, thank Him for making dialysis available to us, and NO SNAKE-OIL MEDICINES!!!!

Best wishes,
Mavis

In 2017 I answered an ad in the paper inviting people in the community to contribute to a booklet called "Words of Wisdom," to be handed out to the high school graduates. Feeling that I did have a message to share, I answered the ad, and my article was accepted. Mine was serious, while many of the contributions were short and/or humorous. I am including it in this section and calling it a letter. In a way, that's what it was.

To the Graduates: It's All About Choices

As you carve your niche in the world as an adult, it will become progressively more evident to you that it is up to you to take care of yourself, because no one else is going to do it. How successful you are at this basic task, and what you make of your life, will depend largely on the decisions that you make, the choices both large and small. Your happiness and success in life depend on whether you decide to go to college and how well you face responsibility there; on your work ethic; on how well you take care of your health; on the friends you choose to spend your time with; on whom you marry, if you do, and how carefully you choose that person; on whether you always obey the law; and on how you treat other people.

Don't fill your life with regrets. Don't be in the wrong place at the wrong time; for example, if a place may get raided, don't be there even if you are innocent. To be there marks you as guilty. Actually, there are a lot of places where you should not be, even if they are not likely to be raided.

Always be functional and able to drive legally; be available and able to act in a crisis—maybe even to save a life. Do not be impaired or under the influence so that you are not able to act. An accident can affect the rest of your life—even ruin it—if you are guilty of breaking the law on drinking and driving. Just ask those in prison because they were driving while intoxicated and someone was killed. Ask the family of the person who was killed.

Choose your friends carefully, and spend your time with people who are uplifting, not with those who will drag you down.

The most concise rule for living ever uttered is to treat others as you would want to be treated. Think what a difference it would make in the world if everyone followed that rule.

The previous year I had answered the request for articles for the Winthrop "Words of Wisdom" booklet, but submitted it too late. It was shorter, but I think it adds a good point:

What Is a Truly Successful Life?

How do you define a successful life? As a thoughtful young adult, you will be thinking about this and defining your personal goals.

The most common definition of a successful person is one who has worked hard, made a lot of money, and lives a life of ease. A more thoughtful definition might allude to the setting of personal goals, and the achievement of them through lofty means. A still deeper meaning of success involves our beliefs about the meaning of life, and the reasons we are here. These deep thoughts can lead you to more defined goals.

Common answers to these philosophical questions are that our purpose is to help others and to enjoy life. Religious people say that we are here to glorify God. The common thread here involves our relationship with others. If we achieve success with that, we will enjoy life—even though we may not have a lot of money.

I believe that would be a successful life!

A Big Decision

Dear Family,

Last night I finally came to a hard and sad decision, the big one for the elderly. For a while now, I have realized that my ability to drive safely has lessened. I don't believe that I have slowed down much in reaction time, or that I fail to grasp situations. It is physical—I can't turn my head, and/or body, enough to see the traffic flow adequately. I have realized that I have had a problem for quite a while now, and I have been trying to address that problem and improve my performance in several ways, realizing the danger. I bought a seat for the car (just a flat round disk) that turns easily on the car seat. It helped some. I have been doing neck muscle stretches to try to improve my mobility. I gained a very little. Arthritis does not give in much, no matter what you do. I have learned to position my car at an intersection so that I can see better in both directions; it is often not enough. I have avoided certain intersections. I have trouble getting off our road. (Remember Lawrence's constant "Watch out for those left-hand turns!" I have trouble with some right-hand turns also.) I have paid very close and constant attention to my driving. I don't know what else I could do to become a safe driver again.

Day before yesterday, I drove to Winthrop to see my doctor, without any problem. I had to go back yesterday to get my flu shot, and almost had an accident on the way home. I can't blame it on anyone else; it was completely my fault. I never saw the car. I had stopped at Hannaford in Winthrop, and then drove to the intersection with Route 202. As I drove, I observed the oncoming traffic on 202, and nothing was coming. At the intersection, I looked carefully again, and then made my turn to the left, toward home. There was a CMP truck coming in the right-hand lane, but there was plenty of room for me.

As I turned, I looked in my rearview mirror, and all was clear. Then I heard a loud, close horn blasting at me, and saw a car to my right, just barely behind me, with nowhere to go. I had come into his lane right in front of him, and he couldn't go to the right because the CMP truck was there. I pulled left and sped up, and somehow we did not collide. I never saw that car until I heard the horn.

It really shook me up, and I am forced to consider that it is not safe for me to continue just trying to avoid these dangers. I just can't express how much I hate giving up this part of my self-care and independence, and having to call on Anna and Scott more than I have been.

My license expires in a few weeks, on my 86th birthday. I think I will renew it so I can drive on my road to the greenhouse, and maybe water the plants at the cemetery next summer. I will keep my car for now, and Anna and Scott will use that to take me to my appointments.

I will listen to your comments, but I will not continue to drive and put other people, as well as myself, at risk. I have had a wake-up call and warning, without anything bad happening. I need to stop driving before I have an accident, instead of after. I hope you understand.

With lots of love,
Mother/Grammie/Mavis

Widowhood

Dear "Barbara,"

I was just thinking of you again, and wondering how you are getting along, since we are both struggling to find our way out of this thick depressive fog, which is grief and widowhood.

Lawrence died Feb. 5 last year, so it has been well over a year now, and I am really doing very well finding my way. I still have good days and bad, but the bad ones are getting fewer and less intense. I will never stop missing him, and I am still apt to cry over a song or a dear thought. I am so lucky to have my children nearby, as they call or visit daily. Those who live away also do their part. I use e-mail often.

My brother is a retired minister, but I never could be that. I don't feel that I can advise people on how to live. Once in a while, though, I may pass along suggestions for something that has helped me to live more happily. Please forgive me if I overstep.

To fight off depression, I find that counting my blessings and pleasant experiences, no matter how small, really helps. It works best if done daily, maybe when going to bed. My list may include things like seeing some spring flowers coming up through the snow, or a robin hopping along, hearing from a friend, getting a good doctor's report, getting a compliment, seeing a smile from a stranger. First thing in the morning, I try to remember to say to myself, "This is the day that the Lord has made; let us rejoice and be glad in it." I try to replace negative thoughts with positive ones all day long.

Equally important is keeping busy. After Lawrence died, there were a zillion ends to tie up, especially since he was a twenty-year veteran. It took weeks—months—of phone calls, letters, forms to be made out, and checking on progress. It was good for me to have things to accomplish.

I have a narrow wall (about 36 inches wide) between the French sliding doors and the picture window, now devoted to memorabilia, and I call it a "memory wall." At the top is the flag that was over his coffin, then our wedding picture (1949), a picture of us in 1991, the President's letter of thanks to deceased veterans' wives, pictures of his big accomplishment—the greenhouse, a picture of our six children, a picture of the entire family—34 of us then, and a picture of us on his 90th birthday. Hung up for the last time is his Army officer's cap. It gives me pleasure and comfort.

Just keeping busy is not enough. I feel that being interested in something is essential. Depression makes that hard, if not impossible. I have a quilt I am finishing, and I just finished getting the records ready for my visit to the tax accountant. I am going to pack away my warmest winter clothes soon and get out the early spring ones. I enjoy reading the paper and a few TV shows. Each person would have his own interests, but taking one's mind off the sadness is healthy. After all, our husbands would not have wanted us to be sad forever. How would you want your husband to feel if you had gone first?

My intent here is kind, and I hope you don't feel that I am intruding. My very best wishes to you!

With love,
Mavis

Some Sage Advice

Dear Family,

As I sit here waiting to see if I am to have any more hob-goblins demanding "Trick or treat," I feel like passing out some advice, being the sage octogenarian that I am. (Ahem!)

When the Fed raises the Prime interest rate, the rates on interest-bearing accounts go up fast. Credit card accounts carry extremely high interest rates—bad enough right now, but they will be much higher then. If anyone is carrying a balance on their credit card accounts, now is the time to pay those off—highest rates first. Borrowing at a lower rate to pay them off might be necessary. Be very careful in any borrowing! Do not jeopardize your home, for instance. Understand what you are agreeing to.

Vow right now to stop adding to your debt. If you can't afford to pay for "it" by the time the credit card bill comes—DON'T BUY IT! Vow that you will pay each month's bill in full, and do not throw away all that money you pay in interest. You can cut your excess spending a lot if you give it a little thought.

My dear husband and I would have been rich long ago if we had not paid out so much of our money for interest. If added up, it would amount to a small fortune! And we never were ones to spend for a lot of "things"—clothes, cars, boats, parties. There were times that I needed new shoes, for instance, but I waited because the children had to have coats. Later in life we were rid of debt, and we spent a lot on travel, but we even did that on a budget. Don't allow much of your money to go for interest payments! It is wasted money.

Second subject: Don't ever run for office unless you have a very tough hide! You will have not only constant criticism and blame, but you may have to face the law, with accusations from enemies. What a horrible life! I prefer peace and quiet and a friendly environment; how about you?

Next: Don't let down your guard for a minute when you are driving. The faster you go, the less time you have in an emergency to make necessary adjustments, or to stop. I'll never forget the good advice I got from a very smart man when I was worriedly training for my first driver's license. He said, "If you are going slow, nothing very bad can happen." Of course, I wasn't on the super highway, but even there you can keep the speed down to a safe rate. I have always said that 80 is too fast—there is no reaction time.

Last: Live your life so you will have no regrets. Actually, that is probably impossible—but you can try. Do what you know is the right thing to do. You will be happy doing it. Love and value your family, your mate, your children—and TELL them you love them. Life is so much better when you have people to love, who love you. Friends are wonderful, also, but too often they come and go. It is family members that you are with for the long haul. Be polite, thoughtful, and loving toward them. It pays off.

No more trick-or-treaters—guess I'll go get supper.

Love always,
Mother/Grammie/Mavis

On my 90th birthday, my family gave me a party. One of the things we did was to have questions asked of me, which I answered the best I could without preparation. My great-grandson, age 12, has had a lot of hardship and sorrow in his young life, and he asked me a very deep question about ways I have found to get through hard times. After the party, I decided to add to my answer by sending him the letter below.

Some Big Answers

Dear Great-grandson,

I believe your question at my party Saturday night might be stated as "How does one get through the bad times?" Your question was the deepest and most profound question asked, so thank you for that. I knew right off that I really needed more time to prepare an answer to such a serious, and important, question. I'm afraid my answers didn't address HOW one develops character, and gains strength, and learns how to deal with difficult situations. Unfortunately, they usually don't just go away.

About my own experiences, remember that as children, Uncle Guy and I didn't feel deprived or poor. During the Depression, most people were in similar circumstances. Today's modern conveniences hadn't even been invented yet. We didn't say, "Oh, I wish I could just turn a faucet and get hot or cold water." Our water came from the spring, which my father brought in two pails daily. That's the way it was, and we didn't know any different. (We were delighted, though, when we finally got a radio. It was a car radio, with a car battery sitting beside it for power.) Any unpleasant conditions we experienced were simply accepted as being the way things were. Acceptance is the key here. If no change is possible, acceptance is necessary. Sometimes, of course, change is possible, but knowing the "how" becomes the challenge.

The kind of difficulty in life that you were referring to, tragedy and sadness, comes into everyone's life, for some a whole lot more than for others. But there are many richly joyful times, too. The bad times are when one needs strength to cope and get through it. Death, of course, is a common occurrence. It sometimes takes a person a long time after the death of a loved one to get through the grief, and get to the place where they have accepted that the person is gone, and they can feel happy again in everyday life. There is nothing wrong with feeling happiness at the same time you are grieving. In fact, it will help the process and make you a healthier person mentally.

There is a goal involved in grieving: It is to build a happy, healthy life without that person, instead of forever grieving and wishing him or her back. One will always remember, always wish he or she were still here, but will have accepted reality, ready for a whole and wholesome life again.

They say that what doesn't kill you makes you stronger. That is how you build character—by facing up to circumstances with a positive "I can" attitude. You know how to build physical strength. You exercise muscles and they respond. Inner strength is the same. Practice acting with courage, not fear. Life is a series of choices. Choose the path that you know you should. Don't let temptations get hold of you—avoid regrets. They are very sad thoughts! And, they prevent normal growth of inner strength, unless you manage to learn from them. When we do make mistakes, we should learn from them.

Building character means constantly trying to be the best YOU that you can be. Follow the rules, be kind and helpful to others, actually feel that other people are just as important as you are, and give them whatever you can to help them with their demons and problems, without interfering or overstepping. Follow the Golden Rule: Treat others as you would like to be treated.

One's attitude in life produces or prevents happiness. What is happiness? It is simple. If you are thinking happy thoughts, you feel happy. If you are having sad or unhappy thoughts, you feel sad and unhappy. Now, tragedies and sad things have to be given lots of thought in order to process them and find one's way through them. Those are going to be sad thoughts. It is very important to try to balance them with positive, pleasant, grateful thoughts—even if you have to list them on paper. This is not just for sad times—it should be at least a weekly habit, if not a daily one. I don't claim that it will cure depression, of course, but it can help with mild depression, and improve mental health generally.

Think positive—think "I can!" Accept what you must. Remember you have a right to be happy, so think happy thoughts.

I hope this adds a little to my answer of Saturday night. I hope it may help as you grow to manhood.

With lots of love—and confidence in you,
Grammie L.

Not One of My Grandchildren

Hello, my dear grandchildren,

It has been quite a while since I have written you a grand-motherly letter. The events of this past week have inspired me to tell you how I feel. You older ones, I didn't want to leave you out; but yes, I do know how old you are! Please don't take offense!

Most all day yesterday, Grampa and I were glued to the televi-sion as the authorities closed in on the nineteen-year-old "Boston Bomber" who, with his brother, took it upon himself to hurt a lot of people, kill some, and upset the whole country—maybe the whole world—and for what?

Every time they showed that boy's face, I felt grief that such a normal-looking, youthful, promising, innocent face could belong to someone who could do such a terrible thing.

Think of those runners who were injured. Think of the work and effort they had put in to prepare for this race, how much strength and ability it takes to run 26 miles, how eagerly they had awaited the big day of this marathon. Now think of what those two men's actions have done to them and to their plans for the future. Some had a foot blown off, and several had amputations. So much for future races, or even normal walking, for them. It's horrible!

The more I saw his picture on the screen, the more I began to identify with his family. That young face belongs to someone's grand-son. How must that grandmother be feeling? How about his parents and siblings? What a good way to spoil lives—and not just their own!

When a baby is born into a family, there is happiness and joy. The child is a blank slate, ready to start learning. Everyone cheers as he or she learns to smile, turn over, sit up, stand, walk, and talk. Most families try to teach the child as much as possible, in order to prepare him for a productive adult life. Every society, human and some animals, have to socialize the young—bring them up—to maintain the integrity of their society, and to maintain the principles on which they function. What has gone wrong when young men like these brothers can do such serious harm, going so far away from what their society should have taught them?

We may learn that there were other influences in this case, like terrorists to whom they listened. If not, then why, why, why? Did they crave attention? Did they want to shame their parents, or get even with them for wrongs, real or imagined? Were they mentally ill?

As I have said in the past, when you get up to mid-teens and beyond, it is time to stop blaming your parents, because you are becoming in charge of your own life then. It's up to you, and to you alone, to take responsibility for yourself and how you "turn out." No matter how bad the parenting has been (or is perceived as having been), a person should no longer blame his parents or anyone but himself, because he is, by that time, the one responsible for himself.

That doesn't mean that any person can say, "If I am in charge of myself, then what I do is no one else's business." It is very much the business of others. You know the old saying, "No man is an island."

A society of people has to have rules and laws to enable them to live together in safety. If you notice, most laws have one reason for being: preventing people from doing harm to each other. That's what it comes down to; that and rules that ease the frictions of living together.

I have pride in all of you, and faith in you to continue to make us proud. You have an honorable name to live up to, that of a respected grand old family. Those of you whose surnames are different still have that responsibility; you have the same genes. Whether you have our name, our genes, or you joined our family by marriage or when your parents signed the adoption papers—every one of you has the solemn duty and responsibility to conduct yourselves as good citizens—good people.

You are all wonderful people. I have all possible trust and faith in you, so don't take this letter the wrong way. I don't fear that any of you will be bombers! I'm just communicating with you concerning my feelings brought to the surface by these brothers. What a tragedy when a person goes wrong!

Much love to all of you always,
Grammie

Guilty, and on Drugs

My very dear grandchildren,

It has happened again. Why do I find myself feeling sorry for a murderer, who is on the front page of today's paper, with 3-inch high letters spelling "Guilty"? This man killed a county sheriff's deputy. He didn't deny that he did it. He couldn't remember much about it. Why? He was so high on drugs at the time that the defense used that fact to claim that it was manslaughter, not murder. A determination of murder could send the guilty one to jail for the rest of his life. They claimed that he was so out of his mind that he could not have planned to kill the police officer or even know what he was doing, because that would be criteria for calling it murder. The jury found him guilty of murder.

We all feel terrible for the victim and his family. Why should I also feel bad for this young man? He did kill another human being! It is because of what he has done to his life, his future. He is only 30. His age is about like that of three of you, my grandsons. I know nothing of where he was before this, in living his life. But now he cannot pursue any of his dreams. He can't date, find a wife, buy a house, have children, travel, go dancing or to weddings or parties, go to the office, or work with wood, siding, or insulation. He cannot buy a car, go to family reunions, or have a cottage on the lake, go fishing, or own a boat. He cannot have horses, or cows, or a company of his own. The American Dream is not for him.

I know a murderer has to pay for his crime, and I don't feel bad about that. I feel sorry because a young person has messed up his life. It makes me realize how devastated I would feel if it were one of you. I am so proud of all of you, and of how well you are doing. I shouldn't worry, and I really don't.

261

I have to assume that he would not have done it, if it were not for the drugs. Maybe he was not to blame for being addicted. We all know that happens, way too often. But did he try to get help? If he was at fault, in that he used recreationally and never tried to stop or go for help, then he is responsible for wrecking his life. The scourge is so widespread, and leads to such awful outcomes! Way, way too many lives have been ruined or lost. Most people don't realize the strength of addiction.

It is not just drugs. Too much alcohol can take away your God-given judgment, too. You know that it can cloud your mind and allow you to mess up your life. You should know your own limit and never go over that, or not drink at all. You should always be able to react and meet emergencies and drive legally. Parents should never allow themselves to be unable to take good care of their children and ensure their safety and well-being. Problems involving alcohol have caused a great deal of sorrow over the years, because of the too common abuse of it.

Young people, take note; and those of you who are parents, teach your children: Treat drugs like the poisons that they are! Do not try it that first time! The possible horrible consequences make it not worth the risk. If you become addicted innocently, or in any way, get the help you need to kiss the problem goodbye. No, it won't be easy. Remember, though, "No man is an island." There are those who love you. Life is hard enough at its best. Why make it worse? But life is a gift that can bring much pleasure. I implore you: Please don't ruin yours!

Much love to all of you,
Grammie

2020 note: I have made more quilts since 2016—a total of five quilts for my grandchildren, six for my children, and two for me.

Each One a Favorite

My dear Grandchildren,

I want to say a few words of explanation to all of you, my grand-children, in case you feel that I am showing favoritism in giving a hand-made quilt to one grandchild, when I don't have one for each of you. Believe me, I sincerely wish I was able to make one for every one of you.

Favoritism is a funny thing, for me. It hovers over one person, and then over another. Or it doesn't really exist, but is only the feeling of love that I have for the one on my mind at that time. Each one of you is special to me, each for different reasons—or for no reason in particular, except that you are you.

Love also is a funny thing. No matter how much you love one person, that doesn't prevent loving another person, or any number of people, any amount. Think of a young child who learns he is going to have a new brother or sister. He may be afraid his parents will love him less when the baby comes. But we know that the parents will keep right on loving him just as much, and will love the baby, too. There is no limit to the amount of love we can feel, or the number of people for whom we can feel it. I have plenty of love for all of you.

So don't connect his gift with the amount of love I have for each of you. In my remaining years, I will probably work on another quilt, or more than one depending on my health and length of time. I have two others that I made, both of which have some faults, but which are pretty. I am using those at present, but those will be up for grabs someday.

When your Grampa died, I had a quilt in the making, more than half finished. Somehow I couldn't settle myself down to work on it again for many months. "Luke" had been away for a long time, and I missed him. (I have missed each of you when I haven't seen you for a long time.) This need I had—or have—for family was even more keen in those early months of emotional vulnerability after your Grampa died. I am very happy that, while he was away, "Luke" had begun attending church with his cousin, had found value in the Christian faith, and had been baptized. When he came home, I was so happy. Looking at the unfinished quilt for the thousandth time, I decided to finish it and give it to him.

This quilt is not of heirloom quality because it is not hand-quilted. It is the pattern called "Wild Geese," with triangles of cloth placed to hint at the shape of geese, flying in a row—that is, several rows. "Wild geese" is kind of like "Luke" and his travels and his love of Nature, fishing and hunting, wouldn't you say? "My heart knows what the wild goose knows..." (an old song).

I truly wish I had fourteen quilts for my fourteen grandchildren! I love you all—lots! One child in each family can inherit the quilt I made for his or her father or mother—my child. The remaining grandchildren will have to have something else to remember me by.

Love to all, always,
Grammie

A tragic accident, caused by an intoxicated driver, took the life of the fiancé of one of my granddaughters. He was not the driver. I did not attend the funeral, but instead wrote this to my granddaughter, and her mother, father, and brother. To protect their privacy, I have not used their real names.

A Tragic Accident

Dear grieving family,

"Don" came into your lives to visit, not to stay. You are now grateful for the time you had with him. He left with you a very real part of himself—his son. Our loved ones can be snatched from us, as this very young man was, but the past itself, and its memories, cannot. Those are yours to keep forever.

You are strong individuals, and your strength will serve you well, as you now continue your lives without him, but with your memories, and with his son. You can and will be strong for each other, and for the little one. You also have us—the rest of your family, who love you dearly, to add to your strength and to act as a safety net.

Concentrate on the positive, and look for the good in your lives. Be thankful for what you have, and especially for this child, and for each other. You will find that you can be happy again. Grief has great strength, but does not preclude happiness. Our spirits are capable of many, perhaps unlimited, numbers of emotions and feelings, almost at the same time. It is okay to be happy, and it should be your goal, but it will take time. The raw edges of grief soften with time. Having that little boy to enrich your lives will help, a lot.

My thoughts, prayers, and love are with you,
Grammie/Mother/Mavis

Responsibilities of a Role Model

My dear Grandson,

Many years ago, there was a song called "What a Difference a Day Makes." I often think of that at times like this. I know that you, too, are experiencing shock and grief in your family's loss of "Don." I can't tell you how sorry I am. I am eternally grateful, though, that you and your sister and her son were not in that car, as you could have been.

One of the saddest parts of this is that a child will not have his father in his life as he grows up. You and your father will be male role models for him, though, which every boy needs. You must do your best to show him what it means to grow up to be a good man. Children copy what they actually see more than do what they are told. They need good examples set for them.

An example of this comes to mind. When I first met your Grampa, he was home from the war, and he occasionally smoked a pipe. I didn't like it, and he soon quit; but the real reason that he quit was because he didn't want to set a bad example for his younger brother. He told me that.

You are a fine man, and so is your father, and you both will help that little boy to grow up whole and happy, as he develops a strong ethical and moral character with good values.

I wish I could scream at all my grandchildren not to take chances in ways that they know better than to do! Usually there are things to learn from these horrible accidents. I don't know any of the details of what caused this one—and please know that I am not passing judgment—but we all know that many, if not most, of them are caused by speeding, or driving after drinking or using drugs, or by texting and phoning, which are distractions. Driving is serious business, not a big game. Wearing a seat belt is an absolute "must," and buckling up should be habitual before starting the motor. Every time! Now that you and others have seen what may happen, maybe someone else will avoid an accident because they learned from his death. You could all help your friends not to take chances. You can keep others from driving drunk, for instance. Take their keys, if necessary.

Please, please, my dear, take care of yourself. I love you so much!

With loving sympathy,
Grammie

I wrote this after my granddaughter's fiancé was killed in the car accident, and the driver was sentenced to a jail term. I have supplied different names, not their real ones. "Pat" is the name I gave to that granddaughter. The letter is to another granddaughter, also; they are the only grandchildren I have who are parents. The deceased young man is "Don," and the driver shall be called "Hal."

Teach the Children

Dear Granddaughters,

You are the mothers of my only great-grandchildren so far. Because of Don's death, and this week's sentencing, I have been doing a lot of thinking about the world we live in, how hard it is to always make good decisions, what an uphill battle bringing up children is, and many related thoughts.

I didn't know Don well, and I never met Hal, who was the driver that night. I think Don was a good person, and would have been a good husband and father. I am impressed with Hal's remorse and effort to do the right thing now.

It is a fact that young people have the feeling that they are invincible. The alcohol and drug scene is too nearly universally accepted as normal. But that doesn't excuse or help what happened. This substance abuse is far, far too common. It causes a tremendous amount of trouble.

I want to make a couple of points: 1.) Hal has done something that will affect the rest of his life, and he is deeply sorry. I believe that a person in such a situation feels better if he is punished. Paying the debt to society relieves the suffering from the conscience somewhat. That is something for you to consider as you feel badly for him and his punishment. 2.) That said, Pat, I agree with you that severe punishment in his case would not be fair or advisable, and I admire your courage in speaking up to the judge, saying what you feel your fiancé would have wanted you to say. The only value of a harsher punishment is that it may serve as a deterrent to others. I don't think that works very well.

The whole awful thing is the result of poor decisions, not all on Hal's part. How can we keep my great-grandchildren's generation from making poor decisions, growing up in this world as it is?

First I want to say that you are both good mothers—I am constantly impressed—and you both have very valuable assistance from your parents, the children that Grampa and I brought up. Your children have a better chance than many. But they are surrounded—bombarded—by societal influences that harm rather than help. Practically everything they see or hear imprints on their minds that anything is alright if it feels right, or if they want to do it. There are few ideals being taught in movies, videos, music (lyrics), books, conversations, daycare, school, or anything else that comes into their lives. Most teachers try, but it is not enough. The concept of right versus wrong has been badly blurred. Too few parents consider what their own example is teaching their children, or consider what system of rewards and punishment might help the child to develop a conscience, by which he can live productively and learn to make good choices. It seems that, for many years, each generation as a group has done a poorer job than their parents did of socializing their children to be good citizens in the best sense of the words. Having good morals to guide decisions isn't much of a priority these days.

So what could or should be done? We are not going back to the days when mothers stayed home and spent all day most of the time with their young children, or when many people lived on farms, and the children worked right alongside their parents, and were not out ramming around nights. They were not apt to have friends who were bad influences. Under those conditions, the children grew up knowing how their parents felt about issues—about right and wrong, about fairness, honesty, kindness, alcohol use, and everything else that came up. Church was a huge factor in the children's lives. Church and Sunday school were wonderful helps in the effort to raise children to be good people. Children adopted what they learned from these sources, and lived by what they were taught. That is key—they were taught!

Parents need to talk and talk and talk to their children. They must spend every minute they can with them in order to seize every chance they get to speak up against something in a movie or book, or what someone said, and take every teaching moment they can find. Yes it takes a lot of effort, especially when you are tired or feel the need for time for yourself. But it is vitally important.

I would think that those who are concerned with this Don/Hal tragedy, which has affected so many people, would learn from it. Grampa and I grew up in families who didn't use alcohol at all. My family, being churchgoers, in those days considered drinking to be a sin. As you know, I am a teetotaler, and while I don't see drinking as a sin, I do deplore the evil that the abuse of it causes. Such suffering! My very strong feeling is that a person—that's everyone—should not drink an amount EVER that would keep him from driving or functioning. What if you are suddenly faced with an emergency? What if your child needs you? As you have seen, making a poor decision, not only about alcohol and drugs, can change your life and that of many others, tremendously.

You are good mothers, so I will spare you anything further. I am "preaching to the choir." I hope I have not offended in any way.

With much love,
Grammie

Recipe for Savory Stuffing

Dear Kristin,

You have always loved the stuffing I make, and I promised you the recipe. It is an original recipe, which I developed over the years from one I saw in the Sunday paper.

<u>Mavis Longfellow's Savory Stuffing</u>
—For a 20-pound turkey—

A day or two before making the stuffing, bake a batch of biscuit dough. Of course, you don't need to cut out the biscuits because you will be crumbling the bread anyway. Just cook the dough in a pan.

Cook 1/3 cup finely-cut onion in about 1/2 cup water while combining ingredients below. Watch that they do not boil dry. Add water if needed.

Bread is best if not too fresh. Crumble into very small pieces, enough to equal 8 cups. Put in large bowl.

Mix together in medium bowl:
3 beaten eggs
1/3 cup cooking oil (Popcorn oil, which is butter-flavored, probably tastes best.)
1 cup unsweetened applesauce
2 or 3 tablespoons Bell's Seasoning, or ground sage, or (best) a combination (Some may like more of this seasoning. Sage is stronger than Bell's.)
1/4 teaspoon celery seed
1/8 teaspoon garlic powder

Dash of black pepper
Dash of thyme

Mix well.
Add cooked onions, and any water left from cooking them.
Mix all with bread crumbs. I put the giblets in the neck cavity and then fill both the neck and body cavities with all of the stuffing, if bird weighs about 20 pounds.

Enjoy! Love,
Grammie

Have a Great Year

Dear Grandchildren,

What's that groaning I hear???? "Another letter from Grammie!"
It's that time of year again when most of you are going back to school, some off to college for the first time, or returning, or even heading to grad school. Even my two youngest grandchildren are in high school. To those of you who are not in school anymore, I include you also, because what I want mainly is to wish you all a good year!

Hopefully, learning never stops, but in school at any stage it becomes formal and disciplined. If you are out of college, consider taking a course—often—in something you are interested in. Learning is a lifelong challenge. Your "job," at school age and way beyond, is to learn as much as you can about as many areas of living in our world as you can. Education adds exponentially to your enjoyment of life. So if school is for you this year, sharpen your brain along with your pencils, and give it your very best! We all know it's not easy, and some of it won't be interesting, and some instructors will be unfair; but don't lose sight of your goals!

I especially want to urge you to make good choices. As adults, or getting up near that age, you are constantly making decisions, some of which will turn out to be very important to your life. This is your life, and as adults you are responsible for yourselves. The quality of your future depends strongly on your choices.

Don't take foolish chances. That would be a very poor decision! Don't be where a tragedy is apt to happen. Don't be one of those who, after an earthquake, watch the sea recede and then are surprised when the tsunami comes in!

The people who were killed or injured when the Indianapolis stage collapsed didn't make a poor decision in being there. There was no way they could have known that might happen. If we do anything at all, we are taking a gamble. Every time you ride in or drive a car, you are gambling that nothing bad will happen. And chances are it won't.

However, the young man in our newspaper today who was driving to work—probably late—and lost control of his car doing 80 mph, slammed into a tree, and died—he was taking a foolish chance.

Don't be where bad things have a bigger chance of happening. Don't be where there may be riots. Don't be where illegal activities are going on. Don't be caught in a "sting," or selling drugs. You might see your name in the paper, if caught as a patron of a house of prostitutes that was broken up. Oh, yes! They do print names! Don't be anywhere that the police might come in and arrest everyone there— you too are guilty by association! Don't ever drink too much. You never know when you may need to be fully alert and not impaired. Don't ride with a poor driver, or one on alcohol or drugs. Life is the easiest if you play it straight and don't try to get away with anything. Having a clear conscience, knowing you are doing what you should do, is the very best way to be happy. Don't fight it.

And oh, yes; choose friends carefully. I believe I have mentioned this before.

Have a great year!

Love,
Grammie

It Pays to Try

Dear Grandson,

I do so appreciate your talking with me on your last visit—Sunday—about your "new" life. My only regret is that I didn't invite you to talk some more, if you wanted to.

I can only imagine how hard it is, but I have faith in your courage and tenacity. You are a man—a good man, and a very intelligent man. Years wasted in this short life cannot be brought back. I am so proud of you for grabbing onto this opportunity—in fact, for *making* this opportunity—to improve your life. Life is richer with education. But that decision is ahead of you. First things first. (I started college when I was 39. Those twenty years before that would have been better if I had had the benefits of a college education.)

You are removing barriers that prevented the rich life you surely desire—a life with a wife and children, a good job that is interesting, friends that help you, not drag you down, an interesting life that contributes and makes the world a better place. (That's what I hope they put on my tombstone—"She made the world a better place.")

That life holds happiness and contentment.

Every person in this world could be a better person. Even the best make mistakes. (I sure do, and suffer with guilt when I do!) We should learn from our mistakes. Everyone should continue throughout their entire life to improve themselves, and to recognize those things that hold them back. I believe you do, and that you know what you must do to get firmly on track, and stay there. You are doing great. I hear good things about you.

Thank you SO MUCH for telling me that you are purposefully trying to improve your life. You have my fervent prayers, and my belief in you. I love you, my grandson, maybe more than you can know.

You are flying back home today. Have a safe trip, and be happy as you progress in your new life! Set reasonable goals for yourself, and rejoice in your success.

Much love always,
Grammie

Making Fudge

From Grammie, to my granddaughters.

Use a pan with a heavy bottom, larger than you think you need; the milk and sugar rise while boiling.

Set out an extra pan in case the fudge starts to burn. You will know if it begins to burn, because little brown specks will show up as you stir. Immediately remove from heat and pour into the spare pan, but don't scrape any of the burned portion as you pour. A few specks will not spoil the batch. Don't answer the phone or do anything that takes you away from stirring for more than a few seconds.

Know what evaporated milk is. It is not condensed milk, which is very sweet and the base for many desserts. Evaporated milk is regular milk from which water has been removed. I use it for cream soups, like fish chowder, and for a creamer for coffee or tea. Many recipes call for it. Shake the can well first.

First, gather everything you will need. Measure the peanut butter and fluff into a bowl, coating the measuring cup and bowl first with butter, oil, or Pam cooking spray. Those ingredients will slide out of the cup much more easily, when you are ready to add them. Set out the mixer, all ingredients, a spoon and spoon rest. Butter or spray the pan you will pour it into. Some people line the pan with foil which they have buttered or sprayed. This recipe makes what I would call a double batch—two 9" x 9" pans, or a 13" x 9" pan. A 9" x 9" pan will yield thick pieces. Don't begin cooking until everything is ready to use.

Most fudge recipes require a candy thermometer, but this chocolate fudge recipe says to boil seven minutes, from a good fast boil, instead of saying boil to the soft ball stage. If using a thermometer, clip it to the side of the pan, but don't let it rest on the bottom of the pan. The handle will slide up or down for proper position. Do not try to use a very hot burner, as it WILL burn! I have thrown out many a batch and started over! Good fudge takes a long time to make, slowly.

As for most cooking success, practice makes perfect! (Call for advice.) Good luck—and enjoy!

Love,
Grammie

See recipe below.

Steve and Carol Bruce's EZ CHOCOLATE FUDGE

Boil for 7 minutes, stirring almost constantly:

½ cup butter
One 12-ounce can evaporated milk (1½ cups)
5 cups sugar
Remove from heat and beat in:
One 12-ounce bag semisweet chocolate chips
1½ tsp. vanilla extract
1½ cups (18 ounce jar) peanut butter
1½ cups marshmallow (7-ounce jar equals 2 cups)

FOR REALLY CREAMY FUDGE, BEAT WITH ELECTRIC MIXER—very important.
Pour into pan, or pans, cool, and cut.
Enjoy!

Recipe for a Good Marriage

My dear Grandchildren (yes, all of you!),

Last year I had no plans to make this "letter from Grammie" an annual thing, but I have been thinking about a "recipe" which I would like to share with you all. I have been working at perfecting the principles of the "recipe" since July 2, 1949, the day Grampa and I were married. This is a serious subject, but I hope you will enjoy the humor I have tried to enlist to make some points.

First, let me explain my choice of title. Notice I am not calling it "Recipe for a Happy Marriage," but instead "Recipe for a Good Marriage." PEOPLE are happy or not according to their personalities, philosophies, attitudes, and determination. A relationship can be satisfying, good, rewarding—or not. For one to be happy, one must have satisfactions for needs. Happiness is defined differently by different people. I think it simply is contentment, not necessarily a euphoric state. I maintain that a MARRIAGE is not happy or unhappy, but a PERSON may be; thus, my title.

Two of you, my grandchildren, are already married. The rest of you may also make possibly the most important choice of your life, and then work out problems—which are always discovered on the journey.

RECIPE FOR A GOOD MARRIAGE

INGREDIENTS: Begin with two adults of similar education, maturity, interests, religion, and goals. Make sure they are attracted to, and interested in, each other. Examine carefully and cull for selfishness, meanness, dishonesty, abusiveness, bigotry, arrogance, lack of manners, a poor bringing-up, and inferior character in general. Discard poor-quality ingredients. Choose new raw materials carefully. ("You can't make a silk purse out of a sow's ear!"—an old saying.) Quality of the raw ingredients is of utmost importance. Check that neither is hauling too much baggage.

MARINATE: Marinate the two for many months or a few years of getting well acquainted, being together, weathering difficulties, solving problems, and maturing together instead of growing apart. Check constantly for character flaws and possible difficulties. Start over with new raw materials if it becomes advisable. Don't waste time on poor ingredients once that is determined.

SIMMER: Once engaged, turn up the heat a bit, to make sure they are compatible and have learned to love each other enough that each desires the other's happiness. Each must be willing to compromise. Be sure that the maturity and unselfishness have aged and developed adequately. Check to see that both consider that they are equals. Add new spices to improve flavor whenever indicated.

FORM, SHAPE, AND TIE TIGHTLY: The process is done— but actually just beginning—at a sincere, meaningful, and honest wedding, in which each promises that the marriage will last a lifetime. There is no room for an attitude of "me first." Both must sincerely promise to unselfishly take care of the other.

PRESERVE: Over time, with the wear and care of daily living, the flush of excitement will diminish. Make sure that the love is still nurtured and the marriage is constantly nourished for both. Enjoy satisfaction and fulfillment, in all ways, by the aspects of married life—THROUGHOUT THE YEARS!

My love to you all,
Grammie

Do's and Don'ts

Don't go with a girl who is grouchy;
Don't marry a man who is mean.
Don't live with someone with big problems
And "baggage" that spoils your life's dream.

Take the time to find out what the faults are;
Make sure your life's goals are the same;
Solve problems before they ARE problems;
Then marital joy you'll both claim!

I wrote this for my grandchildren and other young people in June 2017.

Some people who live to reach some advanced age are asked what the secrets are of successful living. No one has sought my wisdom on the matter, but that isn't stopping me from expressing my opinion!

Rules for Young People

1. Decide which team you are on. (We used to call it good and evil.) If you are not intentionally on the side of improving life and helping others, then you are on the other team.

2. Live so that you can be proud of yourself, not ashamed. If you do something wrong, do what you can to make it right, without making it worse.

3. Recognize your blessings, and think about them with gratitude. This will raise your mood and keep depression and anxiety at bay, and make your personality more pleasant. Nobody enjoys a complainer.

4. Plan ahead and be ready, but be flexible.

5. Don't take foolish chances. Don't give in to the urge to show off in an unsafe manner. Earn praise and recognition for other, more admirable reasons.

6. Be willing to work hard. Work is often its own reward. "As ye sow, so shall ye reap"!

7. Take care of your health. You know how.

8. If you have a gift, in music, art, sports, or anything, develop it and use it to enrich the lives of others, as well as your own.

9. Make the most of the intelligence you were dealt. Stretch it by associating with intelligent people, studying everything you can to add to your store of knowledge, and become educated within your abilities. Read all you possibly can, but not just light and frothy works.

10.   There is no more concise, expansive, or wise piece of advice than the well-known Golden Rule. It really says it all: "Do unto others as you would have them do unto you." Just let it be your guide in all your decisions. It works for married partners, in work and school relations, and in any relationship you can name. One person shouldn't do it all, though. Both sides should try to be fair. There are usually peaceful ways to solve, or help to solve, these problems. Show love and caring for others.

11.   Related to the above, if something you want to do—your "good"—is going to be someone else's "bad," weigh carefully what you choose. If you give in this time, perhaps it will be your turn to have your way next time. Husbands and wives should be sensitive to how important certain choices are to their mate. They should each be trying to make the other happy.

12.   Ridiculing religion or believers is ignorant. People need their faith, and should not have to defend it. Smarter people than you have embraced some form of religion.

Grammie

Family Discussions

My very dear family members (that's all 35 of you),

There is a very divisive issue in our country right now, with no good solutions. We are "darned if we do and darned if we don't." I refer to the school shootings.

I feel compelled to warn you against letting such an emotional problem harm any of our so-valuable loving relationships within this family. There are differences of opinion among us, and rightly so. There are 35 of us, and no two people, even such as a married couple, will agree all of the time. But they still love each other, and they learn ways to avoid the damage that differences in points of view could bring.

Let's think of ways in which we all agree. We agree that there is a big problem that we should try to address. The division comes in our different ideas of how to do it. Nothing is going to work 100%. If you look at the two extremes, without prejudice, both sides are right and both sides are wrong.

The basic premise is that each individual has the right to his or her own opinion. The second truth to remember is that arguing never accomplishes anything, and usually makes each participant firmer in his original belief. When you argue about something you are saying, "I am right and you are wrong." People don't like to be told they are wrong. And both parties may get angry. Anger hurts relationships. Always avoid it. Married (or unmarried) couples have to find ways to discuss things without anger, because there will often be problems that have to be resolved, and it is up to the two of them to find a solution. Not true of a national problem—an angry, harmful argument between two people is not going to accomplish anything that it will involve millions of people to even partially solve. But a loving family bond will be harmed.

How do you avoid arguments and anger? When you know you have a difference of opinion in a serious matter, or think you may, the best way is to not talk about it. You would not be allowing the other person his right to his own opinion. (I realize there may be exceptions—times when you need to keep someone from making a big mistake, like jumping off a bridge.)

Please love me even when I disagree with you; I ask the same for each of you. We must agree to disagree. You probably don't know where I stand on this particular issue because I have not tried to convince any of you of my belief. To my six children: Since you have been adults, I have not challenged any of you on things that I believe and you don't, or vice versa. You have the right to your own opinions. I make sure you know where I stand on morals, religion, right and wrong, and character traits, though. But I would never argue with you about it.

For the continuation of a safe haven in our happy family, then, please always guard love and respect.

Unconditional love to each of you,
Mother/Mavis/Grammie/Grammie L

This letter was to my granddaughter, an expectant mother whose husband, the father of all three children, was just lately out of the picture. She had two young boys, and this baby is a boy, too.

The Road to Higher Ground

My dear, you have no idea how much it meant to me to get that e-mail from you! You are doing so well handling your life challenges. You are going to get to "higher ground" one of these years, as the boys get a little older. You are so fortunate that your parents are willing and able to give you a hand up through this part of life. There are some women who have to manage alone through similar situations. They and their children pay a price. We are very fortunate to have such a helpful family.

A new baby brings so much joy! I will say what I preach to everyone: Our feelings respond to our thoughts. Think happy and positive thoughts, and you will be happy. That means counting your blessings, having hopes, and being like Pollyanna, who tried to see something good in all happenings.

An old hymn will give encouragement and hope, and point us in the right direction to use our inner courage to get things accomplished. (See below.) Higher ground can symbolically mean whatever you need it to mean.

> "I'm pressing on the upward way,
> New heights I'm gaining every day.
> A higher plain than I have found,
> Lord, plant my feet on higher ground!"

Most people have hard things to do at times, some worse than others, of course. My last few months have been no picnic. I have had all these years to build up defenses and learn courage, and I still have needed to discipline myself to find and use those techniques. Life isn't always easy, but over time we can build up defenses.

I went through labor and childbirth six times. Pregnancy and childbirth can be a joyous experience in spite of the discomforts, and contractions. I found it tremendously satisfying to my feelings of fulfillment as a woman. And I enjoyed my little babies so much!

I think about you a lot every day. When the baby is coming, if I know about it, I will be cheering you on. I am cheering for you anyway, whether I know when you go into labor or not. I am very proud of you and your abilities! You can do it! And you will make it to "higher ground," where the road will seem straighter and the sunshine brighter. Be happy!

Love you lots,
Grammie

In times like these I just wish I could gather my children in a big hug and make it all better. I hate to think of my grandchildren and great-grand-children growing up in a world that is not as safe as ours has seemed for so long.

This is a letter to my children, right after 9/11/2001, regarding security:

Play the Hand You Are Dealt

My Dear Children,

Out of the blue, literally, our world has changed. We are suddenly aware of the dangers around us—in our own country, where we are accustomed to feeling safe. The safety net which we assumed we had is suddenly gone. September 11, 2001, will go down in history as the day of our wake-up call.

Historically, though, the world has never been a safe place. There has always been danger—from wild animals, from Mother Nature (tornados, lightning, fire, etc.), from war, and from disease. Too often the danger has been from other people. Homo Sapiens has survived, though, and as a group we have kept the ability to enjoy life, to smile and laugh and sing, to work toward goals, to keep a degree of mental and physical health, and to help others along the way. Enjoying periods of perceived security and safety has certainly helped. Those of us here now have been fortunate to have lived during one such time for many years.

I remember when I came face-to-face with the realization that there actually is no such thing as security. When the Korean War began, men were needed for the armed services, and the Reserves could be called up. It was inconceivable to me that my new husband, who was in the Reserves, could be taken away to fight another war. He had just gone through one, serving in combat on the front lines in Germany. Surely God wouldn't allow this to happen; it wouldn't be fair. Slowly, as I struggled against the worry, it dawned on me. Nowhere have we been promised fairness. Bad things happen to others; they can happen to me. There just is no guarantee. Your father didn't have to go, as you know, and I had gained a new awareness. Security is a state of mind, aided by a lack of adverse conditions for a sustained period.

You play the hand you are dealt, and make the best of it.

This is not to say you cannot improve your lot. There are things you can do to maximize your health. You can live where the crime rate is low and the schools are good. You can avoid places where violence may break out. You can drive safely, and be careful in and on the water. You absolutely must obey the law. A smart person will avoid being in dangerous situations.

People should take care of their mental health. We need to think about pleasant things, and count our blessings. Some of us find strength from a higher power. We can help others. We can engage in goal-seeking behavior. We need to enjoy daily life—a scenic hike, a visit with friends, a good meal; we should smile and sing, love and laugh, enjoy the children and each other. We need to make plans for the future and remember pleasant memories. Every time we feel too engrossed in our present national situation, or other worries, we should purposely change to pleasant thoughts—not easy, but possible.

I haven't personally learned much about handling tragedy because, thankfully, I have been largely spared the dreadful things that some people face. One thing I have learned concerns grieving the death of a loved one. Grief is persistent, can't be avoided, and is a form of personal work which is necessary in order to rebuild one's life without the deceased. However, it becomes morbid when you suddenly realize that you feel guilty that you have been enjoying something. Grief and joy can both exist, in turn. It is healthy to enjoy as much as you can, because grief, being unavoidable, will persist, and its work will be accomplished. Very seldom does it fail.

Keep life as normal as you can. Your regular rituals and schedules can be enormously comforting.

So here's to life, and as much pleasure as we can reasonably get out of it. Here's to our country's success in routing those who are harming us. Here's to more peaceful, carefree, and happy times. Here's to vast improvement in the hearts of men and women, and to a more civilized world, where people get along, and where right triumphs over wrong. Most importantly, here's to our own ability to cope and make the most of our lives in whatever circumstances we find ourselves. Life can be beautiful!

Here's to you, with love,
Mother

SECTION 3

Christmas Poems, Plus

Beginning in 2009, I wrote a poem or two each year to send along with my Christmas cards. I have gathered them here, by date. I have also included a couple of other Christmas articles and poems.

The Magic of Christmas

'Twas the week before Christmas and all through the town
The mothers were weary, their patience worn down.
The children were hyper the last day of school,
Their letters to Santa sent well before Yule.

The youngsters go sledding, cheeks red as a rose,
Or skating or skiing, bundled up to the nose.
They're dreaming of presents, and goodies to sup,
Their eyes, how they sparkle! Their faces light up.

We really love Christmas and this time of year;
The magic, so merry, and the music we hear.
There's color and beauty and treats to the sight,
Red flowers and costumes and lighting at night.

Card sending, and baking, and gifting we share;
The planning, and shopping, and wrapping—we care!
To pageants and concerts and churches we go,
Bell Ringers and parties, and TV's best show.

A live tree inside, oh! The fragrance it brings!
We trim it with mem'ries and lights—many strings.
And then there's the music, sung year after year
To bless us, and nourish, and coax a glad tear.

Poinsettias in their beauty bring joy, so we hear.
They've gone out to most homes at this time of year.
Their redness, their brightness, their softness, their charm,
They speak to the family and their love so warm.

The stories of angels that sang in the night
Announcing to shepherds who shivered with fright,
Great visions of wonder 'neath stars in the skies.
Then gifts to the Baby, by three men so wise.

These stories are ancient, yet they do their part
To celebrate Christmas, and touch every heart.
We all long for peace, all over the Earth;
It's closest at Christmas, the time of Christ's birth.

The good will we practice and feel at the Yule
Is really best known as the old Golden Rule!
If only we used it all year, you would see
What a wonderful life and new world it would be.

Yes, we love it; each Christmas is food for the soul!
It brings us all closer and helps us feel whole.
We love all the magic, and let me be clear—
We wish "MERRY CHRISTMAS" and "HAPPY
    NEW YEAR"!!!!

(2009)

The Memories of Christmas

How blessed are the memories of Christmas long ago—
Our children 'round our Christmas tree, and gifts our love to show,
The simple joy the children knew, the wonder in their eyes,
Their happiness at Christmastime, worth more than any prize.

Now mem'ry is a funny thing, the way an image clear
Is etched forever in the mind, on cue to reappear.
I have an image bright as day, of one such specialty,
Long decades past, my two-year-old, and our new Christmas tree.

No lights were on within that room, but still the tree was bright,
With muted light from the next room, where we sat that cold night.
'Twas bedtime for my little girl. She so enjoyed tree-trimming!
She hugged me tight and listened to the carols we were singing.

I reached to get her jammies as she stood there naked, free.
She broke away with impish laugh and ran back to the tree.
That image I remember well with each new Yule tree grand,
My baby running, bare, with joy, before the tree to stand.

With every year of age I add, my mem'ries bring more joy.
Refreshing was their innocence, each little girl and boy.
I hear the snow slide off the roof—"That's Santa!" children knew.
I thrill again to Bible tales and carols, old but true.

Our memories bring back again our loved ones, gone but dear.
Rememb'ring them still makes us smile, but also brings a tear.
Enjoy your Christmas mem'ries then, that bring your past joys near,
And have a merry Christmas and a happy brand-new year!

(2010)

The Beauty of Christmas

The time is the nineteen-thirties; the place, a farmhouse near town;
There's Daddy and Mama and Grandma, and children from school
    age on down.
Yes, I am one of those children. Let's say I'd be about five.
It's Christmas, and all of my senses with pleasure are coming alive!

I hear the winter wind whistling, I feel the icy cold air,
I smell fresh bread from the kitchen, enjoy creamy cocoa in there.
Can you smell the roasting chicken? With gravy and stuffing, too?
Fruit pies bubbling hot from the oven, and cookies "For Santa
    and you!"

Do I smell the scent of the woodstove? A whiff of the Christmas tree?
The balsam stands tall in the parlor, a fir from our woodlot, you see.
But the sights—oh, the visions of Christmas as seen through the
    eyes of a child;
They all thrilled my soul with wonder, as beauty on beauty piled!

My eyes were aglow with the color of baubles and tinsel galore,
Each with its own special story; and the presents we made, or
    saved for.
Those days were deep in the Depression; no money for extras
    stores sell!
(No power, no indoor plumbing, no TV, computer, or cell.)

We had what we really needed, but extras were cause for glee.
The little saved up for Christmas bought mostly necessities.
I might get some mittens and stockings, snow boots, or a hood
    for my ears.
No money for new coats or dresses—hand-me-downs again
    this year!

I mentioned we didn't have power. No bright bulbs lit up the tree.
By lamplight 'twas even more lovely, muted glow of simplicity.
The icicles, heavy like silver, were made of some metal, you see.
In the magical glow of the lamplight they were etched in
    my memory.

Today's trees, brightly lighted, maybe all white or all blue,
Can really not hold a candle to the beauty my childish heart knew.
So don't tell me "Too commercial!" (It is, if that's all you see,
    though.)
Truly, Christmas is a time to show loving, and to remember the
    long ago!

The Spirit of Christmas has always, ever since the manger birth,
Been all about love, and fulfillment, and beauty in Heaven and Earth.
It shines through its shadow so subtle, and shouts in silence to tell
To souls that can worship through wonder, and to hearts that in
    gratitude swell.

Stand in awe of Creation's greatness, of the wonders of Earth
    and beyond,
Then take to your heart the meaning of the message of each
    Christmas morn.
So enjoy your Christmas blessings, show your love to those you
    hold dear,
Make memories now for the future! Merry Christmas and Happy
    New Year!

(2010)

Tell It Now, at Christmas

Tell somebody something, if
You have something to tell;
Make somebody happy or
Try their fears to quell.

There's no time quite like Christmastime
When love is felt with zeal.
The lack of love hits some folks, too,
So tell folks how you feel!

Tell ladies they are beautiful;
Tell men they really rate;
Tell everyone who's doing well,
They're helpful, wise, or great.

Thank someone who's been kind to you
And helped you where you live.
If words have left a bitter taste,
It's time now to forgive.

If someone needs a boosting up
When really feeling down,
Think of the joy of helping them—
And get needed stars in your crown!

The most important words of all
Are often overdue
These three short words that mean so much
Are these words: "I love you!"

So have a Merry Christmas
Greeting people, as a start,
And know you've helped yourself also—
Your loving soul and heart!

(2011)

The Peace of Christmas

We often speak of peace on earth, at this glad time of year.
But do we mean the end of wars? That won't come yet, I fear.
To make the world a better place, a perfect dream hoped for,
The human race will have to learn to solve things without war.

We hope someday we'll have that peace; it starts with you and me.
It can reside in everyone. Enjoy it; it is free.
Embrace peace now in thought and act, no room for fear or hate.
World peace begins within each heart, and ends at Heaven's gate.

When you are walking in the woods, with beauty all around,
The breeze is sighing through the trees, but there's no other sound;
Except a chipmunk chatters here, or birds sing over there.
But silence, hand-in-hand with peace, has banished every care.

Imagine sitting by your fire, watching glowing coals,
As man and wife you're holding hands, and peace speaks to your souls.
There is no thought of bills or ills, all problems now shall cease;
Just tranquil love, serenity, and ultimately peace.

You're sitting in a pew at church. The choir sings of grace,
And hope and joy. Your burden's lift; the uplift you embrace.
You're free of care while Love Divine renews the needed lease
That sends you forth to life's hard chores, remembering that peace.

You're listening to music sweet. It calls your very soul.
The melody, so beautiful, the harmonies control
Your very being, bringing tears responding to the strength
Of beauty; its effect on you is peace and joy at length.

You took the kids out camping. Now you're gazing at the stars
Without bright lights—amazing! Is that Jupiter or Mars?
There's nothing like a starry night to bring you down to size.
Your heart is filled with humble peace midst wondrous starry skies.

It's Christmas Eve. Your busy day won't end for hours, I bet.
So much to do for Christmas morn! Has the Sandman been here yet?
You creep upstairs just to make sure the children are asleep.
Angelic faces, sweet and pure—your heart this peace shall keep.

Long ago in Bible school we learned a song of joy.
"Down in My Heart," it sang of peace for every girl and boy:
"The peace that passeth understanding, down in my heart."
I speak of times that bring you peace; they're only just a start.

So here's our wish for Christmastime, it's not white snow or drifts;
Or feasts, or families fraught with care, or those expensive gifts.
We wish for you good health, good cheer, that fear and ills will cease,
We wish you joy and precious love, and lasting Christmas peace.

(2012)

"We Need a Little Christmas"

There was a song some years ago that said it best of all;
"We Need a Little Christmas" is the title I recall.

The snow, the cold, the short gray days would make a dull December;
Christmas perks our spirits up; its beauty we remember.

It's time to get in touch with friends—hear news, get Christmas cheer
From relatives you seldom see, but whom you still hold dear.

The mailbox yields up pretty cards and notes from friends afar,
And all the folks not lately seen; you've wondered how they are.

These days with Facebook, e-mail, texts, and tweets and phones
    so smart,
Some keep in touch, but still a card seems special—heart to heart.

The act of giving gifts brings joy to givers, big or small.
To make a loved one happy is the best part of it all.

Surprise and pleasure mixed with love lifts spirits and brings smiles.
Generosity on top of joy—unselfishly it piles.

Christmas for the children is most wonderful to see!
They so enjoy this holiday, they're good as they can be!

The children are so happy that their faces fairly glow.
Left-over childhood happiness can still be ours, we know.

There's an element of childhood still within each grown-up mind;
That's why we still can feel the joy that Christmas helps us find.

It's soothing once again to hear the story of the birth
In Bethlehem; and shepherds' fear, as angels sang on Earth.

Some folks who've suffered recent grief, or loss, or pain, or fear
Will not find joy, but greater pain, when Christmas comes this year.

They need us most in their sad days; we've happiness to spare.
Remember them; console them now, as Christmas love you share.

The spirit of good will on Earth takes root at Christmastime
Through family, friends, and far beyond—someday through
   all mankind!

We hope your season's peaceful, now that Christmastime is near.
Enjoy a "Little Christmas," and a happy brand-new year!

(2013)

Christmas Eve

It's Christmas Eve—a magical time of warmth, and love,
    and memory.
This holy night, some went to church and others stayed with family.
The lights within, the lights without, say "peace" in
    houses everywhere.
Young faces beam, old faces smile; and all hearts glow with
    Christmas care.

You've gifts to wrap, stockings to fill, and this toy's not
    assembled yet;
And after that you'll bake the pies, put cranberry jell to boil and set.
Stuffed turkey oven-ready, too, must be before the sun's first ray.
Its fragrance as you rise and shine will fill the house on
    Christmas Day.

Oh, don't forget the snack and milk that Santa surely will enjoy.
The kids will see the crumbs he left and hope he left an extra toy.
There're still a zillion things to do before old Santa comes this year.
But first, tradition in our house bids us to join with family dear.

Since nineteen hundred seventy-three we've gathered on this
    winter night
At daughter Anna's home, for soup and hearty party food just right.
We've dressed in red, or maybe green, the house is decorated fine.
Each person feels the love and peace in all our family, down the line.

We admire the tree, tomorrow's gifts, the groaning table,
    tempting smell;
We've all looked forward all year long; "A fav'rit!" so the
    grandkids tell.
It's just the families in Maine who get together Christmas Eve.
Except the year our daughter, Dee, had our tree Santa's gifts receive.

The children worried Santa would not know just where they all
 had gone.
It worked just fine; gifts on our tree when they got up on
 Christmas morn.
When they were done we put our gifts around the tree, until
 the time
Our clan all gathered here for gifts and dinner—precious day
 so fine!

Another year our Alice dear had their tree early, drove to Maine.
And once, their dad in hospital, both girls arrived and also Wayne.
All fam'lies there for Christmas Eve! We all were gathered
 except Dad.
But he came home on Christmas Day—the nicest "present"
 anyone had!

One early year when video was newly on the home-set screen,
We watched the Grinch steal Christmas, and sometimes another
 wholesome scene.
And then our grandkids said good night; they hung their stockings,
 time for bed.
Our Seth, who'd lately learned to read, sat down with us and
 nicely read

"The Night Before Christmas" (appropriate). In two more years his
 sister read.
Book done, they dawdled, left a plate of treats with milk, "For HIM,"
 they said.
They each could take a gift—just one! Some years joined us in
 Christmas song.
Then off to dreamland, until morn. "Sooner bed, sooner morning"
 helped along.

Our first such Eve as man and wife, were not with fam'ly—far away.
'Twas fine, just us; we lit a fire—used fireplace first time, that day.
Our cozy rent was happy 'til we looked outside, saw fire trucks!
No knock or call, so maybe, perhaps, 'twas neighbors' fire; it couldn't
    be us!

Each year after that we spent this Eve with my folks, sharing gifts
    on their tree.
There soon were children, each two years there'd be a babe in
    our family.
Their grandfolks gave them gifts, like dolls, kits, teddy bears, and
    also Risk.
They served us supper, before the tree, of soup, spaghetti, or
    tomato bisque.

With children small, this day meant work: wrap presents, cook—a
    love-based job.
Before we left for Grammie's, are they washed and dressed?
    Corral the mob!
I then changed clothes, and combed my hair. Then off to Grammie's
    as arranged.
Later when I checked my shoes—one black, one brown, I'd just
    half changed!

With passing time come changes, sad. Kids grow and leave us,
    sickness, loss;
But also glad—new babes, success. So hope and pray for luck of
    the toss!
Find joy in times like Christmas Eve that make life sweet, with
    mem'ries dear.
May this Christmas be your merriest, its memories bring a glad
    new year!

(2014)

Christmas Grief

The joy went out of everything
Last winter when my husband died.
Our family watches over me
And proves that love shall still abide.

Last Christmas was our 65th,
Together every single year.
Age 92—we can't complain—
But still we wish he could be here.

Now Christmas season's here again.
It's been my favorite time of year.
It's different now that he is gone.
There'll be no joy for me, I fear.

Where is the joy I wrote about?
The Christmas beauty, Christmas peace?
I think I won't put up a tree,
"Bah! Humbug!"—that will be my speech!

I catch the strains of "Silent Night,"
The "Merry Christmas" greeting, too,
The Story—wise men, shepherds, birth—
I start to realize this won't do.

The family gathers here each year;
They will again, for life goes on.
I feel the love, I see the sights,
Hear sounds, smell fragrances, sing songs.

I try anew to prize each day;
I look for "good" in everything.
The memories come flooding back;
I laugh, I cry, I sometimes sing.

"Good" proves its magic; joy sneaks in,
Along with grief that's still with me.
One's memories can't be snatched away;
Our memories help us trim my tree.

With muted joy I welcome Yule;
Its beauty now brings peace to me.
My memories of Christmas Past
Sustain me, and my family.

Yes, grief is strong—will have its way!
But gentle joy will whisper, too,
In love, in giving, memories—
The Christmas Spirit, ever new.

I came to realize one more thing:
Grief, joy, and love can all live here.
So I'll enjoy this favorite time,
With loving family gathered near.

I wish you joy this Christmas, then.
My Christmas blessing now comes clear.
Again you have my sincere wish:
"A blessed Christmas and new year!"

(2015)

Christmas Joy

In life there are so many things that bring us joy, both great
    and small:
A smile, a word, a taste, a smell, success, award, spring peepers' call,
Sunrise, sunset, a lake so blue, a tree, a rose, a violet,
A rainbow bright, new car, old home, old friend, campfire, a loyal pet,

Young love, a wedding, baby's birth, babe's grip on fingers that
    he finds,
A song that stirs the very soul, a book that satisfies our minds.
There's motherhood and apple pie, sunshine of summer, pure
    white snow.
There's love of many different kinds, for many people that we know.

Some people fail to find the joy that Christmas brings to most of us.
They rave "Commercial!" "Hectic!" Yes, we know it can be quite a fuss.
But there is more, much more, to make each bleak December bright
    with joy.
There's beauty, warmth, true love, and peace, a feast, a child's bright
    eyes, new toy.

The greatest blessings in our lives are friends and family, far and near.
It's only right that we should like to give them gifts because
    they're dear.
A gift can say "I love you,"…or…"I thank you," "Welcome,"
    "Sorry," "Praise,"
"I'm glad you're in my family," "I think of you on happy days."

Make someone happy; know it's true that your day then is
    brighter, too.
Look on the bright side; find the good; say "thanks" for blessings
    granted you,
A Baby born in Bethlehem was the first Christmas gift, it's clear.
Enjoy this season; spread joy, too. "Merry Christmas, glad new year!"

(2016)

Christmas Comes in Wintertime

Each season has its symbols strong that speak of that time's charm.
In spring it's lacy new green leaves, spring peepers, days so warm.

In summer it's the great outdoors, the lake, long days, and heat;
While fall is crisp and colorful, with weather hard to beat.

Then, tiptoe soft, the first snowflakes seem gentle, peaceful, pure,
Then vicious, hateful, wild with rage—non-ending, we feel sure!

Yes, winter, that's not hard to say! It's always dark and cold.
There are snow and icy roads and walks—and boredom, truth be told.

Yet there are blessings to be gleaned, think skis and skates and trails,
And snowmobiles and quaint snowmen the kids build—never fails!

But now, remember Christmastime, which brings us love and cheer,
Courts us with warmth and pleasant times with friends and family dear.

Beginning with the Christ child's birth, His teachings spread worldwide.
We know that gift of love to be for us a life's work guide.

At Christmastime we celebrate, amidst the cold and snow,
With lights, and feasts with loved ones, and with gifts our love to show.

Enjoy the lift, the lilt, the love—that's Christmas—time most dear!
Enjoy its blessings, everyone—"Merry Christmas, glad new year!"

(2017)

Christmas Love

The kids are excited; their parents also, because Christmastime
    is in view!
For kids it's the presents they're going to get; for parents there's
    so much to do.

There are cards to be sent, a letter with most, cleaned house
    to decorate.
There are parties and visits and telephone calls, before that
    special date.

And then there are presents—the anguish they cause; they need
    to be just right!
Hints launched, hints recalled, lists made and remade, and budgets
    getting tight.

There's cooking and shopping and shopping again. It's cold and the
    car is balky.
There's frost on your scarf and your eyelids and nose, the path to the
    finish line rocky.

So why do we do it, year after year? For the kids? That's one
    big reason.
We keep Santa alive after hundreds of years to brighten their
    Christmas season.

I remember the thrill of my childhood belief, hearing snow sliding
    off the roof,
I knew it was him checking if we were good, or his spies giving
    Santa the proof.

In my childish innocence, Santa's name was up somewhere close
    to God's;
Christmas morning we found his cookie crumbs, and knew that he
    found our reward.

Why else do we do this? Well, imagine this: This month without
  Christmas? No!
So bleak, so cold, so dark, so dull! We need Santa's "Ho-ho-ho!"

We need the lights, the songs, the smiles. We need the church and
  its tale
Of the birth of the Christ in a manger bed, and the love He taught
  without fail.

Yes, love, that's the reason we do it all. The Christmas cards keep us
  in touch
With people we love who live far away. We enjoy their letters
  so much.

Aunt Nellie, who's ninety, and Freddie and Sue, a sister you see
  twice a year,
This is a way to tell them you care, maybe share with them a tear.

You try to turn the tear to a smile, show care and love, help out.
The lights and music lend beauty and peace. And that's what it's
  all about.

The presents are given to show your love, and bring happiness at
  this time.
Yes, that's the way it's always been: Love and happiness—yours
  and mine.

Love is caring, love is helping, and giving, too. And that's what
  we want to show.
It's love that makes the world go round, and makes it worthwhile,
  you know.

So do all you can to bring happiness home, to your loved ones
    far and near,
You'll enjoy what you gain, and they will too—Merry Christmas and
    happy new year!

(2017)

Christmas Happiness

Life is not a bed of roses, yet there are some here and there,
Among the thorns and weedy posies that are times of deep despair.

Keep your eyes out for perfection; happy thoughts mean happy you,
Steer you in the right direction, bring those roses into view.

Take a tip from Pollyanna; look for good in everything.
See that glass half full! That manner of glad thought makes our
    hearts sing.

Humans have a spiritual life side; nourish it with tender care.
Happy thoughts provide a frame guide; you can take it now
    from there.

Happiness—can you define it? One aspect is always there.
Optimistic outlook won't quit, happiness potential fare.

Christmas is a happy season; opportunity is here.
May you find each happy reason for a wonderful new year!

(2018)

Christmas Memories

Do you remember gifts you got for Christmas years ago?
Well, how about the ones you gave, the special ones, you know?

One year I got a sled, next skates, then skis beneath the tree.
Where in the world did they get the cash for gifts for Brother
    and me?

One gift now rises in memory. I guess I was fourteen.
It was Christmas Eve, with many things my Dad must choose between.

You see, my Gram would stay with us, then visit other folk.
That year she chose to see her kin near Cape Cod—that's no joke!

My father worked the evening shift at the shipyard during the war.
He didn't get home 'til midnight, after his shift was o'er.

We waited for him that evening, then opened our gifts—
    stars beamed.
We then drove Gram to her daughter's—it took all night it seemed!

The gift I got from my brother, Guy, that night so long ago
Was a record album so wonderful, of songs I loved to know.

Another year Lawrence surprised me, after my casual hint.
I thought he wouldn't do it; what if it cost a mint?

But on the tree was an envelope with a silly poem for me,
"'Three wise men' would get it"—whatever could it be?

Since there was "no room at the 'inn,'" to the garage went our
    "three wise" sons.
They brought in my present, my grandfather clock, mid jovial
    laughter and puns.

So now it's your turn to remember your Christmases past so dear,
And please do know that I wish you "Merry Christmas and
    happy new year!"

(2018)

We Need Christmas

Why do we give presents, and celebrate each year
When late December rolls around, and air is crisp and clear?
We celebrate the birthday of a very special One,
Who told us how to live in peace and follow what He's done.

The angels sang; the shepherds quaked to see the wondrous glory!
They told their tale (we hear it still)—the timeless Christmas story.
"Peace on Earth, good will to men" was promised to us all!
Word soon spread the Messiah had come, to cure humans' fall.

So where is this peace, good will among men? They haven't appeared
    in view.
The world is fighting constantly, and neighbor with neighbor, too.
But wait! He brought the answer on how to achieve this peace!
He spent his short life teaching it. If followed, the fighting would cease!

He told us to "Love thy neighbor," and give deference to all men.
He said to do unto others what you would want from them.
He told the sort of person to be, loving and forgiving.
He said to be a peacemaker, gave other advice for living.

To sum it up, a four-letter word that's spelled L-O-V-E.
You have to think of others; respect and care are key.
He didn't fail to bring peace to Earth; He tried to teach us to change!
It's we who have failed to claim our due—no one but ourselves
    to blame.

Just think what a different world it would be, from families to
    nations, worldwide,
If people would practice acting with love, together, to turn the tide.
So—that is why we give gifts and joy, to show love to those we
    hold dear.
To everyone I send this wish, "Merry Christmas and Happy New Year!"

(2019)

317

We So Need Christmas

The wind is howling, snow pelts down, it's freezing cold, and gray.
Our spirits flag, our faces frown, on this December day.
"Bah! Humbug!" says it all right now, with all we have to do
Before the holiday—but how? It will arrive on cue.

You're out shopping—takes so long—so many things to buy.
You faintly hear a Christmas song, from a store nearby.
Just at that time you meet a friend. She smiles, "Let's go for tea."
You feel a glow, some worries end, her visit helps, you see.

All around, in every store, the lights and sounds are joyful.
It begins to raise your spirits more, and even make you hopeful.
Nearby family comes to help, as you decorate the tree.
You sing, and think of the rest of them, and others you soon will see.

The joy will bubble over, too. The family will be smiling.
You'll go to church—you always do—remember the tale beguiling.
And then you'll know the reason why, as the wondrous day draws near,
We need the Christmas spirit nigh, to bring a great new year!

(2019)

An Angel—a Dream?

'Twas the night before Christmas, her last one on earth;
    she'd had all the treatments and tests.
She accepted her fate, happy child since birth, helped others,
    and gave life her best.
She was only thirteen, but wise for her years.
    She was one of those children who care;
She tried to do right, and collapsed into tears when scolded,
    but that was so rare.

Dad and Mom somehow knew that her time here was done;
    they should have their Christmas tonight.
Dad helped her from bed to a chair to rest on, placed a pillow,
    turned on Christmas lights.
They had presents for her, a music box, pink robe and slippers, and such.
She valued each thing and gave them her thanks;
    something else she wanted so much…

She wanted a Bible, hadn't asked; just the same—a package—
    lo, and behold!
Wrapped neatly, no writing, except that her name on the cover
    was printed in gold.
'Twas the Bible she wanted, pages all edged in gold;
    she wanted to know what it said
About dying—the words of God, she was told—and Heaven.
    She went back to bed.

Her mother sat with her, so sadly that night,
    read the verses to her about Heaven.
They'd keep up a vigil, help her with her plight,
    throughout the last hours she was given.
She happily, wearily, closed her eyes.
    Then a light shone bright in her room.
"Is this a dream? Am I now going to die?"
    An angel appeared very soon.

319

She was radiant to see, and dressed all in white.
    All fear just faded away.
When she spoke, it was music, and all was right.
    She said, "Yes, Dear, this is the day!
"Each life on this Earth has hardships, but hope.
    Miracles aren't granted often.
"But God has promised to help you cope,
    and the evil things he will soften.

"He has given you meds and vaccines to help
    prevent illness and help you get well,
"People had it much worse with the hand they were dealt,
    but His love has helped all, you can tell.
"Our God has looked down and He saw you here, suffering,
    and in need of His love.
"He wants you in Heaven where He'll wipe every tear;
    you'll be happy in Heaven above.

"There'll be folks that you know there, waiting for you.
    They know that you're coming, you see.
"And you'll wait in pleasure and happiness, too, for more loved ones;
    together you'll be."
Her parents arose after dozing that night, keeping vigil
    for their dying child.
They knew it was over, her pain and her fight;
    their sadness consuming and wild.

The girl's last Christmas was a loving time
    with family and presents and more.
But especially having that Bible so fine,
    which was what she really longed for.
She's happy now, as the Bible says,
    with mansions and beautiful scene;
No pain, no tears, throughout these days—
    but was the angel a dream?

(2019)

One Colorful Character and His
Special Christmas Gifts

A colorful character—I've got one of those; been married to him for eons. Two of his most illustrative capers involved his creative gifts to me on a couple of Christmases, many years ago.

We owned a greenhouse/garden center, and did a lively holiday business selling poinsettias and other plants, and other seasonal plants in the springtime, summer, and fall. One of our family jokes every now and again was that he was going to give me a plant from our greenhouse—the plants I watered and cared for daily—as a Mothers' Day present, or for Christmas or my birthday. We both understood that it was a joke, since I could have one of those anytime—I was a half owner—and it wouldn't be much of a gift.

Just before this particular December 25th, Lawrence made the same old joke. I thought little about it until the 24th, when he came in carrying three sleeves (in which plants are wrapped to protect them from the cold) with plant pots showing at the bottom and plant hangers sticking out at the top. He actually put them under the tree! I could only hope there would be something else—no matter how inexpensive—that was my "real" present. I was sure he had actually done it this time. The family thought it was hilarious that he was actually giving me plants for Christmas!

However, when I finally unwrapped them, I found inside those three sleeved plant pots—three lovely pantsuits! I was so pleased!

The other creative gift came a few years later. I had mentioned to him that while shopping I had seen a beautiful grandfather's clock on sale, but which still cost more than we ever spent on gifts for each other. I put it way in the back of my mind. I didn't see any package for me from him under the tree, but was surprised, when all the other presents had been opened, to receive an envelope. Inside was a message in the form of a poem, but it didn't name my gift. (I won't embarrass anyone by revealing the poem here! Its literary value may have been somewhat lacking!) It gave hints and clues, but I still didn't understand. It said the "three wise men" would have to bring it to me from the "manger" because there was "no room at the inn." He insisted that I should guess, and finally I did! It was the much-admired grandfather's clock, and our three sons' strength would be needed to bring it in from the garage (the "manger") where he had stored it until Christmas for lack of room in the house (the "inn"). He wanted to keep it a secret from me, and he surely succeeded.

Care, time, thought, and effort, prompted by love—that's what makes a gift special. No amount of money spent can ever equal the value of those ingredients.

Christmas and Peace

You've heard it: "Christmas is for the kids"; "too commercial"; "too much work"; "a hyped-up holiday to make money"; "Bah! Humbug!" We all may have voiced these sentiments at times, because each of them holds some truth (except the last one). Throughout the Christmas season, hopefully we find more meaning and more pleasure than this. Treasure togetherness, the memories, the beauty, and peace.

"Peace on earth, good will toward men," is what the biblical account says the angels sang that night. Peace on earth? Where is it? There is war, fighting, hatred, shootings, horrible crimes in every part of the globe. What happened to the prophecy? But *inner* peace? Over that we do have more control.

Surely everyone has heard of the Golden Rule, which states that we should do as we want to be done by. Probably all have heard "Love thy neighbor." Maybe even "Blessed are the peacemakers" is familiar. Surely everyone knows whose teachings these were? That baby, born in Bethlehem, grew up and spent his short life trying to convince us that peace on earth would be possible, if we human beings would only learn to treat each other with respect and love. We (too many of us) ignored the wisdom of His words, and have not made improvements necessary to bring much change. Are we humans even capable of the unselfish, loving level necessary to achieve peace worldwide? Some are; some are not.

Christmas is a time when most people do enjoy the unique joy—and yes, the feeling of personal peace—that our special celebrations, the music, and the bright beauty bring. We sincerely mean our greetings of "Merry Christmas!" We enjoy being with loved ones, and watching the little ones. We treasure the cards from people with whom we have stayed in touch over the years. The gifts, especially those given, but also those received, do seem to be a symbol of love. Giving is a way of showing love.

Why can't we show more love the rest of the year? Of course it is complicated, but I believe it is basically because of our instinctive greed and selfishness. Certain instincts are necessary for our survival. A newborn baby knows instinctively how to eat. Taking care of oneself is also necessary for survival. Self-preservation therefore is natural and instinctive. The maturing process as a child grows can be, and should be, influenced toward feeling respect and concern for others, also—the vital factor.

Actually, humans do have a natural feeling of love for other people. It begins with a baby's first smile in response to a kind face, and he continues to respond to others, and to want their company. Most people grow up with the ability to love others, and the willingness to step back sometimes to accommodate someone else's needs. The greedy and self-centered ones may cut down anyone or anything that stands in their way. They have a philosophy of hate, with love only for themselves, if that. It sometimes seems that today's society as a whole is too much of a "me first" one.

Is Christmas for the kids? It surely is, but for all of us, too. Is it too commercial? Yes, if one pays attention to that. Is there too much work? It's up to each of us to plan and simplify and assign ourselves enough time. Bah! Humbug? Never! It's a beautiful, wonderful time for enjoying personal peace. Whether or not one sees Christmas as a religious holiday, it's for showing love. You want to make someone happy, so you give them a gift. What is wrong with that? It should be a joyous, loving, thoughtful season. Besides, what would bleak December be without Christmas? Have a merry one!

A Christmas Story—the Saga of L.B.

The year was 1945. The place was Germany,
Where many German prisoners were under the care of L.B.

Finally off the carnage trail, and out of officer school,
The war now over, he must not fail, he had to follow through.

At the manly age of twenty-three, he found himself in charge
Of a POW camp, post-war, with responsibilities large.

He had just replaced the officer who skimped on calories.
"Calories? What's that?" he asked. (He had some facts to seize.)

Now Lawrence was a sensitive man, and he was kind to others.
He had a good heart, and ran the camp as if the men were
    his brothers.

When Christmas came, all thoughts were of home, and how
    all longed to be there,
American boys, so far they had roamed, and German men
    in their care.

Well, some of the Germans had families nearby. They had
    the courage to ask him,
"Can we go home for the holiday? Our question is
    more than a whim."

They promised they would surely return, once their time was over.
His own heart was full, for his home did yearn. If they failed,
    he had no cover.

They could have been the very men who had shot at him in combat;
Yet they were young, just like him; in the seat of power he sat.

He said they could go to their homes for a while, but must return
    by the deadline.
His own head at stake, his worries a pile, he hoped
    it would turn out fine.

The time was up, the holiday done; several men had gone, so eager.
He asked the guard, had all returned? He replied, "Every man
    came back, Sir!"

SECTION 4

The Last Word

In this short section I am including two articles that I wrote recently, that I consider rather special for a conclusion.

I extend a warm "thank you" to the readers of this book. I sincerely hope that it brought enjoyment and possibly more, as my legacy.

Move Mountains and Count Your Blessings

When people get to be as old as I am, they are expected to be overflowing with wisdom and interesting life stories. We are asked about our secrets for a long and/or happy life. I don't feel very wise, but I get by; I gripe about the losses of "the Golden Years," but I do get along quite well, and I am happy.

My secret to a long life? I don't think there is one. First in importance would be to inherit good genes; next would be to maintain a healthy lifestyle. Good luck helps; so could prayer. No secrets there, but I can tell you a few things, like moving mountains and counting my blessings, that have made me happy.

To be happy is largely up to you. It is important to stay positive, which is helped a lot by recognizing your blessings and all the good things in your life. We have a holiday, Thanksgiving, dedicated to counting your blessings and feeling gratitude for them. Taking note of pleasant things—often—is good for emotional health. Your thoughts dictate how you feel. Happy thoughts equal happy you. You can raise your spirits, remedy boredom, and even help mild depression, by consciously listing in your mind all the pleasant things you experience, big blessings or small—a compliment, a smile, a sunset, a robin—whatever pleases you. Also important are helping others, playing nice (see the Golden Rule), and avoiding regrets. Love, laughter, and music fit in near the top. Staying positive does make us happy!

Tragedy strikes all too often in this life. I have been lucky—blessed. But problems? Yes, plenty of problems, and work, sometimes seemingly impossible. But we have attempted to move mountains, and have sometimes succeeded. That has made me very happy!

Raising six children was not easy, but you can't imagine the exponential joy and reward. Either because of us, or in spite of us, every one of them is a person to be proud of. I am proud of their children also, and I treasure each of those grandchildren. There are 37 of us now, counting spouses, grandchildren, and great-grands, and we are a very close family. Coming from several states, we vacation together twice a year. They visit me singly also, and visit each other. Now that I am dealing with a few demons of old age, they are right on deck, as needed. I am so lucky, especially compared to so many who face their last years alone. We had a big family, with great rewards. I am so blessed, so happy.

One of my most challenging periods of time was the five years I spent getting my college degree, beginning at age 39, when the University of Maine came to Augusta. I had a husband and six children at home. Life threw most everything at us during those five years. My father-in-law died of a heart attack. My mother-in-law needed home care, and we all pitched in until her death. Both of my parents died of cancer after long illnesses, with the need for care. I needed surgery, which I was able to schedule between semesters. My youngest child started school; my oldest child began college. During those five years, two more started college. I was mother of a bride, with time happily spent. My daughter went with her new husband to Morocco for ten long months, which included Christmas. Still these five years stand in my memory as a wonderful time of growth—stimulating, challenging, fulfilling, and happy!

Probably the most visible accomplishment we can claim is building the largest greenhouse range of its kind in the state. We had worked for nearly thirty years at the old place, operating a small greenhouse business, with pansies grown in the field and gladiolas to sell as cut flowers. There was so much work! The kids worked some with us. When we moved, we dropped the field-grown crops, making me happy.

We finally got clearance on the funding to build the new greenhouse range on the last day of 1976. That winter of 1977 was harsh, but our family put all efforts into getting ready to open in the spring. My husband and our oldest son worked daily from day one; our college boy came home on break to help out. Our college girl put herself through school, with practically no help from us. We had two kids still at home, and they helped after school. I was teaching, and we were living on my wages. We commuted during all those months, but moved to Manchester in the fall. We all did our best, and then some. The seeds were planted on time for the spring season; we held open house before the carpenters finished the salesroom; the employees were hired and were transplanting, and were filling the benches as soon as the carpenters built them. We "moved our mountain." It was an anxious, yet happy, time.

We had a successful business, which we built with high ethical standards, with honesty, generous care for our employees, and fairness and concern for customer pleasure. We made every effort to be sure that a customer never left unhappy. We ran the business for ten years and then sold it to our son and his wife, the son who had been working with us from the start, and who was our general manager. They have done a marvelous job, and they continue with the ethical practices we established, and the values embraced by all of our children. We often hear, "I just love this place!" I am proud and happy.

So treat yourself occasionally to a bowl of ice cream, snuggle up by a cozy fire, read a book with a happy ending. Choose TV shows and movies that make you happy. Laugh often. Put on some music, and sing along. (Be sure some is the toe-tapping kind.) Invite the whole family for a home-cooked dinner or barbecue, but tell them ahead of time that politics will not be discussed, or anything on which there is serious disagreement. Insist they be polite. Take one day at a time; learn the line from the Irish song "Come by the Hills" (by Celtic Thunder and others on YouTube): "The cares of tomorrow can wait 'til this day is done."

You can add these things to the blessings you count. Be happy!

Final Last Words—Who Am I?

S ometimes I "come to" with a start, with the thought, "I am 90 years old! How did I get so old? Have I done my 'work,' or have I left a lot undone?"

I have used the spoken word only marginally, because I believe that, to persuade people, you need to first avoid turning them off, and I have wondered if my message, which I hopefully have passed on to my children and their children, has been understood. I am much better at writing than at talking. I would truly like to have been of value in this old world.

What more should I have done, in my most important role— bringing up our children? Of course, I think they are wonderful people. There is very little I would change.

Unfortunately no one is perfect. That includes me.

Do I have regrets? You bet I do. And I suffer over them, some a lot more than others. I regret shortcuts I had to take in raising my children, things I would do in a different way if put back to do it over, things I might have done differently in my teaching career, and ways I might have done better in my marriage. No, I am not perfect. And my conscience sometimes gives me grief. On the other hand, I know better than anyone what my reasons were at the time, for the things that I regret.

The world today is vastly different from the world in which I grew up. Some people want constant change, but not all change is for the better. Some things never change, though, even though factors are so different. Our relationship with other people always has been, and always will be, the most important thing to negotiate. Showing love and respect could solve every relationship problem in the world, from personal to national to worldwide. Of course, "it takes two to tango." Everyone's efforts would have to be reciprocated.

Young people—do you know the Twenty-third Psalm by heart? How about the Lord's Prayer? Do you know who Paul was, and what his name was before it was Paul? How about Noah, Moses, David, Jonah, Job, Daniel, Ruth, "three Hebrew children"? What do you know about Mathew, Mark, Luke, and John? Who had the coat of many colors? (Don't say Dolly Parton, who wrote the song by that name.) Do you know there are two "Testaments" in the Bible—the Old and the New, and what each is about? Do you know what the Ten Commandments advise?

I believe this history should be part of every child's education, because most educated and literary people do know about it. Things that we know are used to understand other things that we learn, which builds knowledge exponentially. Such knowledge of our past human history is sadly lacking these days, but could be valuable in building a good mind, and character. The Bible is a book full of treasures, and certainly not just history.

Do people these days still know the Pledge of Allegiance? Is it still recited every morning in school, right hand over the heart, attention on the flag of our country? Back in the 1930s, the students in our elementary schoolrooms took turns reading a passage from the Bible each morning, too, and then bowed their heads and said the Lord's Prayer. This was public school, not a religious institution.

I had a religious upbringing, and took it very seriously. I can only wish everyone had this blessing in their lives. Attending church would be a good first step toward a richer life. There may be things about the faith that we have trouble accepting, but we don't want to "throw the baby out with the bath water."

If there is a Heaven, as promised, I want to be there, with no more parting, no more tears, no more pain, maybe on streets of gold—but the gold is one thing I wonder about!

Who am I? I hope this book helps to answer that question—maybe for me, too.